MEXICO'S
BAJA
**PUERTO VALLARTA, MAZATLAN
MANZANILLO, COPPER CANYON**

FODOR'S TRAVEL PUBLICATIONS

are compiled, researched, and edited by an international team of travel writers, field correspondents, and editors. The series, which now almost covers the globe, was founded by Eugene Fodor in 1936.

OFFICES
New York & London

Fodor's Mexico's Baja & Puerto Vallarta, Mazatlán, Manzanillo, Copper Canyon:

Editor: Andrew E. Beresky
Area Editors: Jim Budd, Maribeth Mellin, David Zielinski
Maps: Mark Stein Studios, Pictograph
Drawings: Michele Laporte

Jim Budd, Mexico City bureau chief for Murdoch Magazines (*Travel Weekly, Meetings & Conventions,* and *Incentive World*), has lived in the Mexican capital since 1958. A former editor of *The Mexico City News* and the Spanish-language business magazine *Expansión,* he has concentrated on travel writing for the past 16 years.

Maribeth Mellin is an assistant editor of the *San Diego Magazine* and a frequent contributor to *The Los Angeles Times* and other regional and national publications.

David Zielinski, a writing instructor at the University of California at San Diego, travels frequently to Baja California and throughout Mexico.

FODOR'S

MEXICO'S
BAJA

PUERTO VALLARTA, MAZATLAN
MANZANILLO, COPPER CANYON

FODOR'S TRAVEL PUBLICATIONS, INC.
New York & London

Copyright © 1987 by Fodor's Travel Publications, Inc.

ISBN 0-679-01469-1
ISBN 0-340-41972-5 (Hodder & Stoughton)

First Edition

MANUFACTURED IN THE UNITED STATES
10 9 8 7 6 5 4 3 2 1

CONTENTS

FOREWORD

Baja California isn't just for Californians anymore. Originally discovered as a playground, sportsfishing haven, and campers' retreat by southern Californians, this long, slender finger of Mexico is now enjoyed by all as a tourist destination. Also covered in this book are other delightful places in northwest Mexico. For the sun-and-sea worshipers, there are the nearby Pacific Coast resorts or Manzanillo, Mazatlán, and Puerto Vallarta. And for the truly adventurous, there's the Copper Canyon, Mexico's "wild west," which boasts a most spectacular train excursion.

While every care has been taken to ensure the accuracy of the information contained in this guide, the publishers cannot accept responsibility for any errors that may appear.

All prices quoted in this guide are based on those available to us at the time of writing. In a world of rapid change, however, the possibility of inaccurate or out-of-date information can never be totally eliminated. We trust, therefore, that you will take prices quoted as indicators only, and will double-check to be sure of the latest figures.

Similarly, be sure to check all opening times of museums and galleries. We have found that such times are liable to change without notice, and you could easily make a trip only to find a locked door.

When a hotel closes or a restaurant produces a disappointing meal, let us know, and we will investigate the establishment and the complaint. We are always ready to revise our entries for the following year's edition should the facts warrant it.

Send your letters to the editors of Fodor's Travel Publications, 201 East 50th Street, New York, NY 10022. Continental or British Commonwealth readers may prefer to write to Fodor's Travel Guides, 9–10 Market Place, London W1N 7AG, England.

FACTS AT YOUR FINGERTIPS

PHYSICAL FEATURES. Geographically, northwestern Mexico is a reflection of the entire country. It is a region of vast deserts, cragged mountains, and lush jungles.

Baja (Lower) California dips like a moonscaped finger into the Mexican Pacific. Separated from the mainland by the 150-mile-wide Sea of Cortés (also called Gulf of California), Baja is 800 miles of desert, longer than the Italian peninsula and, for the most part, empty. (Despite their names, both Baja California and the Gulf of California are located in Mexico.)

Although only 30 miles across at some points and 140 miles at its widest, Baja is a peninsula whose two coasts are separated by soaring mountain ranges, with one peak more than 10,000 feet high. The 28th parallel is the line where the states of Baja California Norte (North) and Baja California Sur (South) meet. Down near the tip of the peninsula, a monument marks the spot where the Tropic of Cancer crosses the Transpeninsular Highway and the tropics really begin.

The Tropic of Cancer hits the mainland just above Mazatlán. To the north lie coastal farmlands and the Great Sonora Desert. Mazatlán is surrounded by some of the richest agricultural country in Mexico, but, not too much farther south, the mighty Western Sierra Madre comes tumbling down into the Pacific, and cultivated fields give way to the jungle. Puerto Vallarta and Manzanillo nestle on bays surrounded by mountains.

Mazatlán is in Sinaloa, a state that borders on Nayarit. Puerto Vallarta begins where Nayarit meets Jalisco. Below Jalisco, where the coastline curves eastward, is the tiny state of Colima and its port, Manzanillo. North of the Pacific resorts and inland is Mexico's "Wild West," the rugged Copper Canyon in the state of Chihuahua, which boasts one of the most scenic rail routes in the world. These areas, along with Baja California, are the regions covered in this book.

CLIMATE. In such a huge expanse of country, weather can vary as much as the landscape. The border areas share the climes of Southern California. They are pleasant enough in the winter but best when a summer sun shines. The beaches at Ensenada and San Felipe draw their biggest crowds from Memorial Day through Labor Day.

Southern Baja bakes during the summer, although, thanks to air-conditioning, the vacationers still come. Winter days can be downright nippy on occasion, and nights often are cool.

The mainland Pacific resorts tend to be a tad cooler in summer and warmer in winter than those in Baja. Summer is the rainy season on the mainland, but the rains usually amount to no more than brief but intense afternoon showers.

1

In autumn, the Pacific hurricanes can be devastating, raking mainland points and sweeping across the Sea of Cortés to batter Southern Baja.

FACTS AND FIGURES. People set this region apart from the rest of the country. Much of Mexico is Indian and Mestizo, inhabited by families who have lived in the same little villages since long before the *conquistadores* arrived. Not so the northwest. Almost empty throughout most of its history—much of it still is—the area attracted settlers from Europe, Asia, and the United States at the turn of the century. Immigration from abroad is much more restricted now, but new people continue to arrive, mostly from central Mexico. The American influence is felt more strongly here than in any other part of the republic.

The border strip of northern Baja is densely populated; Tijuana alone has more than a million inhabitants. Yet below Ensenada, the desert stretches vast and empty. La Paz, with about 150,000 residents, is the only city of any size. The two settlements at The Capes are little more than villages.

Across the Sea of Cortés, Mazatlán bustles, its population nearing the half-million mark. Mazatlán is primarily a shipping center and shrimping port. It has its resorts, but tourism is only one facet of the local economy.

The same can be said of Manzanillo. Smaller, with some 150,000 inhabitants, Manzanillo is mostly a harbor, its airport the gateway to self-contained resorts along the coast.

Puerto Vallarta is a village, albeit a big one now. The town still looks like the quaint fishing settlement it once was, and the native population clings to ancient customs and traditions.

The Copper Canyon is sparsely populated, with the vast state of Chihuahua, largely desert or rugged mountains, containing only about three million inhabitants, including tribes of Tarahumara Indians and colonies of Mennonite farmers.

LANGUAGE. Spanish, of course, is the official language, but every other person throughout the northwest seems to have at least some grasp of English. Baja's border areas are virtually bilingual, and The Capes appear at times to be an American outpost.

WHERE TO GO. The ocean and the sea are the big attractions of Mexico's northwest. The sun and the sand, magnificent fishing, perhaps a bit of hunting, but, most of all, a chance to sample the good life as it is lived in Mexico all combine to bring the visitors in. Millions, of course, get no farther than the border towns, but almost everyone who has seen a bit of Mexico wants to see more.

Beyond Tijuana, Ensenada is the closest resort town, just a 90-minute drive from the border. A favorite with weekending Californians, Ensenada is a delight. Hotels, to be sure, are not the hedonistic playpens found farther south, but they are clean, comfortable, and fun. The beach is not much, but fishing is good, Ensenada billing itself as the Yellowtail Capital of the World. Many of the restaurants are excellent, and the nightlife is the best in Baja.

San Felipe is more of a drive, being 125 miles south of the border at Mexicali. Up near where the Sea of Cortés begins, tiny San Felipe attracts weekenders, campers of the recreational vehicle/trailer crowd. The beaches are nice and offshore fishing is good enough, although there are only a couple of first-rate hotels in town, and San Felipe tends to be mobbed on long weekends.

Trips to anyplace else in Baja probably, although not necessarily, will involve a jet plane/prop plane flight.

Loreto, a good 700 miles down the peninsula, is a wonderful place to escape from civilization without sacrificing any of its comforts. The first capital of the Californias, sonambulant Loreto one day may be a truly major resort area—the Mexican government has invested millions in the hope that it will be—but, thus far, it has but one luxury hotel and a few cozy inns. The setting is spectacular, but other than fishing, playing tennis on some of the best courts in Mexico, and soaking up sun on a stony beach, there really is little to do.

The same might be said of The Capes: Cabo San Lucas and San José del Cabo. The difference is there are more hotels and more restaurants, but not many more. Deep-sea fishing, a pricy sport, is the big activity on The Capes, and the lifestyle is pretty much upscale.

La Paz, capital of Baja Sur, lures those with more modest budgets. Fishing costs less here, as do hotel rooms, and there is more to do. La Paz is the only Baja city of any size south of Ensenada.

Over on the mainland, Mazatlán is nearly as wild and spirited as Acapulco. It is also much less expensive. Probably the most reasonably priced major resort area in Mexico, Mazatlán packs in college kids and pensioners plus big contingents of sports enthusiasts, for here, too, the deep-sea fishing is great.

More fashionable is Puerto Vallarta, which boasts some of the finest hotels on the Mexican Pacific. Much of Puerto Vallarta's appeal is its charm, for the cobblestoned village is Mexico as it is supposed to be—quaint and delightful. The big hotels are spread out along the beaches north and south of town.

Manzanillo is more an airport than a final destination as far as most vacationers are concerned. The airport is the gateway to self-contained resort properties that attract guests who want to check in and stay put.

The Copper Canyon slices through the Sierra Madre Occidental, whose peaks soar to some 9,000 feet in the Mexican state of Chihuahua. In this volume, we follow the route of the breathtaking Chihuahua-Pacific Railway (a century in the building) from Los Mochis on the coast 400 miles inland to the city of Chihuahua.

TOURS. Organized tours are available in the United States to all the major resort areas of northwestern Mexico. One can sign up for a half day of shopping in Tijuana to a week or more of sportsfishing off Mazatlán. Even for experienced travelers, group tours and prepaid packages have much to recommend them. Going with a group, especially on a chartered aircraft, means that you will be paying considerably less than you would be if you traveled independently, although you may sacrifice some flexibility. Prepaid packages cost a bit more than group travel, but they give you more freedom.

In addition to lower costs, group tours and prepaid packages have another advantage: travelers are given a helping hand when they arrive, if they need it. Independent travelers have almost nowhere to turn in case of an accident, theft, or illness or simply when a hotel reservation is not honored.

When considering a package or group tour, it is important to study the fine print carefully. Those going abroad for the first time will appreciate the hand-holding that group travel provides, but missing a plane—especially if it is a charter—may mean losing the price of the ticket. Packages may include more or less than you want. Free tennis will do you no good if you don't intend to play, and you may not want to spend a day away from the beach on a jungle excursion.

Among the items to check when considering any group tour or prepaid package are these:

• Is airfare included or only land arrangements? Often when the price is limited to land arrangements, the operator may still be able to offer attractive airfares.

• Are taxes and tips part of the deal? If not, how much will they add to your costs?

• Are all meals, some meals, or no meals included?

• If a rental car is part of the package, will it be air-conditioned with automatic transmission or a standard-shift subcompact cooled by opening the windows? Are taxes, fuel, and insurance extra?

• Does the operator specify in which hotel you will be lodged or hedge by mentioning only "luxurious" or "superior" accommodations?

• What is the tour operator's responsibility for getting you home on time? Charter flights have been known to be cancelled. When that happens, who picks up the tab if you must stay an extra night or obtain space on a scheduled carrier?

Tours and packages are sold through travel agents. It is important to find a reputable agent, preferably one who is a member of ASTA, the American Society of Travel Agents. Travel agents depend largely on repeat business and word-of-mouth advertising, so they try to keep their clients happy.

Planning also involves deciding when to go and what to carry. Find out what the weather will be like at various destinations when you are able to make your trip. Peak travel periods, such as long weekends or the Christmas holidays, can be hectic and accommodations may be overbooked. As for what to carry, Mexican resorts are delightfully informal; men can leave their jackets and ties at home. Light raincoats may come in handy during the summer months; in winter, a sweater is good insurance against chilly nights.

TOUR OPERATORS. A number of organizations, known in the trade as "wholesalers," offer a variety of package programs to Baja California and Pacific mainland destinations (many hotel chains and airlines also have package programs). As mentioned previously, group tours usually offer the lowest prices and even individual packages are much less expensive than an itinerary in which transportation, accommodations, and sightseeing excursions are purchased individually. Most tour operators market their packages only through retail travel agents, but since not all retailers handle all tour operators, you might wish to contact the various wholesalers to see what they have available.

American Express Vacations, 100 Church St., New York, NY 10007; 800–241–1700.

American Leisure, 9800 Centre Pkwy, Houston, TX 77036; 800–231–5804.

Baja Adventures, 16000 Ventura Blvd., Encino, CA 91436; 800–543–BAJA.

Baja Expeditions, Box 3725, San Diego, CA 92103; 619–297–0506.

Betanzos OK Tours, 323 Geary St., San Francisco, CA 94930; 415–421–0955.

Cartan Tours, 12755 Hwy. 55, Minneapolis, MN 55441; 800–422–7826.

Club Med, 3 E. 54th St., New York, NY 10022; 800–CLUB–MED.

First Family of Travel, 3530 Forest Lane, Dallas, TX 75234; 800–527–6366.

Firstours, 1341 W. Mockingbird Lane, Dallas, TX 75247; 800–423–3118.

Flyfare, 300 E. 42d St., New York, NY 10017; 212–661–3100.

Fun Sun Pacific Tours, 7700 Edgewater Dr., Oakland, CA 94621; 415–633–1633.

Funtastic Tours, 13614 Midway Rd., Dallas, TX 75244; 800–527–0126.

Garza Tours, 14103 Riverside Dr., Sherman Oaks, CA 91423; 800–423–3178.

Horizon Holidays, 2204 Garnet Ave., San Diego, CA 92109; 800–537–7869.

Intersol, 3303 Harbor Blvd., Costa Mesa, CA 92626; 800–421–5365.

Mexican Representatives, 3355 W. Alabama, Houston, TX 77098; 800–231–6333.

Mexico Travel Advisors (MTA), 1717 N. Highland Ave., Los Angeles, CA 90028; 800–421–4037.

Sunam Reservations, 7777 E. Hampden Ave., Denver, CO 80231; 800–525–3504.

Thompson Vacations, 401 N. Michigan Ave., Chicago, IL 60611; 800–621–6400.

Tour Express, Box 5710, Denver, CO 80217; 800–525–1948.

Town & Country Tours, Box 32307, Phoenix, AZ 85064; 800–528–0421.

Westward Adventures, 13982 Euclid Ave., Garden Grove, CA 92643; 415–495–6383.

TOURIST INFORMATION SERVICES. Mexican Government Tourist Offices are located at: 405 Park Ave., New York, NY 10022 (212–755–7261); 233 N. Michigan Ave., Chicago, IL 60601 (312–565–2785);

2707 N. Loop West, Houston, TX 77008 (713–880–5153); and 10100 Santa Monica Blvd., Los Angeles, CA 90067 (213–203–8151).

Sadly, these offices have only a limited amount of information and it tends to be vague and general. Travel agents and airlines serving northwestern Mexico can be much more helpful.

TIPS FOR BRITISH VISITORS. National Tourist Office. 7 Cork St., London W1 (tel. 01–734–1058/9). **Insurance.** We heartily recommend that you insure yourself to cover health and motoring mishaps, with *Europ Assistance,* 252 High St., Croydon CR0 1NF (tel. 01–680–1234). When you need help, there is a 24-hour, seven days a week (all holidays included) telephone service staffed by multilingual personnel.

Money Matters. It is best to provide yourself with U.S. traveler's checks or dollars, since they are much easier to change than European currencies.

Electricity. Usually 110 volts. You should take along an adaptor, since razor and hair-dryer sockets are usually of the American style, taking flat-pronged plugs.

Tour Operators. *Mexican Holidays,* 23 Eccleston St., London SW1 (tel. 01–730–8640) will put together a holiday to any part of Mexico, especially to suit your requirements.

Swan Hellenic, 77 New Oxford St., London WC1A 1PP (tel. 01–831–1616) offers a 17-day tour looking at the art treasures of Mexico, accompanied by a tour manager and a guest lecturer. £1,785.

TAKING MONEY TO MEXICO. Traveler's checks in $50 and $20 denominations are the best idea because payment in cash (and these checks are as good as cash) is appreciated and may even qualify for a discount when shopping. Greenbacks are accepted almost everywhere, but carrying large amounts of currency is not a good idea on any trip. Credit cards, especially those issued by banks, are honored by most large establishments everywhere except in Southern Baja. Because telephone communication is difficult in this state, even around The Capes (which makes calling to check on a card a near impossibility), some hotels and restaurants decline to accept credit cards. When cashing traveler's checks, be frugal; getting pesos for dollars is easy, but getting dollars for pesos is not. Banks and exchange houses *(casas de cambio)* offer the best rates; hotels charge a hefty commission. Tickets, travel documents, and valuables should be kept in a hotel safe deposit box.

INSURANCE. All kinds of policies are available, from those that cover air travel (often included automatically when a ticket is paid for by credit card) to health, accident, and lost baggage. Since baggage insurance may be difficult to obtain and more difficult to collect, the best bet is to lock your luggage, make certain that identification appears both inside and outside, and check nothing of great value; carry documents, traveler's checks, and the like on board.

It is wise to review your health and accident policies to see whether you are covered abroad and how you can collect if any expenses are incurred. The Mexican Social Security Institute offers policies that include ambulance service, medical care, and hospitalization for about $3 per day; hotels can provide all data. Other organizations worth looking into are these:

• *Carefree Travel Insurance,* 9 E. 37th St., New York, NY 10016 (212–683–2622). Policies, available from many travel agents, include emergency medical evacuation.

• *International SOS Assistance, Inc.,* Box 11568, Philadelphia, PA 19116 (800–523–8930) has fees from $15 for 7 days to $195 for a year.

• *International Association for Medical Assistance to Travelers,* 736 Center St., Lewiston, NY 14092 (716–754–4883) and 188 Nicklin Rd., Gueplh, Ont. N1H 7L5, Canada (519–836–0102).

Trip cancellation insurance, available from travel agents, is an excellent idea when cancellation would otherwise result in the loss of deposits, the cost of air tickets, etc.

Motorists in Mexico should always carry third-person coverage; without it, an accident may be followed by a stay in jail while responsibility is determined. U.S. insurance is not valid in Mexico, but Mexican insurance may be obtained at the border. One source is Sanborn's Mexico Insurance Service, Box 1210, Dept. F, McAllen, TX 78502 (512–682–3401).

HOW TO GET THERE. By Car. More foreign tourists drive into northwestern Mexico than into any other part of the country. Mexico 1, the Transpeninsular Highway, runs the length of Baja California, starting at Tijuana (just south of San Diego) and going all the way to The Capes. Mexico 3, out of Mexicali, is paved only down to San Felipe, 125 miles below the border. Mexico 3 links San Felipe to Ensenada and Mexico 1. The route to mainland Pacific-coast resort destinations is Mexico 15, which starts at the Arizona border and goes down through Mazatlán; motorists who are bound for Puerto Vallarta and Manzanillo pick up Mexico 200 at Tepic. (For more on driving in Mexico, see *How to Get Around.*)

By Air. Tijuana, Loreto, La Paz, The Capes (Los Cabos), Mazatlán, and Manzanillo are all served by direct flights from the United States. Promotional fares are frequently available, and package prices are often lower than the cost of an ordinary ticket. With rates changing so frequently and so many specials (two for the price of 1½, midweek discounts, etc.), it is wise to consult a travel agent when saving money is important.

Travelers with flexible schedules sometimes can benefit from the last-minute efforts of tour and charter operators to fill their planes. A number of brokers specialize in discount sales; they charge an annual membership fee usually under $50. Among these are *Stand Buys, Ltd.,* Box 2088, Southfield, MI 48037 (800–621–5839); *Moments Notice,* 40 E. 49th St., New York, NY 10017 (212–486–

0503); *Discount Travel Club,* 114 Forrest Ave., Narbeth, PA 19072 (800–458–5200); and *Worldwide Discount Travel Club,* 1674 Meridian Ave., Miami Beach, FL 33139 (305–895–2082). At times, charter and tour operators advertise last-minute specials in Sunday newspaper travel supplements; some of these are more reliable than others.

By Bus. Coach tours to Tijuana and Ensenada depart San Diego daily, and there are weekend trips to San Felipe out of Calexico (see sections on these cities for details). Also available are coach tours that go down the entire Baja peninsula with an option of flying home; since departure dates vary, it is best to check with a travel agent about them.

Tres Estrellas de Oro operates a scheduled service the length of the Baja peninsula from Tijuana south. *Transportes del Norte* has frequent departures from Nogales, on the Arizona border, down the mainland Pacific coast. First-class and luxury *(de lujo)* vehicles may not live up to their name (leg room is limited and the air-conditioning may not work), but they are remarkably cheap (about a dollar for each hour of travel). Seats are reserved and must be purchased at the depot, usually on the edge of town. There are no stopover privileges. If you want to stay overnight in Ensenada, you buy a ticket for Ensenada and another for Loreto or wherever you intend to get off next. Language is less of a problem in the northwest than elsewhere in Mexico; there always seems to be someone who speaks English. Even so, bus travel in Mexico can be monumentally confusing and appeals primarily to the adventurous or travelers who are watching their pesos.

By Ship. Carnival Cruise Lines' *Tropicale* sails out of Los Angeles every Sunday for Puerto Vallarta, Mazatlán, and Cabo San Lucas, and Admiral Cruises' *Stardancer* follows a similar route, with Friday departures October through May. Sitmar, Princess, and Epirotiki are among the other cruise lines with sailings to Baja and mainland Pacific ports, mainly during the winter. Admiral Cruises also offers three- and four-night cruises from Los Angeles to Ensenada throughout the year aboard the *Azure Seas.* Within the region, overnight ferries cross the Sea of Cortés between Mazatlán and La Paz as well as between Cabo San Lucas and Puerto Vallarta; cabins with bunks are available at very low prices, but these are not luxury liners. Tickets must be purchased at the ferry terminal on the day of departure.

HOW TO GET AROUND. By Car. Baja California and the mainland Pacific coast of Mexico are visited by more foreign motorists than the rest of the country combined. The scarcity of unleaded fuel south of the border is a matter of concern, but many drivers report that for short hauls there is little to worry about. Nevertheless, it makes sense to check with your mechanic before subjecting your car to Pemex, the only brand of gasoline available in Mexico.

Ferries, carrying both passengers and motor vehicles, plow the Sea of Cortés to connect Baja with Mexico's mainland. The ferries operate between La Paz and Los Mochis, Mazatlán, and Puerto Vallarta. There is also a ferry between Cabo San Lucas and Puerto Vallarta.

Motoring is a marvelous way to see and get the feel of the country, but it is not for everyone. Not only is the language different, but the measurements are in kilometers instead of miles. Highways are only passing fair, road signs are few, and distances between some towns (and gas stations) are great. And there are other points to consider:

- Mexican insurance should be regarded as mandatory, since uninsured motorists involved in accidents may be jailed until responsibility is determined and the damages are paid. U.S. policies are not valid in Mexico, and Mexican insurance, available at the border, can run up to $150 per month.

- If you enter Mexico with a car, you must leave with a car; possession of a vehicle is noted on your tourist card. If an emergency arises and you need to fly out, the car must be left in the care of Mexican customs—a complicated and sometimes costly procedure.

- Nighttime driving should be avoided. Free-grazing cattle, which are enough of a menace during the day, are just one factor to consider. The misery of being stranded by a breakdown is another. During daylight hours, Mexican highways are patrolled by the Green Angels, government-operated trucks staffed by English-speaking mechanics whose services are free. (There is a charge if parts must be replaced, and tips are gratefully received.)

- As was mentioned, gas stations frequently are far apart. Any half-empty tank should be filled at the next opportunity. Neither credit cards nor dollars are accepted at most Pemex stations. *Lleno* (YEH-no) means "fill it up," and *aceite* (ah-SAY-tay) will get the oil checked (several U.S. brands of motor oil are available, as well as Pemex's *Faja de Oro*). If you want the tires checked, indicate *las llantas* (lahs YAN-tas); the windshield is *parabrisas* (PAR-ah-BREE-sas) and will be cleaned only upon request. Service station attendants expect a tip; the equivalent of a dime is fine normally, but double that if oil and tires are checked and the windshield is cleaned. Rest rooms often are filthy.

- Major repairs can be a problem, especially for car models that are not manufactured in Mexico. When possible, seek advice before selecting a mechanic. Hotel people should know who is reliable.

- Road signs, where they exist, are similar to those in the United States, but the wording is in Spanish: *Alto* means Stop; *No Rebase,* No Passing; *Ceda el Paso,* Yield; *Conserva su Derecha,* Keep Right; *Despacio,* Slow; *Tramo en Reparación,* Road Work Ahead; *Desviación,* Detour; and *No Hay Paso,* Road Closed.

- Speed limits are usually 100 kilometers per hour (62 mph) on open highways and 40 kph (25 mph) in town. Although these limits are rarely enforced, they should be obeyed; Mexican highways are not engineered for high speeds. In many towns, speed bumps lie waiting to bounce the unwary.

- In many towns, streets are one way, an arrow on building corners indicating the direction in which the traffic flows. Two-headed arrows mean two-way streets. A circle bearing an E with a slash through it (E̸) means no parking. License plates may be removed from illegally parked cars; they will be returned on payment of a fine.

Highway Signs

STOP

YIELD RIGHT-OF-WAY

TWO-WAY TRAFFIC

NO REBASE
NO PASSING

ANCHO LIBRE
HORIZONTAL CLEARANCE

PESO MAXIMO
MAXIMUM WEIGHT (METRIC TONS)

NO
NO PEDESTRIANS

SLIPPERY ROAD LOOSE GRAVEL

DIP

LIMITE
PARKING LIMIT

UNA HORA
ONE-HOUR PARKING

NO
NO LEFT TURN

NO
NO U TURN

STEEP HILL

R.R. CROSSING

NO
NO PARKING

CONSERVE SU DERECHA
USE RIGHT LANE

INSPECCION
INSPECTION

NO
NO TRUCKS

BUMPS

4.20 m
VERTICAL CLEARANCE

PEATONES A SU IZQUIERDA
PEDESTRIANS KEEP LEFT

MAXIMA
SPEED LIMIT (IN K.P.H.)

CONTINUA
CONTINUOUS TURN

NO
NO BICYCLES

TRAFFIC CIRCLE

NARROW BRIDGE

ROAD SIGNS IN SPANISH	DESCRIPTIONS IN ENGLISH
TOPES	Speed Bumps
UN SOLO CARRIL	One Way Bridge
PAVIMENTO DERRAPANTE	Pavement Slippery
PROHIBIDO SEGUIR DE FRENTE	Do Not Enter
VADO	Dip

CIRCULACION
KEEP RIGHT

NO
DO NOT ENTER

SCHOOL CROSSING

SIGNAL

TRAILER CAMP

AIRPORT

HOSPITAL

MECHANIC

FERRY

CATTLE

MEN WORKING

• Minor violations of other sorts usually can be settled by offering to pay the fine to the policeman, who, in Mexican slang, accepts a *mordida* or "bite." Law enforcement officials frown on their people hassling tourists, but it does happen. The equivalent of $5 should settle anything. If it does not and the offense truly is minor, simply be patient, pretend to understand nothing (you may not be pretending), say little, and eventually the policeman should walk off in disgust.

• Leave aiding accident victims to others. This goes against one's instincts, but, under the Mexican legal system, the provision of assistance can lead to unpleasant complications.

Rental cars are available at airports or at many hotels in the resort destinations covered in these pages. Avis, Budget, Hertz, and National, as well as many local firms, have cars for hire. Most readily available are Volkswagen and Nissan standard-shift models, although Ford, Chrysler, Chevrolet, and Jeep vehicles are manufactured in the country. Air-conditioned cars with automatic transmission should be reserved in advance. Along the border, it makes more sense to rent in the United States, where rates are considerably lower; not all agencies, however, allow their vehicles to be taken into Mexico.

 TRAVEL DOCUMENTS. First, bear in mind that to reenter the United States, proof of citizenship may be demanded (foreign nationals will need the appropriate visas). Mexico requires no papers for entering its border areas or for going to San Felipe or Ensenada in Baja California. Just below Ensenada, there is an immigration post where tourist cards are checked. These cards, issued free by Mexican consulates, travel agents, and airlines, are required for traveling into the interior of the country. Usually, they are valid for 90 days and must be presented to the authorities before leaving the country (in other words, don't lose yours). Americans and Canadians do not need passports to visit Mexico but must present proof of citizenship to obtain a tourist card. Other foreign visitors must have a valid passport to obtain a tourist card or visa. Temporary import permits for automobiles are not needed in Baja California but will be required for driving to Pacific coast resorts on the mainland.

British subjects need a valid passport and a Mexican tourist card. A passport may be obtained from the Passport Office, London, from passport offices in Glasgow, Liverpool, Newport, and Peterborough, or from any British consulate abroad. It is valid for ten years. Mexican tourist cards may be obtained from the Mexican Embassy, 8 Halkin St., London S.W.1, or from your travel agent; or, if already abroad, from any Mexican embassy and national airlines. Students wishing to study in Mexico and business travelers must inquire at the consulate for additional requirements. A passport or another proof of citizenship must be presented to reenter Great Britain. There is no limit on the amount of money carried out of the country for pleasure travel.

TRAVEL AGENTS. One should select a travel agent with the same care as one chooses a physician, attorney, or stock broker; a vacation trip is, after all, a large investment, the costs, one hopes, exceeding those for one's medical and legal expenditures during a year.

In North America, the services of a travel agent are free except for out-of-pocket expenses. The travel agent's earnings are based on commissions paid by tour operators, airlines, hotels, and car rental firms. Although this situation leads some travel agents to tout costly holidays and organizations that pay the highest commissions, a good agent seeks to provide value and satisfaction for clients, counting, in return, on further business and word-of-mouth recommendations.

European travel agents simply charge their clients a small fee and thus may be less biased in their suggestions.

In addition to honesty, a good travel agent should be familiar with the area in question and be able, for example, to tell interested female clients where the men are as well as to advise honeymooners on the places in which romance best flourishes and not pack a weary executive off to a hotel in which music from the lobby bar seeps into the rooms.

Group tours and prepaid packages usually are purchased through travel agents. Because many are available, it takes an expert to know which program will best suit an individual client.

Membership in the American Society of Travel Agents (ASTA) is a good indication that a travel agent is a professional who knows his or her business. Many states require agents to be licensed, which is additional protection for the consumer. In Canada, Britain, and other countries, good travel agents belong to associations that police the ethics of their members.

WHEN TO GO. With the exception of border areas, the Baja and mainland Pacific coast resorts covered in this volume are winter resorts. The high season—with its high prices—runs from mid-December through Easter Week. The Christmas and Easter holidays, long weekends, and *carnival* time in Mazatlán (the week before Lent) tend to be exceptionally crowded, and some hotels have been known to overbook. Summers usually are very hot in Baja but pleasant on the mainland, although there may be some rain in the afternoons. Pacific hurricanes blow up, starting in late summer, and continue through early autumn.

WHAT TO TAKE. Resort wear is about all that will be needed, although a sweater could come in handy during winter evenings and light rainwear is essential for summer when afternoon showers become downpours. None of the resort areas is dressy enough to expect a man to wear a jacket and tie. Before stocking up on vacation clothes, remember that resort wear is one of the best buys in Mexico.

Airlines permit passengers to check two bags and tote a bit of hand luggage on board. Checked baggage should be locked and identification tags attached. Carry valuable documents, costly cameras, and jewelry with you (expensive jewelry should be left at home). Porters usually are available, but not always; bring no more than you can carry. If possible, pack one bag inside another; if bargains in the shops are too good to resist, you still will be able to carry them home.

Cameras, including still, movie, and video, may all be brought into Mexico, along with 12 rolls of film for each. Kodak fairly well dominates the market, so if you prefer another brand, bring it. When not in use, cameras should be kept locked in luggage or checked with hotel security.

Other handy items are insect repellent, a small flashlight, two or three ball-point pens plus a notebook, tweezers, facial tissues, and a sewing kit with a few spare buttons. These items are available in Mexico, but they usually are needed most when they are not at hand. Liquids, whether perfume or detergent, travel better in plastic bottles.

WHAT IT WILL COST. The price of a holiday in this area depends on where you go as well as where you decide to stay and the season you make your trip. Summer costs less than winter, and Mazatlán is less expensive than Puerto Vallarta. Here is what a couple might spend during a busy winter's day in Cabo San Lucas:

Double room at a *First Class* hotel	$75
Buffet breakfast, light lunch, cocktails and drinks with dinner	60
Rental car (Jeep)	55
	$190

SEASONAL EVENTS. January and **February** are the best months for *whale watching* in La Paz, The Capes, and Gray Whale National Park at Scammon's Lagoon near Guerrero Negro in Baja. February is usually the month for *carnival,* the pre-Lentan Mardi Gras celebrated in Ensenada, San Felipe, La Paz, and especially in Mazatlán. Feb. 5 is *Constitution Day,* a national holiday.

March is *Fiesta Month* in Mexicali and San José del Cabo. It is also the time for the *Long Beach-to-Cabo San Lucas Regatta. Benito Júarez Birthday,* Mar. 21, is a national holiday. *Holy Week,* just before Easter, is a time when everyone in Mexico tries to get away to the beach.

April is when the *Rosarito Spring Fair* takes place just south of Tijuana. It is also the month of the *Newport-to-Ensenada Regatta.*

May 1 is *Labor Day,* a national holiday, and May 5 marks the anniversary of the *Cinco de Mayo Battle,* when Mexican troops routed the invading French in 1862. *Fiesta Week* starts May 3 in La Paz and the final week of the month in Puerto Vallarta.

June 1 is *Navy Day,* celebrated in all Mexican ports. June also is the month for the *Baja 500* off-road race.

August is the date for the *Annual Fair* in Tecate on the border. The *Mazatlán Fishing Tournament* usually is held the final week of the month.

September 16 is *Mexican Independence Day,* but festivities get going the night before with fireworks and parties that outblast New Year's Eve. The *Loreto Festival* takes place the first week and the *Ensenada Festival* is the final week.

October is the date of the *Tecata Pamplonada,* or bull chase, when the toros tear up the streets as they race toward the ring.

November 2, All Souls Day, or the *Day of the Dead,* is a time for remembering the departed. It is an oddly merry occasion, with candy skulls sold on street corners and picnickers spreading blankets in cemeteries. Nov. 20 is *Revolution Day,* a national holiday. November is also the month of the *Baja 1000* off-road race down the length of the peninsula and of the *Marlin Tournament* on The Capes.

December means Christmas and Christmas means *posadas,* a string of parties held nightly from Dec. 16 through Christmas Eve. Dec. 12 is the *Feast Day of Our Lady of Guadalupe,* patroness of Mexico. *New Year's Eve* is celebrated as grandly in Mexico as it is throughout the rest of the world.

 BUSINESS HOURS. The *siesta* is still a time-honored tradition in Mexico; throughout the northwest, shops and businesses close for two to three hours, anywhere from 1 P.M. to 5 P.M. Each establishment makes its own rules. In the evening, shops and many offices stay open until 8 P.M. They open between 9 A.M. and 10 A.M. Banks are open from 9 A.M. to 1:30 P.M. weekdays. Most shops are open Saturdays, but many close on Sundays.

 HOTELS. The Mexican Tourism Ministry uses a star system to classify hotels (full-length mirrors, color TV, and dial phones help win five stars) and allows maximum rates to be established accordingly. Here we consider five stars, *Deluxe;* four stars, *First Class;* three stars, *Moderate;* and two stars, *Inexpensive* (we do not recommend one-star properties). A few very special establishments qualify for a rating of *Grand Turismo* and are allowed to charge as much as they please; these we consider *Super Deluxe.*

Authorized rates vary from destination to destination. With inflation rampant in Mexico, they may have risen somewhat by the time you read this. Prices are listed in each city section and are for a double room without meals unless otherwise noted.

DINING OUT. Seafood is the specialty throughout the area covered by this book. Generally, prices are quite reasonable, although not so much so in Southern Baja, which is far from sources of supply (steaks are flown in from the United States).

Meal hours are somewhat later than in the United States. The usual routine is to enjoy a big breakfast, have a light lunch about 1 or 2 P.M., and then go out for a big dinner somewhere after 8 P.M. Menus are usually in English as well as Spanish, but when ordering, it helps to speak slowly to make certain you are understood. Dress is casual, up to a point (the more elegant places will not admit customers in shorts).

Nightlife starts late; few discotheques open before 10 P.M.

 TIPPING. Baffling in any foreign currency, tipping is even more confusing in Mexico, where the annual inflation rate has been running at 100% for the past few years and the value of the peso has been tumbling compared to the dollar. The 15% rule is fine for restaurant checks; otherwise, keep the exchange rate in mind (what, at the moment, is the equivalent of a dollar) and hand out pesos accordingly. Large tips are unnecessary, but let your conscience be your guide. The following is suggested as a guide:

Bellboys—$1 should be sufficient.

Porters—Equivalent of 25¢ a bag.

Maids—$1 per day.

Taxis—No tip expected, but 25¢ will win a smile.

Car watchers—Between 10¢ and 25¢.

Shoe shiners—No tip expected.

Service station attendants—When tires and oil are checked and the windshield is cleaned, 25¢; otherwise, 10¢.

Tourist guides—A minimum of $1, $2 for a half-day tour, $5 for a full day, $20 to $25 per person for a week (more if the guide has been especially good, less if not).

Bus groups—For the driver, up to $1 a day per person.

 SHOPPING. Travelers leave home to see the sights, but when they get back, they talk about what they bought. In northwestern Mexico, shopping opportunities are remarkably varied.

All Baja California is a limited duty-free area (tobacco and liquor not included), and the federal sales tax is only 6% compared to 15% in the rest of the country. Cosmetics and foreign fashions are among the best buys, and La Paz and Tijuana are the best places to find them.

Tijuana features a remarkable selection of handicrafts from all over the country. Shopping is one of the big attractions in that border city, as it is in Ensenada. Cabo San Lucas does a big business with cruise ship passengers, which means that prices are high and the quality is low. Both Mazatlán and

Puerto Vallarta boast excellent shops; resort wear and local art are among the best buys.

Stores usually have fixed prices, but many smaller boutiques may be willing to negotiate (ask if they give a discount, what rate they give for dollars—it may be higher than banks are paying—or what the price will be if payment is made in cash). At markets and outdoor stalls, bargaining is the rule.

Bargaining, to be sure, is an art. Probably the best results come from a sad smile and a slow shaking of the head, which indicates the article is appealing but too expensive. When asked what you would be willing to pay, offer half the original price, but avoid speaking aggressively. Your offer may produce a counter-offer; it surely will if you start to walk away. Then the battle of wits begins.

 TIME ZONES. The northern half of Baja California down to the state line is on Pacific time. Mountain time is used in Southern Baja and on the mainland Pacific coast, including Mazatlán. Puerto Vallarta is where central time begins; Manzanillo and all the rest of Mexico is on central time. Mexico uses standard time throughout the year.

ELECTRIC CURRENT. All Mexico has the same 60-cycle, 120-volt system as the United States. Power failures are common, however, and flashlights come in handy.

 TELEPHONES. The most important fact to bear in mind is that international telephone calls are exceedingly expensive, but reasonable when made collect (all this has to do with taxes, a bit complicated to go into here). Collect or not, long-distance calls must be placed by hotel operators; credit card calls are not always accepted. Local calls may be dialed directly from most hotels and are free.

Although not on a par with the United States, the Mexican telephone system is good. In Baja California, however, little or no service is available outside the larger cities. Some hotels in The Capes have no telephone lines.

To call from the United States, you must use the area code 7066 for Tijuana, 70665 for Tecate, 70667 for Ensenada, and 90376 for Mexicali. The international access code for the rest of Mexico is 01152 followed by the local area code: La Paz, 682; The Capes, 684; Mazatlán, 678; Puerto Vallarta, 322; and Manzanillo, 333.

 LAUNDRY AND DRY CLEANING. Hotels can take care of this, usually overnight. In Mazatlán and Cabo San Lucas, where some visitors stay for months, there are do-it-yourself coin laundries. Dry cleaning and laundry establishments can be found almost everywhere, but it pays to ask around because some are much better than others.

STUDENT/YOUTH TRAVEL. Since some special facilities are available, young people who qualify should obtain an *International Student Identity Card* from the Council on International Educational Exchange (CIEE), 205 E. 42nd St., New York, NY 10017 (212–661–1414), or 312 Sutter St., San Francisco CA 94108 (415–421–3472). CIEE also provides information on summer study, work/travel programs, and tours for high school and college students. Canadians should contact the *Association of Student Councils,* 44 St. George St., Toronto, Ont. M5S 2E4 (416–979–2604). This association has a travel bureau and arranges tours for students of more than 50 Canadian colleges and universities.

Other organizations listed below can provide information on low-cost flights, educational opportunities, and other matters for young people who are considering travel to Mexico as well as to other parts of the world.

Institute of International Education, 809 United Nations Plaza, New York, NY 10017 (212–883–8200), administers scholarships and fellowships abroad and provides information on international summer and full-time programs run by American institutions for academic credit.

Arista Student Travel Assn., 1 Rockefeller Plaza, New York, NY 10020 (212–541–9190), specializes in travel programs for students and young adults.

 HINTS TO THE DISABLED. Few special facilities are offered in Mexico, but those who wish details on conditions might contact any of the following:

Society for Advancement of Travel for the Handicapped, 26 Court St., Brooklyn, NY 11242 (718–858–5483), can provide data on special tours for the handicapped and who runs them.

Rehabilitation International USA, 1123 Broadway, New York, NY 10010 (212–972–2707), publishes a list of access guides for various countries.

International Air Transport Association (IATA), 2000 Teel St., Montreal, Quebec H3A 2R4 (514–844–6311), publishes the *Incapacitated Passengers' Air Travel Guide,* which is available free.

 HEALTH. The biggest worry is the upset stomach and diarrhea that seem to plague so many visitors to Mexico. These complaints are less of a problem in Baja California than elsewhere, but visitors to the peninsula are not immune. On the Pacific mainland, avoid any restaurant that looks less than clean; better still, ask hotel personnel which places they recommend (hotel food and beverage outlets are by far the safest).

If illness strikes, call the hotel physician quickly; the trouble usually can be cleared up in a matter of hours. Pharmacies and tour guides also can be helpful in suggesting remedies. If ignored, the discomfort may last for days and self-treatment often only makes it worse.

A few other tips:

- Carry along frequently used items such as nose drops, cough syrup, and vitamins, since the same brands may not be available in Mexico.
- No inoculations are required to visit Mexico, but your physician may suggest preventatives to stave off hepatitis, typhoid, or malaria.
- Bring along extra eyeglasses or contact lenses plus a copy of the prescription.
- Keep insect repellent handy and use it liberally.
- Always carry an identification card that includes an emergency telephone number, your health insurance company and policy number, and your blood type.
- Those who have a serious problem, such as epilepsy or diabetes, should wear a medical-alert or similar tag around the wrist or neck.

 MAIL. Allow two weeks for cards and letters to arrive; mail is slow in this area. Use Mexican stamps in Mexico (some people forget). Postage rates change periodically —often with no advance notice—to compensate for inflation. Post office hours are from 8 A.M. to 6 P.M. weekdays; hotel newsstands usually sell stamps but charge a bit more than the face value.

ENGLISH LANGUAGE MEDIA. *The News,* published in Mexico City, is sold in the mainland Pacific resorts as well as in Southern Baja. *The Baja Times,* published in Tijuana, and *Ensenada News and Views,* are giveaways, handy for finding out what is going on at the moment. Magazines and paperbacks in English are available at most hotel newsstands. Many First Class and Deluxe hotels have U.S. satellite programs on their in-room TVs.

DEPARTURE. A $10 airport tax is slapped on all passengers who board international flights. Once they pay it, passengers clear immigration, where their tourist cards are picked up.

For domestic flights, a more modest airport tax is included in the ticket price. Passengers who fail to show up for a domestic flight on which space has been reserved forfeit 50% of the value of the ticket.

Passengers should arrive at the airport at least one hour before the flight is scheduled to depart. Late arrivers, even those with confirmed space, may be denied boarding. Late arrivers also risk leaving without their baggage.

 CUSTOMS. U.S. residents may bring back $400 worth of foreign merchandise as gifts or for personal use without having to pay duty, provided they have been out of the country more than 48 hours and have not claimed a similar exemption within the previous 30 days.

Most Mexican handicrafts may be brought into the United States duty free even if the purchaser has been abroad only for a few hours (say on a shopping spree in Tijuana). However, because these provisions change, it is wise to check with U.S. Customs in advance. No duty is charged on art or antiques that are

CONVERTING METRIC TO U.S. MEASUREMENTS

Multiply:	by:	to find:
Length		
millimeters (mm)	.039	inches (in)
meters (m)	3.28	feet (ft)
meters	1.09	yards (yd)
kilometers (km)	.62	miles (mi)
Area		
hectare (ha)	2.47	acres
Capacity		
liters (L)	1.06	quarts (qt)
liters	.26	gallons (gal)
liters	2.11	pints (pt)
Weight		
gram (g)	.04	ounce (oz)
kilogram (kg)	2.20	pounds (lb)
metric ton (MT)	.98	tons (t)
Power		
kilowatt (kw)	1.34	horsepower (hp)
Temperature		
degrees Celsius	9/5 (then add 32)	degrees Fahrenheit

CONVERTING U.S. TO METRIC MEASUREMENTS

Multiply:	by:	to find:
Length		
inches (in)	25.40	millimeters (mm)
feet (ft)	.30	meters (m)
yards (yd)	.91	meters
miles (mi)	1.61	kilometers (km)
Area		
acres	.40	hectares (ha)
Capacity		
pints (pt)	.47	liters (L)
quarts (qt)	.95	liters
gallons (gal)	3.79	liters
Weight		
ounces (oz)	28.35	grams (g)
pounds (lb)	.45	kilograms (kg)
tons (t)	1.11	metric tons (MT)
Power		
horsepower (hp)	.75	kilowatts
Temperature		
degrees Fahrenheit	5/9 (after subtracting 32)	degrees Celsius

more than 100 years old, but pre-Hispanic artifacts may not be brought into the United States without written permission from the proper Mexican authorities. Also barred is the importation of products made from animals that are considered endangered species.

U.S. Customs publishes a free booklet, *Know Before You Go,* which spells out the latest regulations and is available from travel agents and airport customs offices.

Canada. In addition to personal effects and the regular exemption of $150 per year, the following may be brought into Canada *duty free:* a maximum of 50 cigars, 200 cigarettes, 2 pounds of tobacco, and 40 ounces of liquor, provided these are declared to customs on arrival. Small gifts may be sent by post if the outside of the package states the nature of the contents and the phrase "Unsolicited gift, valued under $25 in Canadian funds." Up-to-the-minute regulations are spelled out in the booklet *I Declare,* available from travel agencies and customs offices.

British Subjects over 17 years old returning from Mexico (or from any other country outside the European Economic Community) may bring home *duty free* 200 cigarettes, 100 cigarillos, 50 cigars, or 200 grams of tobacco (this exemption is doubled for nonresidents). Also allowed is 1 liter of spirits, 38 proof or more, or 2 liters of spirits less than 38 proof plus 2 liters of table wine. Permitted too are 50 grams of perfume and 9 fluid ounces of toilet water. In addition, £28 worth of goods may be imported duty free.

Prohibited are live animals, fresh meats, plants and vegetables, controlled drugs, firearms, and ammunition.

INTRODUCTION TO BAJA AND NORTHWEST MEXICO

Vast Land of Contrasts

by
JIM BUDD

The immensity of northwest Mexico boggles the senses. Baja California is longer than the Italian peninsula and as empty as the Sahara. Across the Sea of Cortés (Gulf of California), Mexico's Pacific littoral stretches for 2,000 miles. This is some of the richest country in the republic, and some of the poorest. Hernán Cortés, conqueror of the Aztecs, sent his legions to explore these lands early in the 16th century, yet the area defied settlers for hundreds of years. It was only in the late 1960s that the first paved highway reached Puerto Vallarta.

Puerto Vallarta is by far the best known of the resort destinations on the upper Pacific coast. It was something of a vacation hideaway until John Huston chose it as a movie set and Elizabeth Taylor arrived to court Richard Burton in a steamy romance that tingled in the gossip columns. Puerto Vallarta became a dateline in newspapers around the world.

Hollywood brought fame to Manzanillo as well. A Bolivian tin magnate erected a pleasure dome along its shores, and to that dream-world came Dudley Moore and Bo Derek to film "10." Manzanillo blossomed along different lines, becoming not so much a single destination as a gateway to semi-isolated, self-contained resorts.

Mazatlán has a more prosaic history as a playground. One of Mexico's major ports, it was discovered by American sports people back in the 1950s. Mazatlán is located where the Pacific Ocean meets the Sea of Cortés, forming what has been called the world's greatest natural fish trap. Of late, everyone from college kids to pensioners has been finding the way to Mazatlán, but it is still best known for its marlin and sailfish. The sports fishing fleet here is the biggest in Mexico.

The spirit of adventure, not resort pleasures, is what brings tourists to the Copper Canyon. Located in the high Sierra Madre Occidental in the state of Chihuhua, this area of Mexico's wild north is noted for its incredible Chihuahua-Pacific Railway route (billed as the "world's most scenic railroad") from Los Mochis on the Sea of Cortés across the rugged mountains to the capital city of Chihuahua.

Baja: "Cult Destination"

It has only been in recent years that most of Baja became easy to get to. A nearly 1,000-mile-long finger of desert washed by an ocean and a sea, the peninsula captivates. As there are cult films and cult books, perhaps there are cult travel destinations. If so, Baja heads the list.

Long before the rich and famous stumbled on the mainland resorts, they found Baja. Back in the days of Prohibition, when Hollywood was new, the movie crowd learned the joy of having an international border so close by. In Ensenada, Jack Dempsey got involved with a scheme to build a lavish casino, only to see his dreams smashed when the United States legalized liquor and Mexico outlawed gambling. John Steinbeck brought attention to La Paz when he made it the setting for his novel *The Pearl.* Erle Stanley Gardner put aside his typewriter in Baja to battle marlin off The Capes. Dwight Eisenhower became an early fan. Bing Crosby put up some of the money for the first resort hotel in San José del Cabo when the only way to get there was aboard your own plane or yacht.

There are many paradoxes about the American love affair with Baja. During the Mexican War in 1847, U.S. troops occupied the peninsula, but Washington declined to keep it once a peace accord was reached. Yet Americans have been lusting after the land ever since. William Walker invaded La Paz with his private army in 1853, decreeing himself president of a new republic; the Mexicans saw to it that his administration was brief. In 1910, Richard Ferris tried something similar, but with Mexico City's approval. Ferris sought to set up a new republic, which he would name in honor of Porfirio Díaz who had ruled Mexico for 30 years. Revolution brought Díaz down before Ferris got anywhere with his plan. More recent invasions have been peaceful—tourists moving in with no intention to steal.

Prehistoric Dwellers

The *gringo* fascination with Baja California baffles many Mexicans. A vast and empty peninsula, it has, after all, defied mankind for centuries.

There are, to be sure, indications of some prehistoric development in these parts. In the rugged mountains that are the backbone of Baja, explorers have come across scores of monumental cave paintings, many of which are art of remarkable skill—larger-than-life figures sketched in red, blue, yellow, and black. These works date back some 2,000 years; no one can say who did them.

The first exploring Spaniards encountered natives who were remarkable both for their poverty and hostility.

The tale of Spanish penetration into Baja California is a curious one. Within a few years of his conquest of the Aztec Empire, Hernán Cortés dispatched Diego de Becerra to explore what was then believed to be an island west of mainland Mexico. De Becerra ended up murdered by his pilot. Such mutiny might have been a capital offense, but the pilot made sure that it was quickly forgotten by returning with a tale of a wonderful land where seductive maidens spent their days diving for pearls. Ruling over them, he reported, was a queen of enormous wealth whom he compared to a figure in the Spanish fiction of the day, Calafia. The legendary Calafia gave her name to California.

Cortés hurried across the sea that now bears his name to investigate for himself. Around La Paz, where he established the first settlement in 1535, Cortés found pearls, but no seductive maidens, and he departed shortly afterward. The settlement was abandoned two years later.

The rumors about Calafia and her court of beautiful pearl divers, however, lived on. Within the next 150 years many Spanish expeditions to Baja were launched and attempts at settlement were made. All failed.

High Mountains, Vast Deserts

What the explorers eventually learned is that their island is actually a peninsula about 800 miles long and anywhere from 30 to 150 miles wide. Rugged, soaring mountains made it almost impossible to cross. The peninsula was found to have countless coves and bays, many of them with excellent harbors. Offshore lay islands big and small, most of them barren, inhabited only by colonies of sea lions.

With the exception of its few oases, Baja California is desert. The Pacific side, especially in the north, is kept cool by ocean breezes and currents, but the land east of the mountains is hellishly hot in the summer. The farther down one goes, the more desert landscape one encounters. Joshua trees and barrel cactus dot the countryside. Here grow the ciros that appear to be tree trunks minus branches and leaves. Cardon cactus resembles the saguaro of Arizona. There are vast sandy plains on which Arab horsemen might be at home.

Inhabiting this inhospitable land at the time of the Conquest were sparse tribes who called themselves Kikiwa, Cochimi, Cucapa, and Kumyai—hunters and gatherers—survivors. What clothing they wore was made of animal skins.

Arrival of Missionaries

To save the souls of these tribes, the missionaries came. With great difficulty, they established settlements that managed to survive. Padre Eusebio Kino, whose name is revered in Mexico, arrived in 1683, to be followed by Padre Juan Salvatierra, who built a church in Loreto in 1697 that is still in use. This church was the first California mission. In the decades that followed, 23 missions were established on the peninsula.

Those first missionaries were Jesuits. When the Jesuit order was expelled from the Spanish Empire in 1768, Franciscans like Junipero Serra came to take their place. Landing at Loreto, Serra was unimpressed with what he found. Little more than half the Jesuit missions had proved to be successful. The Indians were anything but pacified. Rather than civilizing them, the Spanish clergy seemed to be killing them with imported European diseases. Serra decided that more could be done above the peninsula in the land called Alta (Upper) California.

Independence brought with it a withering of the few missions left in Baja California that had been an arm of the Spanish church until the ties with Spain were severed. Foreign clergymen were deported, mission lands returned to the few surviving Indians, and the churches converted into parish chapels for which there were no priests. Baja, in effect, became empty again—emptier than the Spaniards first found it. It is little wonder that the U.S. troops that occupied La Paz and Mulegé (Loreto had been leveled by a storm and only its church survived) were happy to sail away. Negotiators from Washington could see no point in adding this peninsula to their conquests—a land that one described as "fit only for cactus and rattlesnakes."

Border Goes Ignored

The existence of a new international border was largely ignored for nearly 30 years. In the 1870s, the United States put up a customs station, and across the line in Mexico, a few shacks were erected on what, legend has it, was *El Rancho de Tia Juana* (Aunt Jane's Ranch). The little community was distinguished only by being as far away as anyone in the country could get from Mexico City. It attracted the sort of people who found such distance to be as convenient as having the American border so nearby.

With only some 9,000 people said to be living in all Baja toward the end of the 19th century, the central government made various attempts to allow several individuals and an American-based company to settle the peninsula. A group of British pioneers tried near San Quintin and failed. More successful were a band of Russians, who settled in the Guadalupe Valley not far from the border. Mexicali was founded in 1906 through the efforts of the American-controlled Mexican Land and Colonization Company. Hordes of Chinese laborers were brought in by the Americans to dig the badly needed irrigation ditches.

Then, in 1910, came the whirlwind of the Mexican Revolution.

The Mexican Revolution was followed by Prohibition in the United States. The border area was all but taken over by Americans who would have fought an attempt at annexation as hard as any Mexican. The repeal of Prohibition was a disaster for the Mexican border towns, but within a decade, the United States was caught up in World War II. As thousands of recruits swarmed into San Diego, Tijuana flowered into "Sin City," the wickedest town in the Western Hemisphere. In Tijuana, as in the boot camps, boys were turned into men.

Threat of Invasion

Of more concern to both Washington and Mexico City was the perceived threat of a Japanese invasion. The worry was that Tokyo might land troops in Baja and move north. Some Americans urged the U.S. government to undertake a military occupation of Baja. That, of course, never occurred, but Mexico suddenly became convinced of the need to integrate the peninsula with the rest of the country.

The process has been long, slow, and sometimes paradoxical. To make Baja more Mexican, the government has allowed it to be less Mexican in many ways. The peninsula is a duty-free area beyond the pale of Mexican customs (there are some exceptions). This exemption applies all along the border but, in Baja, it covers two states. The federal sales tax is only 6% in Baja; elsewhere (except in border areas) it is 15%. Dollars circulate as freely as pesos in much of the peninsula, although devaluation has had an effect in this respect.

Large federal investments in dams and irrigation systems have made the Mexicali Valley one of the most prosperous agricultural regions in the country (foreign landholdings have been expropriated). Tender are the grapes grown in the Guadalupe and Calafia valleys that produce some of Mexico's finest wines. Ensenada has become one of the country's largest Pacific coast seaports. Tijuana, no longer a sin town, is still heavily dependent on tourism, but it is an expanding industrial center as well; here assembly plants turn out quantities of manufactured goods for the American market.

Statehood Finally Arrives

Northern Baja became a state in 1952. The south was to remain a federal territory for 22 more years. During that time, seagoing ferries began making overnight trips between peninsula ports and the mainland, while jets started zipping into La Paz from all over Mexico and the United States. It was the completion of the 1,061-mile-long Transpeninsular Highway in 1972, however, that led Southern Baja into statehood.

Tourism is by far Southern Baja's largest industry. There are, to be sure, lush farming areas where the occasional river flows or man has made the desert bloom. Mineral exploitation is beginning to pick up. Oil and gas fields have been discovered and await development. But tourism is where the action is.

Once tourism meant game fishing. Off Southern Baja, marlin weigh in at half a ton, snook grow nearly as long as a man is tall, and a grouper can top 200 pounds. Yet, these days, hooking such brutes is only one of the many sports that are available. Hunting is catching on; ducks, geese, and white-wing doves winter in Baja, and quail are a favorite target. Then there are the joys of tennis, and soon there will be golf. Plus all the joys of the seashore.

Fonatur, the Mexican government agency charged with creating new resorts (it gave the world Cancún), is busy putting the finishing touches on projects at Loreto as well as in Cabo San Lucas and San José del Cabo, the two resort towns at the tip of the peninsula that have come to be known simply as *Los Cabos*—The Capes. Travelers who are not pleased with all this progress will find La Paz—another vacation favorite—little changed. The La Paz that Cortés's men abandoned has been reborn. Although no bustling metropolis, La Paz is the largest city on the peninsula below Ensenada and the capital of Baja South.

Mazatlán, A Nearby Resort

Eastward across the Sea of Cortés lies the splendid port of Mazatlán. Some 750 miles south of the Arizona border, Mazatlán is the major Mexican resort (those in Baja are too small to be considered major) closest to the United States. Here begins what the cruise ship operators are fond of calling, the Mexican Riviera.

The country around Mazatlán was initially as much ignored by the *conquistadores* as was Baja. What changed things was the discovery of gold and silver at Concordia, a few miles inland. To keep out pirates, a small garrison was established in 1576, but it never amounted to much. The action was up in the hills. For more than two centuries, Mazatlán was not much more than a dock and a cannon. It was only in 1837 that the settlement was deemed large enough to warrant a municipal government. Visitors lose precious little time here touring colonial monuments.

Not that Mazatlán is without history. It was blockaded by the Americans in 1847 during the Mexican War, and in the 1860s was occupied by French troops shoring up the regime of the Emperor Maximilian. Emperor Maximilian, an Austrian archduke, worried that his French allies planned to keep the nearby gold fields for themselves. As something of a counterbalance, he invited veterans of the defeated army of the Confederate States of America to build a new life in the area. Even after the emperor was deposed, many of the Johnny Rebs, as well as quite a few Frenchmen, stayed on.

Fishing for Fun—and Profit

These and other immigrants from abroad had much to do with Mazatlán's development as Mexico's largest Pacific port. The railway, which came in during the late 19th century, helped, but so did the surrounding countryside. More than 600,000 acres in the region grow tomatoes, melons, cantaloupe, wheat, and cotton, much of which is shipped to the United States. On top of that, nearly all the 150,000 tons of shrimp that are hauled in from local waters are processed and frozen for the American market.

Yet it is fishing for fun that accounts for Mazatlán's popularity as a resort area. First fishing, then hunting, and, of late, surfing or just lounging on the beach. Mazatlán attracts all kinds of people. One of the big appeals is the price. Some of the best hotel chains in the country have properties along its beaches, as does the largest resort outside Acapulco. Rates, however, are startlingly low, about half what the sandboxes in Cancún are charging.

More "classy" is Puerto Vallarta. Some 200 miles down the shoreline from Mazatlán, Puerto Vallarta is where Jalisco state begins, a stretch of littoral that promoters hope the world will someday come to call the Happy Coast. The Happy Coast is the Jalisco coast with a bit of neighboring Colima tossed in. Manzanillo is in Colima.

Hollywood "Finds" Puerto Vallarta

If little attention was paid to Baja California and the northwest Pacific mainland during their early years, Puerto Vallarta was virtually ignored. There is a tale about how one of Cortés's nephews led an expedition to these shores and gave the *Bahia de Banderas* (Bay of Flags)—Puerto Vallarta sits at the head of this bay—its name because the Indians who came to greet him flew many pennants, but that may be no more than a myth. Pirates are thought to have sought shelter in these parts, and *Playa de los Muertos* (Deadmen's Beach) downtown is supposed to take its name from those swashbuckling times. The isolated village was known to its inhabitants as *Puerto de las Peñas* (Rocky Port) until 1918, when a mapmaker dubbed it Puerto Vallarta in honor of one of Jalisco's more notable governors.

A mapmaker may have given Puerto Vallarta its name, but film director (and sometime resident) John Huston put the town on the map. Huston chose to film Tennessee Williams's *The Night of the Iguana* on the outskirts of the village. Among the stars he brought was Richard Burton. And Burton brought Elizabeth Taylor, which was scandalous behavior in 1964 (Burton and Taylor were married, but not to each other at that time). Gossip columnists and the Hollywood press flocked to report on the naughty goings-on. In between titterings, stories were circulated about the Eden that Huston had discovered—this quaintest of all quaint Mexican fishing villages, with its cobbled lanes and whitewashed, tile-roofed houses. Before long, travel agents were being deluged with queries about Puerto Vallarta, a place many of them had never heard of.

Actually, Huston did not discover Puerto Vallarta. A handful of Americans, some fabulously rich, others in the same tax bracket as churchmice, had found the place some years before. The village already had a street called Gringo Gulch and a clutch of cozy inns to which the traveling cognoscenti hied to escape the rigors of civilization.

Not that Puerto Vallarta was an easy place to escape to. A *Mexicana* DC 3 dropped out of the skies to bounce along a grassy joke of a landing strip three times a week. No roads worth the name linked the village with the outside world. The two or three taxis had been brought in by sea. There was electricity, but lights flickered out at 10 P.M. When Westin Hotels opened its Camino Real in 1970, every room had a telephone but there were no outside lines.

Puerto Vallarta has changed considerably since then. These days, finding a place to park is a problem. Yet the village has held on to its charm. The streets are still cobbled and burro trains still come down from the hills. The grand resort properties dot the beaches above and below the town, and many of the quaint tile-roofed buildings house boutiques and more or less elegant saloons.

Manzanillo Envisioned as Gateway

Manzanillo, at the other end of the Happy Coast, is as much a tale out of a storybook as is Puerto Vallarta. The difference is that Manzanillo has a past.

The port is almost due west of Mexico City and of Veracruz. Cortés envisioned the area as the gateway to the Orient. From these shores, Spanish galleons would bring in the riches of Cathay to be lugged across the continent and hauled aboard great vessels that would carry them to Spain. It was from nearby Barra de Navidad that Miguel López de Legaspi sailed to conquer the Philippines.

As things turned out, Acapulco, not Manzanillo, became the port of call for the Manila galleon, which indeed arrived each year with riches from beyond the seas. Pirates are said to have hovered around Manzanillo during the colonial era, and chests of loot are rumored to be still buried beneath the sands.

With the coming of the railroads, however, Manzanillo lived up to its promise. It became a major port of entry, albeit not a lovely one (it was grubby, to describe it charitably). Out of town a ways, some 40 or 50 years ago, a few seaside hotels opened up. Before cars and planes were reliable, vacationers could at least reach Manzanillo and the sea by train. The jet age, however, seemed to doom the port as a sunny vacation spot. Then came Anteñor Patiño.

Patiño made his millions mining tin in Bolivia. A nice chunk of that fortune went into building Las Hadas (The Fairies), which, as its name implies, is a fairyland sort of resort. The complex was inspired by Moorish villages along the Mediterranean; it took ten years to turn his dream into reality.

Resort Stars in Film

The inauguration of Las Hadas in 1974, the "Gala in White," was the social event of the year. Patiño even provided the funds for the government to build a new airport in Manzanillo, one that could handle his friends' jets. The press came, too, and for a while Las Hadas was better known than Manzanillo itself. The film "*10*" added to the legend. The picture made a star of the resort as well as household names of Bo Derek and Dudley Moore.

It is not surprising, then, that many of the older hotels in the neighborhood began to spruce up. In addition, new places, many of them condo developments, opened, as did self-contained resorts. These resorts are called self-contained because they supposedly have everything on the premises. Guests check in and stay put. The town of Manzanillo is worth a quick look-see, and a zone of shops and restaurants out toward the Santiago peninsula (where Las Hadas is located) is still in its infancy.

For many travelers, Manzanillo is not so much a city as an airport, the last stop before a holiday begins. The Jalisco state line is just a few miles up the coast from the airport. Then comes Barra de Navidad, Melaque, Tenacatita, and Costa de Careyes. In them and in between, often on isolated strips of beach, are the self-contained resorts.

BAJA NORTE

NORTHEAST BAJA

Borderlands, Beaches, and Barren Beauty

by
MARIBETH MELLIN and DAVID ZIELINSKI

The northeastern region of Baja California Norte is a land of surprises, of new and startling vistas in its cities, mountains, lakes, and deserts. There are the comforts of luxurious resorts, the excitement of the big city, and the awesome presence of varied landscapes—the blazing orange sun rising in the east over deserted islands in the Gulf of California, the rugged crags in the volcanic mountains, the sweeping plateaus of productive ranchland; and the rich, black soil of the Imperial Valley farms.

Mexicali, the capital of Baja California Norte, shares the Imperial Valley farmland and the border crossing with Calexico, a small California city. Mexicali is a growing city. New neighborhoods (called *colonias*) crop up steadily in the far-reaching suburbs. Massive new government buildings and sprawling shopping centers appear throughout the city.

As a capital city, Mexicali sees a great deal of government activity. The current president of Mexico, Miguel de la Madrid, is a former governor of Baja California Norte. He has maintained strong ties to this area since taking office in 1982 and has appointed many Baja Californians to important federal posts.

Mexicali Growing Rapidly

Near the center of the city, a number of new government buildings reflect Mexicali's importance as an administrative seat. Their presence is a testament to the rapid growth of Mexicali. More and more people are migrating here from all over Mexico in search of a better life. The current population is estimated to be close to 900,000. Most of the new buildings are located in the vicinity of Anahuac Boulevard and Avenida Independencia, not far from the bus depot and the bullring. The hotels in this area are hosting more and more conventions and business meetings and adjusting their amenities to suit their professional clientele. Bordering the area of government buildings is a neighborhood called *Nuevo Mexicali* (New Mexicali), where some of the city's finest homes and restaurants are located.

The old State Capitol *(El Antiguo Palacio de Gobierno)* is closer to the center of town, almost two blocks from the border, at the intersection of Avenida Obregón and Calle Ulises Irigoyen. The architecture of the palacio reflects Mexicali's past, before the days of massive concrete and glass structures. The palacio is a traditional structure, with archways, balconies, and a quiet park.

The construction of the Imperial Canal in 1902 brought an influx of Chinese immigrants to the region. Their presence is reflected in the faces of the people whose heritage is mixture of Mexican and Chinese. Mexicali is considered to be a center of Chinese cuisine, and Chinese imports fill the curio shops.

Freebooters Take Hold

After the completion of the Imperial Canal, Mexicali began to grow, transformed from the small mining outpost it had been for years. Close to 10 years later, during the Mexican Revolution, Mexicali was taken over by freebooters and soldiers of fortune, who were out to amass as much land as they could; some of these renegade fortune hunters

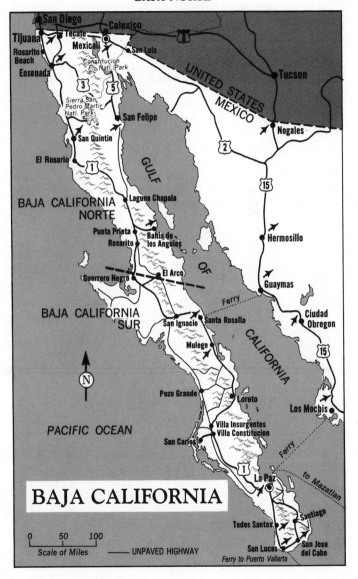

BAJA CALIFORNIA

Scale of Miles
0   50   100
——— UNPAVED HIGHWAY

attempted to create empires of their own, but their power-hungry dreams were short-lived.

During Prohibition, Mexicali earned a reputation as a seamy border town; liquor was plentiful and gambling and prostitution were common. The first major automobile road to Tijuana—an impressive engineering feat in itself—was financed from taxes imposed on these nefarious activities. A steady stream of gringos took advantage of Mexicali's permissive environment until 1935, when gambling was outlawed. Since then, the action has toned down considerably.

Water a Precious Commodity

Agriculture is the primary source of income in this section of Mexico, and the Mexicali area is blessed with some of the world's richest topsoil. But water is precious in these largely desert lands. In 1954, the United States signed a treaty with Mexico guaranteeing a share of at least 1.5 million acres of water from the Colorado River, but the details of this arrangement are still in dispute. (When the Imperial Canal was first under construction, it sprung a leak; water from the Colorado River flooded the area, and it took almost two years before order was restored. In the process, California's Salton Sea was formed. Mexicali has its own salt lake—the beautiful and serene Laguna Salada—whose tip lies about 15 miles east of town, but it is a natural lake, an extension, of sorts, of the Gulf of California.)

Since water is so valuable, it is wise to travel in this valley with a plentiful supply in the hot summer months. The climate here is more or less typical of that found in the low desert regions of the American Southwest—the elevation is sea level and the average rainfall is approximately three inches per year. But in the summer, the temperature can hit 120 degrees. Geothermal energy also is important; the Cerro Prieto generating plant a few miles south of town is the largest of its kind in North America.

As a tourist town, Mexicali is not very popular. It lacks the fine museums, parks, and attractions of Mexico's larger cities and does not have the charm of the small colonial towns. It is more a place to do business and a stopover on the way to the mainland, on the train, which reaches points throughout Mexico and originates in Mexicali. Sometimes referred to as the "Gateway to the Sea of Cortés," Mexicali is the port of entry for travelers to the attractive beaches of San Felipe.

San Felipe Undergoing Development

At the end of Hwy. 5, 125 miles south of Mexicali along some compelling stretches of desert and salt marshes, lies the one-time fishing village of San Felipe. Along the coast, the traveler passes through some of the most desolate desert imaginable. West of San Felipe, on the way to Ensenada, the highway winds through an imposing mountain range—the Sierra San Pedro Martir—whose highest peak, Picacho del Diablo (10,498 feet), is in Baja. Farther south along the Gulf coast, approximately halfway down the peninsula, lies the beautiful Bahia de los Angeles, a secluded bay that is perfect for fishing, camping, and relaxing.

Not until 1948, when the first paved road was completed from the northern capital, did San Felipe become a town with permanent residents. In 1967, a hurricane nearly destroyed San Felipe, but the residents rebuilt most of the town, and the new housing was of much higher quality than it had been before the tragedy. Now, although it is still the home of an impressive fishing fleet (the largest boats are docked three miles south of town within a manmade breakwater enclosure), tourism has taken over as the primary industry, and San Felipe has become a popular getaway spot. Today, this small resort town is undergoing extensive redevelopment. In addition to three newly built luxury hotels and a first-class beachfront hotel in progress, it boasts a new international airport (not yet open for use).

The accommodations range from excellent to adequate. Reservations are necessary, especially during peak seasons, such as Christmas, and on weekends, when the visitors seem to outnumber the locals by the hundreds.

On the way into town, there are at least a dozen campgrounds on the beach that are quite popular and fill quickly during the winter and spring holidays. There are more campgrounds in town, and two large trailer parks between the Hotel Cortés and the popular boardwalk. Dune buggies, motorcycles, and off-road vehicles abound. On weekends, San Felipe can be boisterous, and then some.

San Felipe draws many fishermen, and the ideal time for fishing is in the spring. Launches, bait, and supplies are readily available. Newcomers should know that the game wardens regularly check for valid fishing licenses, which are available through fishing charters and some travel agencies in Mexicali.

Bahia San Felipe has dramatic changes in its tides, which crest at 20 feet. Since the beach is so shallow, the waterline can move in and out up to half a mile. This has been the cause of problems for many fishermen who have tied their boats on shore, stopped in town for a few *cervezas* (beers), and found their crafts high and dry after a few hours. The sea here is often unpredictable. What begins as a glassy smooth surface in the morning can quickly turn rough and high running before noon. The local fishermen are well aware of the peculiarities of this section of the Sea of Cortés. Many of them visit the shrine of the Virgin of Guadalupe *(Cerro de la Virgen)* before setting sail. This shrine sits 940 feet high on a hill at the north end of the bay and offers a spectacular view of the town and the clearly etched desert mountains in the background.

Tecate, a Typical Mexican Town

About 90 miles west of Mexicali on Hwy. 2 is the quiet community of Tecate, a typical Mexican small town on the border. For some reason, Tecate never stooped to offer the vice that many other border towns thrived on. So incidental is the border to local life that the gates are closed from midnight until 7 A.M. Absent are the cheap curio shops that are so thick in Tijuana and, to a lesser degree, Mexicali. Once across the border, the main park *(zócalo)* and the church appear, and a pleasant country atmosphere prevails.

Over 50,000 people live in and around Tecate. Despite its relatively small size, the town is known throughout Mexico for the beer that bears its name. (In restaurants, Tecate beer seems to be the only brand served with wedges of lime; also, some say that this brand, in its familiar red can, connotes more *machismo* than do various other brands.)

The brewery is the one big industry, but farming is also good in this area, especially a bit farther south in the valleys of Guadalupe and Calafia that boast some of Mexico's lushest vineyards, as well as olive groves and grain fields. At 1,600 feet, Tecate enjoys a climate that is warm in summer and cool in winter.

The Mexican government has elected not to develop this area for tourism and has declared it to be part of a special industrial zone. Distinct advantages have gone to U.S. manufacturing concerns that have established large assembly plants in the region. A large instant coffee plant, Nacional Cafetalera, roasts coffee beans from Chiapas and Veracruz and exports them to the United States. On a good day, the plant can process 45,000 pounds of coffee in eight hours.

At one time, a steady stream of mountain water flowed through the valley, and Tecate still maintains an impressive water supply. Furthermore, Indians thrived in this area before the settlers drove them out, and a few tribes still inhabit the land south of town. The government strives to protect these tribes, mostly by not interfering in their affairs; it is rare for anyone to be allowed access to their communities.

Tecate's main tourist draw is Rancho la Puerta, a fitness resort catering to well-heeled Americans. But many residents of San Diego drive down for the day to savor the foreign atmosphere, to dine at one of the many good restaurants, and to stroll around the shops.

PRACTICAL INFORMATION FOR
NORTHEASTERN BAJA

HOW TO GET THERE. Mexicali is located on the border, opposite Calexico, California, in the arid Imperial Valley, approximately 115 miles east of San Diego and 55 miles west of Yuma. Tecate lies on the border between Tijuana and Mexicali and can be reached by car or bus. San Felipe is on the coast, 125 miles south of Mexicali. Most travelers to this section of Baja prefer to drive, but the Mexican bus service is frequent and the airport in Mexicali has international and national flights. San Felipe has an airport that accommodates only small private planes; Mexico Hwy. 5 south from Mexicali is the only other access.

By Air. At the moment, American carriers do not fly into Baja. *Aeroméxico* (800–237–6639) and *Mexicana Airlines* (800–531–7921) fly into Baja from some U.S. airports and from Tijuana and Mexico City. Small planes are allowed at the airport (more like an airstrip) in San Felipe and Bahia de los Angeles.

By Bus. *Greyhound* (619–239–9171 in San Diego) serves Calexico from San Diego four times a day. Return tickets on Greyhound can be purchased in San Diego or at the Mexicali Central Bus Station. Four Mexican bus lines run out of the Mexicali Station: *Tres Estrellas de Oro* goes through Tecate on its way to Tijuana; *Transportes del Pacífico* goes to Mexico City and other points on the mainland; *Transportes Norte de Sonora* frequents border towns in Baja and on the mainland; and *Autotransportes de Baja California* goes to San Felipe, Tijuana, and Ensenada. It is possible to purchase reserved seats on all buses the day before departure, but only at the bus stations:

● Mexicali. Central Bus Station, Centro Civico en Nueva Mexicali, Av. Independencia; 7–2451.

● San Felipe. Autotransportes de Baja California, Av. Mar de Cortés; 7–1039.

● Tecate. Av. Benito Juárez and Calle Abelardo Rodriguez; 4–1221.

By Car. Driving is the best way to see Northeastern Baja. Whether you have a small economy car or a large motor home, you won't have any trouble as long as you stay on the main highway and the paved arterial roads. To reach Mexicali, take California Hwy. 111 off I-8; here, Mexico Hwy. 5 runs 125 miles down the eastern coast of the peninsula to San Felipe (Hwy. 5 ends in town; the road farther south is not recommended for passenger cars or recreational vehicles). To get to Tecate from San Diego, take California Hwy. 94 to the Hwy. 118 turnoff; it's 2 miles to the border from there. Mexico Hwy. 2 runs through Tecate, and the journey east, down the La Rumerosa grade to Mexicali (84 miles) provides some engaging desert scenery. Visitors in this area will not need tourist cards, but should purchase Mexican car insurance at agencies near the border.

The Mexican highways are good, but at times they are poorly banked and the shoulders can be soft. Exercise caution when driving; before your trip to Baja, stock up on spare belts, fuses, hoses, and other necessary parts. Cars should be in top condition for travel in this desert region. Road assistance is provided by the Green Angels, whose sturdy green trucks can be seen frequently looking for motorists in need of help. The Green Angels, who are sponsored by the government tourism office, will perform minor repairs free and sell parts at cost. Most of the Green Angels speak English.

It is not advisable to drive at night in Baja. Cattle wander across the road, and the glare from oncoming headlights combined with the frustration of narrow passing room can be perilous. Be wary of dips *(vados)*. The road from Mexicali to San Felipe contains a fair number of these troughs, and high speeds should be avoided. When it rains, the runoff can sweep across the roads swiftly. Most of the dips are marked with depth sticks. If it looks too deep to cross safely, it probably is; generally, the water will subside as fast as it rises.

Gasoline stations are abundant in this area of Baja, but if you plan to do a lot of driving it is wise to fill the tank frequently since the stations may operate on irregular hours.

By Train. Although there is no train service through Baja, the *Sonora–Baja California Railroad (Ferrocarril Sonora–Baja California)* runs from Mexicali to points south in the mainland interior. The station is located at the south end of Calle Ulises Irigoyen, a few blocks north of the intersection of Av. Lopéz Mateos and Av. Independencia. Trains leave twice daily. The first is the express with sleeping and dining cars; the other is the local, coach only. The fares are reasonable, and there are several travel options. *Camarines* are sleepers for one or two people with an adjoining restroom. *Alcobas* have twin bunk beds and an adjoining restroom and are large enough for four people. *Primera clase* (first class) is fairly comfortable, but travelers sleep in their seats. *Segunda clase* (second class) is not recommended, since it is packed full, with no running water. At press time, a *camarin* for one person to Mexico City cost 49,000 pesos; the journey lasts at least 2½ days.

 TELEPHONES. To call Baja Norte from the United States, dial 70, then the area code and number. The area code for Mexicali is 656 and for Tecate, 665. Tourist offices in Mexico usually have English-speaking personnel, but only Spanish speakers may be on duty in hospitals or police stations. It also would be wise to stock up on a supply of one-peso coins; although these coins are no longer widely circulated, they are still used for pay phones.

Mexicali. Tourist Office: 2–4391; Chamber of Commerce: 2–6160; Police: 2–4443; Hospital: 5–1666.

San Felipe. Tourist Office: 7–1155; Police: 7–1006; Hospital: 7–1001.

HOTELS. Good hotels can be found in northeastern Baja, and their rates are lower than comparable lodgings in some of the more popular sections of the peninsula. The architecture and accoutrements of some of these hotels are in the familiar American style, but others are more charming with Mexican touches. From the stylish resort hotels of San Felipe to the ranchos of Tecate, there is something suitable for every taste and budget. Generally, prices range from $45 and up for *Deluxe,* $25–35 for *Expensive,* $15–20 for *Moderate,* and $15 or less for *Inexpensive.* Because of the instability of the peso, however, these prices and categories are subject to change.

MEXICALI

Expensive

Holiday Inn. Blvd. Benito Juárez 2220; 6–3801. The perennial favorite that incorporates some interesting Mexican touches in its 120 rooms. Most major credit cards are accepted, and full services are provided. The Mexicali Rose steakhouse is pleasant; live entertainment is offered.

La Lucerna. Blvd. Benito Juárez 2151; 4–1000. When the president of Mexico visits, he stays here. There are 200 rooms, including bungalows near the main building, and a specialty restaurant, a coffee shop, a piano bar, and a mariachi lounge.

Moderate

Castel Calafia. Justo Sierra 1495; 4–0222. One of the newest hotels in town, complete with restaurant, bar, and pool. Its 100 rooms are clean and comfortable.

La Siesta. Justo Sierra 899; 4–1100. The 85 very adequate rooms have all the amenities, including movies on cable TV.

Inexpensive

Motel Cosmos. Justo Sierra 1493; 8–1255. A decent motel in the vicinity of some of the better hotels.

Del Norte. Madero and Melgar; 2–8101. The first hotel one sees upon crossing through the border gates; in the midst of downtown noise. Recently renovated.

Montana. San Felipe Hwy., Km 1.5; 6–7705. Another good place for travelers, quiet and outside of town.

Plaza. Madero 366; 2–9757 or 2–9759. In the heart of the city near the international border and the House of Culture; 54 rooms with air-conditioning, full services, and a bar.

El Portal. San Felipe Hwy., Km 1.5; 6–7477. A comfortable place to stop before negotiating the highway south.

SAN FELIPE

This fishing village on the Sea of Cortés is a weekend favorite with Californians. Sometimes it gets crowded, so reservations are necessary during holidays and peak seasons.

Expensive

Castel Playas de San Felipe. Av. Misión de Loreto 148; 2–2822. Reservations: 706–652–2822. This 3-story air-conditioned hotel, on the beach 1 mile south of town, is complete with bar, coffee shop, disco, wet bar, catamaran and boat rentals, pool, 2 tennis courts, volleyball court, and gift shop.

Fiesta San Felipe. On the road to the airport 5 miles south of town; 4–0393. Reservations: Av. Reforma 1200, Mexicali, B.C.; 706–554–0393 or 554–0394. On the beach, with 130 air-conditioned rooms, room service, tennis, 2 pools, restaurant, coffee shop, disco, snack bar, bar, and banquet room.

Moderate

El Cortés. On the beach, one-half mile south of town; 2–1039. Reservations: Box 1227, Calexico, CA 92231; 706–566–8324. Some of the 90 units have beachfront patios. Air-conditioning, pool, launching ramp.

El Capitán. Av. Sur Mar de Cortés. Reservations: Box 1916, Calexico, CA 92231; 706–577–1303. A newer 2-story motel with 40 units, carpeting, air-conditioning, and a laundry.

El Cortés Motel. Av. Sur Mar de Cortés. Reservations: 706–561–8321. In addition to the 77 rooms, this motel has a pool, boat ramp, 2 bars, and a laundry.

Hotel Riviera. Fracc. Sol y Mar; 4–0212. Reservations: 706–577–1186. Facing the bay, this 44-room hotel has 2 bars, a pool, and air-conditioning.

Villa del Mar. Av. Sur de los Cedros; 8–3990. Reservations: 706–577–1004. 50 rooms, air-conditioning, pool, restaurant, and laundry.

Inexpensive

Chapala. Av. Mar de Cortés. Reservations: 706–577–1240. Air-conditioned and carpeted, with 26 units, 12 double and 14 single.

El Pescador. Blvd. Chetumal and Av. Mar de Cortés; 7–1183. Fairly nice air-conditioned rooms, with a laundry and liquor store.

TECATE

Rancho la Puerta. *Deluxe.* Mexico Hwy. 2, west of town; 4–1005. A luxury fitness resort with cottages, tennis courts, and a pool set in beautiful country terrain. Guests usually check in for a week, taking advantage of the special diet and exercise regimen to lose weight and get in shape. Overnight guests are accepted when space is available.

Santa Veronica. *Expensive.* Mexico Hwy. 2, east of town; 5–1636. This ranch where fighting bulls are raised is now also a resort with a large pool and tennis courts. The dirt-road turnoff to the south is approximately 10 miles east of Tecate.

El Dorado. *Moderate.* Benito Juárez and Esteban Cantu; 4–1101. A pleasant in-town motel with a restaurant and pool.

Hotel Mexico. *Inexpensive.* Benito Juárez 230; no phone. A modest hotel between the main park and the bus depot.

El Refugio. *Inexpensive.* Aldrete and Hildalgo; 4–1160. Not the best, but cheap and clean.

 RECREATIONAL VEHICLE PARKS, TRAILER PARKS, AND CAMPGROUNDS. San Felipe is a popular place for campers and recreational vehicle travelers who often settle in along the coast for the winter. Better parks and campgrounds fill quickly during the Christmas and Easter vacations, so it is wise to get reservations early—preferably by mail since many of these places have no phone.

SAN FELIPE

Club de Pesca Trailer Park. One mile south of town on the beach off Av. Mar de Cortés; 7–1180. Reservations: Apartado Postal 90, San Felipe, B.C.; 706–577–1180. A large facility, well groomed, with 120 recreational vehicle and tent sites and all amenities, including a boat launch and store.

Faro Beach Trailer Park. South of town, 6 miles on the airport road, overlooking the sea on Punta Estrella. Reservations: Apartado Postal 107, San Felipe, B.C. Offers 150 sites and complete services, including a pool, tennis court, and bar.

La Jolla Trailer Park. A half-mile west of town at Mar Mermejo and Av. Manzanillo. Reservations: Box 978, El Centro, CA 92243. Only 60 sites in a residential area, with hookups, electricity, water, and sewage. Not on the beach and unshaded.

Mar del Sol RV Park. Adjacent to the Hotel Castel Playas, right on the beach. Reservations: Mexico Resorts International, Box 8193, Chula Vista, CA 92012; 800–336–5454. All amenities, 125 sites, and hotel facilities available.

Playa Bonita Trailer Park. One mile north of town on Av. Mar de Cortés. Reservations: Sonia Alvarado, 208 W. Chestnut Ave., San Gabriel, CA 91776; 800–282–1337. On the beach, offering 35 sites with electricity, showers, and toilets only.

Playa de Laura Trailer Park. In town, on the beach at Av. Mar de Cortés. Offers fishing, 35 sites, hookups, and most amenities (13 sites on the beach itself). No reservations.

Ruben's Trailer Park. One mile north of town on Av. Mar de Cortés; 7–1091. On the beach, 50 sites, hookups, and most amenities, including a restaurant and bar. No reservations.

San Felipe Trailer Park. Beachfront park in town on Hwy. 5. Offers 34 sites, hookups, toilets, showers, and ice. No reservations.

Victor's El Cortes Campground. On the beach next to the El Cortés Motel in town; 50 sites, hookups, all amenities, and game room. For reservations: 706–561–8321.

DINING OUT. Northeastern Baja is not especially known for its cuisine, yet there is good seafood and steak to be had here. Mexicali is best known for its Chinese restaurants, which are so abundant that it is sometimes difficult to find a Mexican restaurant. Tecate boasts one of the better Italian eateries in the region. Lobster and succulent fish abound in San Felipe. Allow $20 for a meal in an *Expensive* place; $15, in a *Moderate* establishment; and under $10, in one that is *Inexpensive,* not including, drinks, tax, or tip. Credit cards are generally accepted in expensive and moderate restaurants along the border, but less so farther south. Abbreviations for credit cards are AE, American Express; D, Diners Club; MC, MasterCard; V, Visa. Many of the inexpensive restaurants have no phone.

MEXICALI

Expensive

Casino de Mexicali. Pino Suarez and Calle L; 2–9966. The most elegant spot in town, part of a private club, where the locals go for a fine night out. Piano bar and Continental menu. AE, D, MC, V.

La Misión Dragon. Lázaro Cárdenas 555; 6–4375 or 6–4400. An eclectically landscaped restaurant, a combination of mission and Chinese palace. Behind its gates are fountains, a huge garden, and a mixture of Oriental and Mexican artifacts. The locals hold large dinner celebrations here, and the Chinese food is top-notch. AE, D, MC, V.

Moderate

Casa Grande. Aquiles Serdán 1692; 2–4073. Paella and other Spanish dishes are the specialties of the house. MC, V.

Cenaduria Selecta. Av. Arista and Calle G 1510; 2–4047. This charming restaurant has been serving traditional Mexican food since 1945. The help is formal and efficient, the menus come in quaint wooden folders, and 2 rows of booths always seem filled with locals enjoying themselves.

Chernest. Pino Suarez 1994; 2–6185. An intimate, romantic spot in the same neighborhood as the Casino de Mexicali. International food and a large, well-lit bar. MC, V.

Chu-Lim. Morelos 251; 2–8695. This spacious Chinese restaurant is a welcome haven from the bustle of downtown shopping. The walls and ceilings are decorated in detailed Oriental panelling, and inside it is large but quiet.

Del Mar. Madero 517–1; 2–8849. An attractive roadhouse specializing in seafood. MC, V.

El Dragon. Benito Juárez 1830; 8–1020. Another of Mexicali's highly regarded Chinese restaurants. AE, D, MC, V.

El Nuevo Pekin. Justo Sierra and Paseo de los Pinos; 8–3730 or 8–3630. One more fine Chinese restaurant that also serves Mexican and American dishes. Family atmosphere. MC, V.

Heidelberg Restaurant. Madero and Calle G. A brand-new place with stained-glass windows and a convivial German atmosphere. MC, V.

Rincón Colonial. Calle F 557; 4–1115. Good Mexican food, specializing in steak. Live guitar music; air-conditioned. MC, V.

El Rincón del Sabor. Larroque and Calle H; 4–0888. A newer restaurant serving good steak and Mexican specialties. MC, V.

Ristorante Italiano. Reforma 1070; 2–9544. A good Italian restaurant in a quiet residential neighborhood. MC, V.

Inexpensive

Casita de Patzcuaro. López Mateos 648. A good place for a light Mexican meal, this is a favorite with regulars headed for San Felipe.

Las Cazuelas. Av. Benito Juárez 14. A nice, clean restaurant serving traditional Mexican dishes. Good combination meals.

Chung Hwa. Av. Benito Juárez 92. A good Chinese restaurant, very popular with Americans.

Gloria. Blvd. de las Americas 502; 6–5530. Specializes in home-cooked Mexican food—tacos, tostadas, chiles rellenos, menudo, and pozole.

Jabba. Reforma 326. A gringo-style hamburger stand offering burgers, fries, shakes, nachos, and crescent sandwiches.

Mei-Sim. Reforma 316. Fast food à la Chinese.

Restaurant Alley 19. Av. Benito Juárez 8. One of the best Chinese restaurants in the downtown area—much worthier than its name. MC, V.

Restaurant Victoria. Av. Benito Juárez 90; 2–2151. Good Chinese and Mexican food, in the heart of the downtown shopping area close to the border.

Restaurant Yaqui-Mayo. Zuazua 478. Near Parque Constitución, this comfortable family-run restaurant offers a wide variety of traditional Mexican dishes, including chimichangas, sopas, tortas, empanadas, and menudo. A satisfying lunch with soup can be had for about $2.

SAN FELIPE

Corona, George's, El Nido, Puerto Padre, and **Las Redes,** all along the waterfront, are fine for tacos, steaks, and seafood. **John's,** 2 blocks east of the bay and just off Hwy. 5, is excellent for all types of Mexican food and lobster. **El Pescador,** on a hillside, is slightly more elegant. All these restaurants are *Moderate* and accept MC and V. The **San Felipe Clam Man,** on the main street through town, is *Inexpensive* and always open. There are also a number of good inexpensive restaurants on the east side of the main street between Hwy. 5 and the postoffice.

TECATE

El Florido. *Moderate.* Km 29-½ Carretera a Tecate. Specializes in Sinaloan-style cuisine and fresh seafood. MC, V.

Passetto. *Moderate.* Callejón Libertad 200; 4–1361. This could be the best Italian restaurant in all Baja. The proprietor makes his own fine wines. Live music on the weekends. MC, V.

Pueblo Viego. *Moderate.* Hidalgo 140; 4–5310. Highly regarded for its Mexican dishes, particularly fare from neighboring Sonora. MC, V.

El Tucan. *Moderate.* Esteban Cantu 1100. An appealing steak house 4 blocks from the border. MC, V.

Restaurant 70. *Inexpensive.* Benito Juárez and Esteban Cantu. The finest Chinese restaurant in Tecate.

Restaurant Intimo. *Inexpensive.* Av. Juárez east of the Chamber of Commerce. Very good seafood in a homey atmosphere.

HOW TO GET AROUND. The ideal way to see the northeastern part of Baja is to drive your **car** or to rent a car in a major city, such as Mexicali. Most U.S. car rental agencies do not allow their cars to be taken into Mexico. Be sure to buy Mexican auto insurance before driving into Baja. A car is necessary in Tecate and San Felipe if you wish to explore the outlying areas, since these two towns are relatively small and provide limited services.

Rental vehicles. Four major rental agencies operate out of the Mexicali airport: *Avis, Budget, Hertz,* and *National* (Avis and Budget also have offices in the city). In the United States, toll-free phone numbers are 800–331–1212 for Avis, 800–527–0700 for Budget, 800–654–3131 for Hertz, and 800–227–7368 for National. In addition, four Mexican car rental agencies make both large American cars and European imports available in Mexicali at the airport: *Central Rent, Ipri-Rent, Plani-Rent,* and *Rentautos de Baja California.*

Taxis. Taxis are easy to find in downtown Mexicali, especially at the intersection of Azueta and Reforma, where dozens of cabs line up. Make sure you negotiate your fare before the start of the trip. Taxis are less available in Tecate and San Felipe, but your hotel should be able to arrange one for you if you wish to explore outside the town.

Buses. The municipal bus service is frequent in Mexicali; there is always a bus waiting in line on Reforma near Melgar. Several bus lines operate out of Mexicali, with service to Tecate and San Felipe. (See *How to Get There* above).

SEASONAL EVENTS. February is the month in San Felipe for *carnaval,* a *Mardi Gras* celebrated before Lent. **March** is the month for the appetizing *Mexicali Chinese Food Festival.* **April** brings the popular *Tecate-to-Ensenada Bike Race,* growing larger each year. **July** heralds the *Tecate Fair,* which runs during the first two weeks of the month. **September** is the month in which Mexico celebrates its *independence.* Mexicali provides fireworks on the night of the 15th, followed by parades and fiestas on the 16th. **October** brings the *Tecate Pamplonada,* a scaled-down version of the running of the bulls in Pamplona, Spain; these huge beasts actually stampede through town to the bullring. Mexicali's annual fair, the *Fiestas del Sol,* is held this month, along with the *San Felipe Bicycle Ride,* which begins in Mexicali with an overnight stop in La Ventana in the desert.

TOURIST INFORMATION. Obtaining pamphlets, maps, and brochures is easiest from travel agents in the United States. Tour operators, car rental firms, and Mexican automobile insurance agencies can provide adequate information. Hotels in Mexico sometimes offer printed information, but only on request. The government tourist offices listed below are open from 10 A.M. until 3 P.M. and 5 until 9 P.M., with no afternoon hours on Sunday.

Mexicali. The *Tourist Commission Office* is at Calle de Comercio 204 in the center of town. The Chamber of Commerce has a new information center at Lopéz Mateos and Camelias about one mile south of the border, not far from the State Theater.

Tecate. The *State Tourist Commission* office is at Callejón Libertad 1305, almost five blocks south of the border crossing. There is also a small office on the southeast end of the main park in a row of other government buildings.

San Felipe. The *Tourist Commission* is a few blocks south of the center of town on Av. Mar de Cortés.

USEFUL ADDRESSES. Mexicali. *Aeroméxico,* Centro Civico, on Independencia just north of Boulevard Anahuac, across from the bullring. *Mexicana,* Madero 833. *Police,* Centro Civico. *Hospital,* Durango and Salina Cruz. *Postoffice,* Madero 491.

Tecate. *Police,* Ortiz Rubio and Libertad. *Hospital,* Venustiano Carranza (no number). *Postoffice,* Revolución and Cárdenas.

TOURS. *Baja Tours* (619–357–0200) in Calexico, CA, operates trips to San Felipe with sightseeing in Mexicali on the way; prices vary according to accommodations, length of stay, and whether fishing is included.

There are also a handful of tourist agencies in Mexicali in which tour information on northeastern Baja can be found; try *Tamez Tours* at Reforma 907 (4–2468) or *Aero-Olympico Tours* at Madero 641 (2–5025).

PARKS AND GARDENS. Mexicali. *Parque Obregón* at Reforma and Irigoyen, and *Parque Constitución* at Av. Mexico and Zuazua are the only two parks in downtown Mexicali. Both are attractive and restful during the day. Obregón is one street away from the border, next to the House of Culture; Constitución is deeper in the downtown area, built around a large music pavilion. The *Mexicali Zoo* is in the *Bosque de la Ciudad* (city park), south of town; the entrance is at the south end of Calle Victoria, between Cárdenas and Independencia. This is a pleasant zoo, but hardly to be compared with its counterparts in many other Mexican cities. Adjoining this park is *Laguna Xochimilco* (the Mexicali reservoir), where there are picnic facilities and pedal-boat rentals. *Laguna Salada,* 13 miles west of town, is an impressive desert lake with boating and picnic facilities and camping at Centinela Beach just off the highway across from the deserted Pemex station.

San Felipe. There is a nice waterfront here, with a seawall, commemorative plaques, and the occasional thatched *palapas.* The lighthouse behind the Shrine of the Virgin of Guadalupe, overlooking the Sea of Cortés and San Felipe Bay, is worth viewing.

Tecate. *Parque Hidalgo,* in the center of town, is a typical Mexican village plaza, similar to the *zócalos* found throughout Mexico. Parque López Mateos on Mexico 3 south of town is the site for dance and band concerts on summer evenings.

 SPORTS. Along the border, the main sporting events are baseball games, bullfights, and *charreadas* (Mexican rodeos). Cockfights are popular during fiestas. Along the coast, fishing is the major sport.

MEXICALI

Bullfights are usually held twice a month from October through May at the Califia Bullring, near the Civic Center on Independencia. At press time, the bullring was closed because of a labor dispute and some sanitation problems. For information, call 2–9795.

Charreadas, the fast-paced Mexican rodeos, are usually held on Sundays once a month during the winter in one of the town's two rings. Call 8–2330 or 8–2320 for information.

Baseball is played by Mexicali's team in the Triple A Pacific League from mid-October through December. Many American players sharpen their talents in this league during their off-season, and the games are exciting, to say the least. Baseball is gaining popularity in Baja. For more information, call 2–4709.

Golf may be enjoyed at the country club in the Campeche subdivision on Hwy. 3 south of town. The 18-hole course is open throughout the year. Although this is a private club, anyone can use the course. Green fees are about $10. For information, call 6–7170.

SAN FELIPE

Fishing is the big sport here, and the Sea of Cortés offers plentiful sea bass, snapper, yellowtail, and other game fish. *Baja Tours,* Box 5557, Calexico, CA 92231 (619–357–0200), runs trips from the border with 2 nights in San Felipe. *The Bent Rod* at 715 El Camino Real, Tustin, CA 92680 (714–838–1420), organizes 5 days on the Sea of Cortés, departing from San Felipe on Saturday mornings aboard 75-foot boats. *Hibet Travel and Tours,* with offices in El Centro, CA, and Mexicali, Baja, can provide additional information on fishing in Baja. In the United States, call 619–353–1695; in Mexicali, call 4–1033.

MUSEUMS AND GALLERIES. *The State Library* in Mexicali at Obregón and Av. E often doubles as a museum of art, holding exhibitions of paintings and sculpture. Particularly interesting is the *Regional Museum* at Reforma 1998 near Calle L. Administered by the Autonomous University of Baja California, this museum provides a comprehensive introduction to the natural and cultural history of Baja. Exhibits on indigenous Indian tribes, missions, and wildlife are especially good. Closed on Mondays.

STAGE, MUSIC, DANCE, FILM. Mexicali's *Teatro del Estado* (State Theater) is located on López Mateos near the government tourist center. Stage hits from Mexico City are often performed, and dance troupes and musical groups, both classical and modern, are often featured. Much of the entertainment would be hard to find in the United States, particularly the excellent jazz bands and dance troupes from Cuba and Russia.

SHOPPING. Northeast Baja is not known as the shopper's paradise. The typical rash of curios is noticeably absent in Tecate, and the curios found in Mexicali are tawdry and shopworn. In San Felipe, you can find the usual blankets, onyx chess sets, and cheap sombreros, but at higher prices than they would be found elsewhere. *Baldini Importers,* at the corner of Calle F and Reforma, in Mexicali, offers a nice selection of imported items, ranging from perfumes and cosmetics to porcelain and cut crystal. There are also dozens of shoe stores in Mexicali; *Tres Hermanos* and *Canada* are the best (boots are a bargain if the right size can be found). Two *outdoor markets* sell produce in Mexicali, one at Obregón and Calle del Comercio and the other at the end of Calle Aldama, a block south of Parque Constitución.

SPECIAL-INTEREST SIGHTSEEING. The Bahia de los Angeles, located over 400 miles from the border, is one of the most beautiful spots on the entire peninsula. For fishing, relaxation, and concentrated getting away from it all, there are few places in Baja that can top this secluded gulf coast paradise. To get there, take Mexican Hwy. 1 south from Tijuana through Ensenada and the Santo Tomás Valley, past the Pacific coast towns of Colonet and San Quintin, turning inland at El Rosario, through Cataviña to the junction 8 miles north of Punta Prieta. The turnoff is paved and easily passable by passenger vehicles. The bay is backed by mountains, and there are a number of islands offshore. The sportfishing is spectacular, and boats can be rented; there are excellent beds of oysters and clams offshore. Trips to the nearby islands are also recommended. The two motels are good, and reservations should be made, particularly during the peak season from late October until May. *Casa Díaz* is adequate, built of rough-hewn stone, offering 15 units and electricity until 9 P.M. (Mailing address: Apartado Postal 579, Ensenada, B.C.) The *Villa Vitta Motel*

is nice looking and modern. The 40 units have air-conditioning, and the motel provides guide service for fishing. (Reservations: Jimsair, 2904 Pacific Hwy., San Diego, CA 92101; 619–298–7704.

On Mexican Hwy. 2 between Tecate and Mexicali, there are turnoffs for two fascinating spots, the **Parque Nacional Constitución de 1857,** and **Cañyon de Guadalupe.** Only the most adventurous and properly equipped travelers should challenge the dirt roads leading to these areas. West of Tecate, the same road that leads to the Hotel Santa Veronica eventually passes through the national park, the surprisingly beautiful Laguna Hanson, and ends in Los Ojos, connecting with Mexican Hwy. 3 that runs east and west from Ensenada to San Felipe. If you take this side trip, be sure to carry extra gas, water, and food. The sprawling pine forests, the verdant meadows, and the pleasant lake make this a good place for hiking and camping. The turnoff for Cañyon de Guadalupe is 16 miles east toward Mexicali from the top of the La Rumerosa grade; at the Pemex station, turn right and follow the signs to Cantu Palms (19 miles from the highway) and Cañon de Guadalupe (35 miles from the highway). The Cocopah Indians once congregated in Cantu Palms, and evidence of their presence—petroglyphs (rock carvings) and grinding holes—can still be found among the rocks. This canyon is beautiful, but not as startling as Cañyon de Guadalupe with its hot springs and cool stream that rushes in from the nearby 6,000-foot-high mountains. Palm trees abound in this oasislike setting, and the campground can accommodate about 30 campers. It is recommended that you visit this area in the spring, when the flowers are blooming and the weather is not yet unbearably hot.

Between San Felipe and Ensenada, south of Mexico Hwy. 3, lies the **Sierra de San Pedro Mártir National Park.** In this mountain range stands the highest peak in Baja, Picacho del Diablo, at over 10,000 feet. Snow atop this peak can sometimes be seen from both Pacific and gulf coast vantage points. The high plateau in this area contains thick forests and streams that run all year through mountain meadows. The Mexican government has an observatory here, where, some say, the air is clearer than anywhere else in the world and perfect for serious astronomers. There are two popular places to stay in this area, the **Meling Ranch** and **Mike's Sky Rancho.** About 88 miles east of Ensenada on Mexican Hwy. 3 (also known as Baja California 16), a dirt-road turnoff leads 21 miles to Mike's Sky Rancho, a resort with cabins, a pool, bar, cafe, and horses. About 11 miles farther south on this road lies the Meling Ranch—a working cattle operation that takes up to 12 guests at a time. From here, pack trips are arranged into the mountains. To avoid winter storms, plan trips from May through October. For reservations at either ranch, write 874 Hollister, Sp. 48, San Diego, CA 92154, or call 619–423–2934.

 NIGHTLIFE. In **Mexicali,** entertainment is provided nightly in the Lucerna and Holiday Inn hotels, as well as at several places along Benito Juárez, including the *Cadillac, El Zarape,* and *Chic's.* Also on Juárez is *La*

Capilla, a disco with live entertainment, and *El Guaycura.* The area by the major hotels has the *Studio 54 Disco* and a quieter spot called *El Piano Bar.*

San Felipe hotels provide music for dancing (usually recorded) on weekends, while live country music blasts at *Cantamar.*

Tecate, for all its sleepy, provincial atmosphere, has a disco called *Los Candiles* at Hidalgo 327 and another at *La Hacienda* on Benito Juárez 861. *El Tucan Bar* at Benito Juárez and Esteban Cantu often has live entertainment.

TIJUANA

Bustling International Border City

by
MARIBETH MELLIN

Just 20 miles south of San Diego, the eighth largest city in the United States, lies Mexico's third largest city, Tijuana. A teeming metropolis of more than 1,000,000 residents, Tijuana can hardly be called a border town. It is a city, yet so unlike a U.S. city that the traveler feels instantly immersed in a foreign country. The language is Spanish, often called "Spanglish" for the local mix of Spanish and English spoken by residents and visitors. The currency is the peso, which fluctuates in value. The residents come from all over Mexico and Central America. The visitors come from everywhere. Tijuana's promoters like to call it "the most visited city in the world."

Tijuana's international border is the busiest and often the most troublesome border to the United States. Border officials know there is no way to stem the flow north and south. Tijuana attracts hundreds of new Mexican residents a week, drawn to border-town wages that far exceed the wages in their native towns. For many newcomers, Tijuana is the last stop before their eventual departure for a new homeland in the United States. The border fence that stretches through the canyons and hills between Tijuana and California is filled with holes the size of people; helicopters and Jeeps patrol these barren landscapes, attempting to deter illegal immigration. But illegal immigrants are not among the thousands who travel through the border crossings each day. Tijuana also attracts hordes of visitors, who come to work and play. Tourism in Tijuana and the neighboring Rosarito Beach and Ensenada practically doubles each year and is easily the area's leading industry. In this sense, Tijuana is most assuredly a border town.

American Influence

As foreign as Tijuana may seem to the visitor, it is steeped in American influence. The border area has served as a gigantic recreation center for southern Californians since the turn of the century. Before then, it was a ranch, populated by a few hundred Mexicans. In 1911, a group of Americans invaded the area and attempted to set up an independent republic; they were quickly driven out by Mexican soldiers.

When Prohibition hit the United States in the 1920s, Tijuana boomed. The spectacular Agua Caliente Racetrack and Casino opened in about the same time as the Rosarito Beach Hotel and Ensenada's Pacífico Riviera Casino were built. Americans seeking alcohol, gambling, and more fun than they could find in the United States flocked across the border, spreading money to fire the region's growth. Tijuana became the entry spot for what some termed a "sinful, seamy playground," frequented by Hollywood playboys and the idle rich. Then Prohibition was repealed, Mexico outlawed gambling, and Tijuana's fortunes dwindled. The Agua Caliente Resort fell into ruin and has never been revived.

The flow of travelers from the North slowed to a trickle for a while, but Tijuana still captivated those in search of the sort of fun that was illegal and frowned upon at home. The ever-growing presence of servicemen in San Diego, particularly during war times, kept the town's sordid reputation growing; visitors of a different adventuresome bent kept pushing inward and southward, discovering new scenes, lifestyles, and cultures.

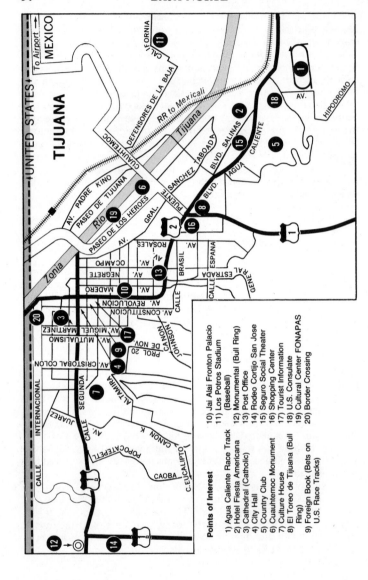

Points of Interest

1) Agua Caliente Race Track
2) Hotel Fiesta Americana
3) Cathedral (Catholic)
4) City Hall
5) Country Club
6) Cuauhtemoc Monument
7) Culture House
8) El Toreo de Tijuana (Bull Ring)
9) Foreign Book (Bets on U.S. Race Tracks)
10) Jai Alai Fronton Palacio
11) Los Potros Stadium (Baseball)
12) Monumental (Bull Ring)
13) Post Office
14) Rodeo Cortijo San Jose
15) Seguro Social Theater
16) Shopping Center
17) Tourist Information
18) U.S. Consulate
19) Cultural Center FONAPAS
20) Border Crossing

"Sin City" Reputation Wanes

Until the toll highway to Ensenada was finished in 1967, travelers going south drove straight through downtown Tijuana, stopping along Avenida Revolución and the side streets for supplies and souvenirs. The free road, still used by those with plenty of time for wandering, curved over the hills through barren ranch land, and eventually turned west to the coast at Rosarito Beach. The toll road, which now bypasses downtown (if you follow the signs carefully), cut down on the traffic through the hills that now are full-sized towns, called *colonias*. Downtown Tijuana wasn't affected much by the toll road, since it took many more years to complete the bypass, and continued carrying on as "sin city" until the early 1970s, when local politicians and businessmen began eyeing Tijuana's resources. From then on, Tijuana paid serious attention to tourism.

Throughout the 1970s and 80s, Tijuana's population and tourism have exploded. In 1970, Tijuana's population was under 300,000; today, it is over 1,000,000. The city has spread into canyons and dry riverbeds, over hillsides, and ocean cliffs. It is crowded, services are constantly affected, and the government is forever dealing with natural disasters such as floods. Many of its residents live in total poverty, in cardboard shacks far from electricity and running water, but many are prosperous. Tijuana continues to attract more and more businesses and factories that employ thousands of Tijuana's residents. Originally, many of the companies operating in Tijuana were based in the United States; now, the Japanese are leading manufacturers in the area.

Tourism Vigorously Courted

Tourism creates jobs and bolsters Tijuana's fragile economy. The city's leaders realize this, and have worked hard to attract visitors. Avenida Revolución, the main street that once housed brothels and bars, is lined with shops and restaurants, all catering to tourists. Brick-lined arcades, park benches, and shade trees encourage tourists to rest and watch the passing scene. Shopping is an adventure; the shopkeepers call to shoppers from their doorways, offering low prices. The restaurants and bars serve excellent inexpensive meals and drinks, which the tourists love. Many of Tijuana's tourists are regulars, who patronize their favorite shops and restaurants. San Diegans often travel south of the border just for dinner and become neighbors of a sort, making lifelong friends in Tijuana.

The Cultural Center speaks for Tijuana's presence as Baja Norte's leading city for in tourism and business. As the capital of Baja Norte,

Mexicali is the state's civic center, but Tijuana is its cultural soul. The Cultural Center's exhibits of Mexican history are the perfect introduction for the thousands of visitors who first taste Mexico at the border. It is possible to wander past the models of Mayan and Aztec temples, Indian pueblos, and missions and get a true sense of the scope of Mexico's land, people, and history. In a way, Tijuana is representative of all Mexico: its variety of cultures, arts, crafts, foods, and faces. Surely, every Mexican state is represented in the faces of the populace.

"The More the Change . . . "

Tijuana's tourist attractions have remained much the same throughout the century. Gambling may be illegal, but horseracing is legal and popular. The recently renovated Agua Caliente Racetrack speaks of that glamorous decade when Hollywood stars gambled and played at the Agua Caliente Resort. The Frontón Palacio (jai alai palace) is equally fantastic, with its fast-paced games, cheering fans, and palatial edifice. Some of Mexico's greatest bullfighters appear at the oceanfront bullring; some of the country's greatest musicians and dancers perform at the Cultural Center. And there are restaurants, more than anyone could count. Eating and drinking are among Tijuana's greatest attractions. A few of the best restaurants from the 1920s and '30s still attract a steady clientele with their excellent international cuisine and reasonable prices. On a more moderate scale, there are scores of seafood restaurants and kitchens that serve great Mexican food, unadulterated for American tastes. Avenida Revolución is like one huge cafeteria, with places for every taste and budget. At night, the streetlife gets rowdy, with tourists demonstrating the effects of Mexican margaritas (much stronger than those in the North).

Shopping is Tijuana's other main draw. From the moment you cross the border, the bartering begins. If you walk downtown, you pass row after row of curio stands; if you drive, workers will run out from auto body shops to place bids on new paint or upholstery for your car. All along Avenida Revolución and its side streets, shops sell everything from tequila to Tiffany lamps; serious shoppers can spend a full day searching and bartering for their item of choice. Shopping has become a major attraction in other areas of the city as well. Shopping centers and malls seem to be multiplying along Boulevard Agua Caliente, near the country club and racetrack. The neighborhoods above the boulevard in Chapultepec Hills are the wealthiest in town; here, one sees Tijuana's history reflected in grand mansions.

Area Gets Glamour

The Rio Tijuana area is quickly becoming the city's *Zona Rosa,* it's glamourous zone. The area is not far from the border, just past the dry riverbed of the Tijuana River along Paseo de los Héroes. This boulevard is one of the main thoroughfares in the city, with large statues of historical figures, including Abraham Lincoln, in the center of the *gloriettas* (traffic circles). Plaza Rio Tijuana, built a few years back, was Tijuana's first major shopping center. It is an enormous affair, with good restaurants, major department stores, and hundreds of shops. The plaza has become a central square of sorts, where holiday fiestas are sometimes held. The Cultural Center is within easy walking distance; the two combined make a pleasant day's outing. Smaller shopping centers are opening all along Paseo de los Héroes; Plaza Fiesta and Plaza de los Zapatos are two of the finest. The Playas Tijuana area, at the oceanfront, is slated for development next. Now the area is a mix of modest neighborhoods and a few restaurants and hotels. The beaches are long and pleasant and visited mostly by locals.

As a tourist spot, Tijuana is visited mainly on day trips or used as a layover for trips farther into Mexico. Southern Californians are accustomed to taking advantage of the lower airfares into Mexico from the Tijuana airport; if you are planning a trip farther into Mexico, you might want to compare the rates from Tijuana. There are plenty of good-quality hotels in the city, and taxis to and from the airport are economical. Some of the hotels offer reduced-rate weekend packages to lure travelers who normally just pass through town on their way to the coast. With tourism predicted to double again in the next few years, Tijuana is sure to continue adding more and more luxury hotels and attractions.

PRACTICAL INFORMATION FOR TIJUANA

HOW TO GET THERE. Tijuana is located just 18 miles south of San Diego, at the busiest international border of the United States. The city can be reached by bus, plane, train, or car; from there, one has the option of traveling farther into Baja by bus or car. Visitors to this area do not need tourist cards if they are staying fewer than 72 hours and traveling no farther than 10 miles south of Ensenada.

By Car. U.S. Interstates 5 and 805 end at the border crossing in San Ysidro; Hwy. 117 leads from I–5 and I–805 to the newer Tijuana border crossing at Otay

Mesa, near the Tijuana airport. Those who visit Tijuana for the day often prefer to park their cars on the U.S. side and walk across the border. Those who drive into Tijuana should purchase Mexican auto insurance, available at many stands along the last exit before the border crossing. On holidays and weekends, there can be a wait at the border when traveling into Mexico; there is almost always a wait coming back into the United States.

By Train. The San Diego Trolley leaves the San Diego Depot downtown every 15 minutes during the day and every 30 minutes after 7:30 P.M. and passes through National City, Chula Vista, and San Ysidro on its way to the border. The trip costs $1.50 and takes about 45 minutes. There are **taxis** on the Mexican side of the border to take you to your destination.

By Plane. *Aeroméxico* and *Mexicana* fly into the Tijuana airport from cities in California and Texas (not from San Diego). Both airlines and *Aero California* fly from Tijuana to other points in Mexico.

By Bus. *Greyhound* serves Tijuana from Los Angeles (213–620–1200) and San Diego (619–239–9171) several times a day. *Mexicoach* (619–232–5049) has several departures from the San Diego Depot to Tijuana. Within Mexico, *Autotransportes de Baja California* and *Tres Estrellas* link Tijuana with other points in Baja. The *Tijuana Central Bus Station* is at Av. Madero and Calle 2 (6–9515).

EMERGENCY TELEPHONE NUMBERS. To call Tijuana from the United States, dial 70, then the area code 668 and the number. To call the United States from Tijuana, dial 95, the area code, and the number. Pay phones in Tijuana cost one peso. A new three-digit emergency dialing system is in effect throughout Baja Norte; *Police,* 134; *Red Cross,* 132; *Fire,* 136. The *Convention and Tourism Bureau* number is 4–2173; the *U.S. Consulate* number is 6–3886.

HOTELS. Tijuana's hotels are clustered in downtown, along Av. Revolución, near the country club on Blvd. Agua Caliente, and in the Rio Tijuana area on Paseo de los Héroes. There are ample accommodations for all price levels, and a number of new hotels are under construction. The *Tijuana Convention and Tourism Bureau* has an office in San Diego that can reserve hotel rooms; call or write Tijuana/Baja Information, 7860 Mission Center Court 202, San Diego, CA 92108; 619–299–8518; 800–522–1516 in California. Categories determined by price for a double room are as follows: *Deluxe,* over $40; *Expensive,* $30–$40; *Moderate,* over $25–$30; and *Inexpensive,* under $25.

Deluxe

Fiesta Americana. Blvd. Agua Caliente 4558; 1–7000 or 800–223–2332. A luxurious high-rise hotel near the racetrack and country club with 430 large, comfortable rooms and a nightclub, specialty restaurant, coffee shop, health club, tennis courts, pool, and travel agency. The hotel often hosts receptions and parties for Tijuana's elite and is a glamorous place to visit for a drink or meal.

Expensive

Agua Caliente Valparaiso. Av. Via Oriente; 3–2908. A motel located by a mineral hot springs, with rooms and suites, restaurant, bar, and pool.

El Conquistador. Blvd. Agua Caliente 7000; 6–4801. The first tourist hotel in Tijuana, close to the racetrack and country club. The 110 rooms are plain, but the restaurant is good and the disco lively and there is a swim-up bar at the pool.

Lucerna. Blvd. Paseo de los Héroes and Av. Rodriguez; 6–1000. A charming, popular high-rise hotel with 178 rooms, 9 suites, a coffee shop and gourmet restaurant, live entertainment in the lounge, a large pool in a pleasantly landscaped garden, and a good travel agent at a desk in the lobby.

Palacio Azteca. Av. 16 de Septiembre 213; 6–5401. A 90–room semiresort operated by the owners of the Rosarito Beach Hotel. Lavish rooftop restaurant, night club, coffee shop, pool.

Paraíso Raddison. Blvd. Agua Caliente 1; 1–7200. A high-rise hotel with strong tourism and convention business; 200 rooms, 36 suites, a pool, Jacuzzi, sauna, spa, restaurant, bar, beauty salon, and car rental.

Moderate

Caesar. Av. Revolución 827; 6–1616. Downtown and noisy, famed for its long bar and for being the home of the Caesar salad. The restaurant is fair; the rooms are somewhat rundown.

Country Club Motor Hotel. Av. Tapachula 1; 6–2301. A motel close to the golf course and race track, with 100 rooms, a restaurant, bar, sauna, and pool.

La Mesa Inn. Blvd. Díaz Ordáz 50; 1–6522; 905–525–9081 in the United States. A Best Western hotel with 95 plainly furnished rooms, but a nice bar, coffee shop, and pool.

La Sierra. Carretera Ensenada Km 1; 6–1601. A 60-unit motel with restaurant, bar, and pool. Modest but a good value.

La Villa de Zaragoza. Av. Madero 1120; 5–1832. A fairly new motel-like establishment, with a good downtown location by the Frontón Palaciot (jai alai palace) a block from Av. Revolución.

Inexpensive

Centauro Hotel. Blvd. Díaz Ordáz 4104; 6–9650. A small hotel with 39 rooms, by the racetrack.

León. Calle 7 and Av. Revolución; 5–6320. A 40–room downtown hotel, just off Revolución. Clean and in the middle of the action, but a bit less noisy than those on Revolución.

Motel Cortés. Paseo de Playas Tijuana 226; 0–6617. A small motel with 51 rooms near the beach area; air-conditioning, bar, and restaurant.

Motel La Joya. Blvd. Díaz Ordáz 2900; 9–1360. No restaurant or bar, but 50 clean rooms, near the racetrack.

DINING OUT. There is no shortage of good eating in Tijuana, from the taco stands on the street to gourmet French and Continental restaurants. The seafood is great; beef and pork are common, grilled and marinated as *carne asada* and *carnitas.* Pheasant, quail, rabbit, and duck are popular in the more expensive places. Lobster and shrimp *Puerto Nuevo style* (grilled and served with beans, rice, and tortillas) are served in restaurants modeled after those at the popular seaside fishing village south of Rosarito. Prices are low in Tijuana; the price for a dinner without tax and beverage averages, for *Expensive,* $15; *Moderate,* $8; and *Inexpensive,* $5. Most of the expensive and moderate restaurants accept credit cards. Abbreviations for credit cards are AE, American Express; DC, Diners Club; MC, MasterCard; and V, Visa.

Expensive

La Escondida. Av. Santa Monica 1; 1–4458. A beautiful restaurant in an old hacienda. The menu features unusual international specialties: a gourmet dining experience. AE, MC, V.

Puerta del Sol. Blvd. Sánchez Taboada 9, Rio Tijuana area; 4–2020. An Argentinian-style steak house featuring baby kid, *churrasco,* and baby beef; pleasant surroundings with Latin American folk music. AE, DC, MC, V.

Reno's. Av. Revolución at Calle 8; 5–9210. Long established; a favorite steak and seafood house for veteran visitors. AE, DC, MC, V.

Moderate

El Abajeno. Agua Caliente 101; 5–6980. A classic Mexican restaurant in an old hacienda; tops for *carne asada,* tamales, and enchiladas, with hot, hot salsa. Mariachi music and a piano bar. DC, MC, V.

Amito's. Calles Brasil and Fresnillo (a block from Agua Caliente); 4–1013. One of several Italian restaurants and possibly the best.

La Langosta Loca. Revolución 914; 5–1313. An attractive seafood house specializing in Pacific lobster and Mexican specialties. AE, DC, MC, V.

La Lena. Blvd. Agua Caliente 4560; 6–2920. A large, new place with a central grill, where chefs prepare unusual beef dishes, such as *gaonera,* a filet of beef stuffed with cheese and guacamole.

Las Macetas. Tijuana Cultural Center; 4–1132. A Mexican restaurant for American tastes; highly recommended for its Sunday brunch, 10 A.M.–2 P.M.

Margarita's Village. Av. Revolución at Calle 3; 85–7362. Twelve flavors of margaritas, baked kid, and other Mexican dishes served by singing waiters. Inexpensive weekend buffet. AE, DC, MC, V.

El Meson Espanol. Calle 4, 1838; 6–2860. Tijuana's Spanish inn, a good place to order paella and other Iberian dishes.

Pedrin's. Av. Revolución 1115; 5–4052. One of Tijuana's best seafood restaurants, located across the street from the Frontón Palacio. The tables along the second-story windows overlooking Av. Revolución are the nicest. The menu includes several different lobster and shrimp dishes, fresh fish, and abalone.

Popeye's. Av. Lopéz Portillo 112; 3–1946. One of few restaurants near the Otay Mesa border crossing; branch of a popular seafood restaurant in Ensenada. Fresh fish, lobster, and turtle.

Rodeo. Blvd. Salinas 1647; 6–5640. An American-style steak house made up like the set of a Hollywood movie. A fun place, though the steaks are none too good.

Tia Juana Tilly's. Av. Revolución at Calle Septima; 85–6024. Tijuana's first Carlos Anderson restaurant, next door to the Frontón Palacio, with a decor reminiscent of certain U.S. chain restaurants. The food is generous and well prepared. Others in the chain are **Tilly's Fifth Avenue,** catty-corner to the original on Revolución, and the **Guadalajara Grill** in the Rio Tijuana area. AE, DC, MC, V.

Inexpensive

Bol Corona. Av. Revolución 520; 5–4708. Popular since its inception in 1934. The bar is a lively place; the restaurant serves excellent traditional Mexican food in pleasant surroundings.

Carnitas Uruapan. Blvd. Díaz Ordáz 550; 1–6181. An enormous, rundown restaurant where the main attraction is *carnitas,* marinated pork served with homemade tortillas, salsa, cilantro, guacamole, onions, and plenty of beer. Patrons mingle at long wooden tables.

Chiki Jai. Av. Revolución and Calle 7; no phone. A tiny Basque place, redolent of the blue cheese served on each table; popular for dishes like squid and fresh fish.

Denny's. Av. Revolución 148; 6–3788. Burgers and fries, along with tacos and tostadas.

La Especial. Av. Revolución 770; 5–6654. Located at the foot of the stairs leading to an underground shopping arcade, this restaurant is a traditional favorite for down-home Mexican cooking at low prices.

Yogurt Vision. Calle 2, 2034; no phone. Healthy snacks, natural shakes, fruit salads, and frozen yogurt.

HOW TO GET AROUND. Those spending just a day in Tijuana are advised to park their cars on the U.S. side of the border and walk or take taxis to their destinations. There is a large lot with scores of taxis just inside the border; from there you can reach the airport, the Cultural Center, the Rio area, or Av. Revolución for under $5. The 1-¼ mile walk to Av. Revolución is an easy one over the pedestrian bypass, past vendors and restaurants. Returning to the United States is more difficult than going into Mexico; at times, the wait at the border can be 2 hours if you are driving. The lines are usually shorter at the Otay Mesa crossing, which is about 10 miles from downtown, near the airport.

By Car. There are plenty of signs at the border to lead you to the main highways and downtown, but once you hit the surface streets, Tijuana can be confusing. There are parking lots along Revolución and at most major attractions; it is advisable to leave your car in a guarded lot. If you park on the street, pay attention to the signs. Your license plates will be removed if you park illegally. Always get Mexican auto insurance before crossing the border.

Rental vehicles. The larger U.S. rental agencies have bureaus in Tijuana at the International Airport. Offices in town include the following:

Avis, Av. Agua Caliente 3310; 6–4004.

Budget, Paseo de los Héroes 77; 4–0253.

National, Av. Agua Caliente 5000; 6–2103.

By Taxi. Taxis are plentiful and cheap in Tijuana. Fares to all parts of the city should be less than $5 per person; be sure to agree on the price before the car starts moving.

By Bus. The central bus station is at Calle 2 and Av. Madero; 6–9515. *Tres Estrellas* and *Autotransportes de Baja California* travel throughout Baja.

 SEASONAL EVENTS. The border areas tend to celebrate Mexican and U.S. holidays. In late **October** and early **November,** the traditional *Dia de Muerte,* or Day of the Dead, rituals blend with costume parties and carved pumpkins. *Christmas* is a bustling tourist holiday with rampant commercialism along the Revolución strip. The traditions of the many states and countries represented in Tijuana's populace are more visible in the churches and *colonias,* or neighborhoods. *Cinco de Mayo* **(May** 5) is more popular with the tourists than with the locals; most celebrations center on drinking margaritas and getting rowdy. Also in May is the annual *Tijuana Home Tour,* a day-long tour of some of the area's finest homes. In **August,** the *Tijuana Fair,* called "Baja California on the March," is held by the Cultural Center in the fairgrounds in the Rio area. Manufacturers and merchants from throughout Mexico demonstrate their wares, alongside midway booths, taco stands, and amusement-park rides. On **September** 15 and 16, Tijuana celebrates Mexico's independence with parades, fiestas, and fireworks.

 TOURIST INFORMATION. Tijuana's *Convention and Tourist Bureau* has made a concerned effort to assist the thousands of travelers who visit the area. In the United States, the bureau operates a San Diego office that handles information and reservations. Call or write Tijuana/Baja Information, 7860 Mission Center Court, 202, San Diego, CA 92108; 619–299–8518, or 800–522–1516 in California. A tourism office just after the border crossing has maps, newspapers, and English-speaking clerks. The *Chamber of Commerce* is located at Av. Revolución and Calle 1; 5–8472. Other tourist information booths are located at the foot of Calle 1, just after the pedestrian overpass across the border; at the airport; and at the intersection of Av. Revolución and Calle 4. *Baja Reservations,* 3939 La Salle St., San Diego, CA 92110 (619–222–9099) can reserve hotel rooms throughout Baja.

TOURS. Tours of Tijuana and Baja are available through *El Paseo Tours*, 563 Third Ave., Chula Vista, CA 92010; 619–585–7495.

 PARKS AND GARDENS. The Rio Tijuana area, although not strictly a park, is lined with grassy medians, trees, and occasional sidewalks that lead from the Cultural Center to Plaza Rio Tijuana. *Guerrero Park,* at Calle 3 and Av. F, is Tijuana's one city park, a couple of blocks of trees and lawn on the fringes of town, of no special interest.

 BEACHES. The *Playas Tijuana,* or Tijuana beach area, is located south of town off the toll road, Ensenada Cuota. The area has been under development for years, but, as yet, there are no major hotels and few restaurants in the area. The beaches are frequented primarily by locals; in the winter, the area is fairly deserted.

 SPORTS. Bullfights usually take place on Sunday afternoons and holidays at *El Torreo Tijuana,* on Agua Caliente just beyond the downtown area, and at the *Plaza Monumental,* the bullring by the sea in the Playas Tijuana area. The season runs May through September. For ticket information, call 4–2126 or 7–8519.

Jai alai games are played in the Frontón Palacio, a palatial building on Av. Revolución and Calle 8. This jai alai palace is an impressive old building, worth seeing even if you don't attend the games, which are held nightly except Thursdays; admission is $2. For information call 2–3636.

Horse racing at the recently refurbished elaborate *Agua Caliente Racetrack* is very popular. Horses race on weekend afternoons; greyhounds race nightly at 7:45 throughout the year. The new Jockey Club and restaurant are quite lavish. At the Foreign Book area, gamblers can bet on races taking place in California and being shown at Agua Caliente on TV monitors.

Charredas, Mexican rodeos in which amateur cowboy associations compete, take place at one of several rings around town on Sunday mornings. Call 4–2126 for information.

Golf is played at the *Tijuana Country Club,* which has attracted U.S. golfers since the 1920s. The club is located on Av. Agua Caliente, just east of downtown. Rental clubs, electric and hand carts, and caddies are available for the 18-hole course; open to the public. Call 619–299–8518 for information and reservations.

 MUSEUMS AND GALLERIES. The *Tijuana Cultural Center,* in the Rio Tijuana area, was designed by the same architect as the famous Anthropological Museum in Mexico City. Movies are shown in the domed theater; the museum houses a permanent anthropological and historical exhibit that is a great introduction to Mexico and mounts occasional art and anthropology exhibits. There is a good restaurant on the museum's lower floor, and the gift shop has an excellent selection of books on Mexican art and literature. The center is open 7 days a week, 9 A.M.–8:30 P.M. Call 619–299–8518 for information.

STAGE, MUSIC, DANCE, FILM. The *Tijuana Cultural Center* frequently hosts dance and music troupes from throughout Mexico and Latin America. The *Omnimax* domed theater has daily showings of *People of the Sun,* an overview of Mexican pre-Columbian history and culture. Call 619–299–8518 for information and schedules.

SHOPPING. Tijuana has always been considered to be a bargain hunter's haven and is gradually opening more and more shopping centers and stores with high-quality Mexican arts and crafts. The traditional shopping area is *Avenida Revolución,* from Calles 1 through 8. The avenue is lined with shops and arcades displaying a wide range of crafts and curios; among the most popular items are woolen rugs, serapes, shawls, silver jewelry, stained-glass lamps, tin mirrors, candelabra and trinkets, pottery dishes and planters, piñatas, paper flowers, leather goods, wooden and wicker furniture, and too many more items to enumerate. Sellers yell to shoppers in the street, cajoling them with promises of low prices. Bartering is expected. The *Drug Store, Maxim's, Dorian's,* and *Sara's* have a good selection of clothing and imported perfumes. *Tolan,* across the street from the Frontón Palacio on Revolución, has a good selection of high-quality crafts. The *Guess Store, Eduardo's,* and *Maya de Mexico* on Revolución have nice sportswear and resort wear, as does the *Ralph Lauren Polo* store on Calle 7. *La Gran Bota* on Revolución has great cowboy boots; *Espinosa,* on Revolución and at the Cultural Center, has fine silver, brass, and glass jewelry. Liquor stores dot the avenue; shoppers get good bargains on tequila, kahlua, and Mexican beers and wines, but may only bring one liter of alcohol back to the United States.

The Revolución shopping area has sprawled down Calle 1 to the foot of the pedestrian walkway from the border, until it is impossible to make it into town without burdening yourself with bargains. The shops in the new Plaza Revolución, at the corner of Calle 1 and Av. Revolución, have crafts of a higher quality than most. If you're spending a day shopping in Tijuana, it works well to begin shopping at the arcades at the end of the pedestrian border crossing walkway, gauging prices as you travel toward Revolución. You may find that the best bargains are close to the border and won't have to carry your rugs and *piñatas* around all day.

Playa Rio Tijuana, on Paseo de los Héroes in the Rio area near the Cultural Center, is a major shopping center with department stores, specialty shops, and restaurants. *Plaza Patria* is a new center on Blvd. Díaz Ordáz near the country club and Agua Caliente Racetrack; *Lamparas y Vitrales de Baja California,*

Tijuana's nicest stained-glass store, has an outlet here. *Plaza Fiesta,* another new center, is located on Blvd. Agua Caliente, across from Plaza Rio Tijuana. Plaza Fiesta has high-quality boutiques, jewelers, and artisans who work in stained glass. Next door, the *Plaza del Zapatos* holds over a dozen shoe stores with designer styles from throughout Mexico, and some shops with beautiful leather goods, including *La Herradura de Oro,* which sells fine hand-tooled saddles.

 NIGHTLIFE. Tijuana has toned down its "sin city" image, and much of the night action takes place at the Frontón Palacio and the racetrack. Several of the hotels, especially the Lucerna and Fiesta Americana, have entertainment. For those who want to experience the seamier side of old Tijuana, several places along Revolución, including *Sans Souci, Regio, Bambi,* and *Les Girls,* have strip shows around the clock.

There are also many bars and discos along Av. Revolución. The nicer ones for disco dancing are *Aloha* and *Regina. El Jardin del Tucan,* at Revolución and Calle 5, is a popular watering hole, day and night, because of its second-story terrace overlooking the action on Revolución. The bars at *Tijuana Tilly's, Bol Corona,* and *Guadalajara Grill* get quite lively at night. The *Oh! Disco,* on Paseo de los Héroes, is one of the most popular nightspots in town for the stylish set. Next door, *Uups!* is a video bar with phones at the tables so you can call the person you're eyeing across the bar.

ENSENADA

Charm Along a Rugged Coast

by
MARIBETH MELLIN

Ensenada is a major port city 65 miles south of Tijuana on Bahia de Todos Santos. The view along Hwy. 1 from Tijuana to Ensenada is spectacular; the paved highway often cuts a path between low mountains and high oceanside cliffs; exits lead to rural roads and oceanfront campgrounds. The Coronado Islands can be clearly seen off the coast of Tijuana; below Rosarito Beach, hang gliders lift off from towering sand dunes. Californians often weekend along this coastline; their new condos and homes appear in resort communities with impressive white villas. Still, much of the coastline is still wild and undeveloped.

A small fishing community, San Miguel, sits on the highway just north of Ensenada; the smell of fish from the canneries lining the highway is overpowering at times. The beach area between San Miguel and Ensenada has long been a haven of moderately priced oceanfront motels and trailer parks, but there are a few luxury hotels under construction now, with more being planned.

Like much of Baja, Ensenada has grown incredibly in the past five years, but it remains charming and picturesque. Juan Rodriguez Cabrillo first discovered the bay in 1542; Sebastian Vizcaino named the region Ensenada—Bahia de Todos Santos—in 1602. Since then, Ensenada has drawn discoverers and developers in a steady stream. First, ranchers made their homes on large spreads along the coast and up into the mountains. Gold miners followed, turning the area into a boom town during the late 1800s; after the mines were depleted, the area once again became pastoral. The harbor gradually grew into a major port for shipping agricultural goods from the ranches and farms in the valleys of Baja Norte. Now it is one of Mexico's largest seaports and has a thriving fishing fleet and fish-processing industry.

Bahia de Todos Santos

The city of Ensenada, the third largest in Baja, hugs the harbor of Bahia de Todos Santos with a long boardwalk lined with sportfishing charters, restaurants, and warehouses. On the northernmost point sits an indoor/outdoor fish market, with stand after stand selling fresh fish, seafood cocktails, and fish tacos. The market is packed on weekends with buyers and sellers; browsers may pick up some standard souvenirs and cheap food and take some photographs of some great scenes. Boulevard Costera runs along the waterfront from the market past the sportfishing pier; after the shops and shacks trickle out, there is a long stretch of palms and rocky coast next to the Plaza Cívica. The beautiful old Riviera del Pacífico, once a glamorous gambling hall and hotel, faces the palms and ocean and recalls the Ensenada of old, where movie stars and politicians from the United States and Mexico drove by in their limousines. Today, the coastal road is filled with Jeeps, vans, and recreational vehicles headed south to the Baja wilderness.

Ensenada's tourist zone is centered one block east of the waterfront along Av. López Mateos. High-rise hotels, souvenir shops, restaurants, and bars line the avenue from its beginning at the foot of the Chapultapec hills for eight blocks to the dry channel of the Arroyo de Ensenada. South of the riverbed is a row of inexpensive motels, across the street from the Tourist Office. The tourist zone spreads farther and farther each year toward `Avenida Juárez, Ensenada's true downtown, where the locals shop for furniture, clothing, and necessities.

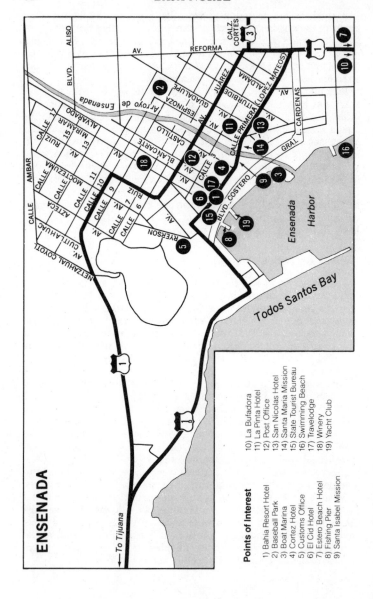

ENSENADA

→ To Tijuana

Todos Santos Bay

Ensenada Harbor

Points of Interest

1) Bahia Resort Hotel
2) Baseball Park
3) Boat Marina
4) Cortez Hotel
5) Customs Office
6) El Cid Hotel
7) Estero Beach Hotel
8) Fishing Pier
9) Santa Isabel Mission
10) La Bufadora
11) La Pinta Hotel
12) Post Office
13) San Nicolas Hotel
14) Santa Maria Mission
15) State Tourist Bureau
16) Swimming Beach
17) Travelodge
18) Winery
19) Yacht Club

The best way to grasp the expanse of Ensenada is to drive up Calle 2 into the Chapultapec hills to El Mirador, the viewpoint. From here, one can see the entire Bahia de Todos Santos, from the canneries of San Miguel south to Punta Banda and La Bufadora. The city of Ensenada spreads for miles below the hills; by checking the scene against a map, you can pretty well figure out how to get anywhere. Behind El Mirador, the hills rise even higher; here are the palatial homes of the town's wealthier citizens.

Weekend Retreat

Ensenada is a popular weekend destination; many of the travelers are repeat visitors who stick with their favorite hotels, shops, and restaurants. The beaches north and south of town are good for swimming, sunning, and surfing; there are no beaches in Ensenada proper. Many hotels have swimming pools; relaxation and tanning are popular sports. Ensenada turns into a real party town on holiday weekends when the young, rowdy crowd spreads from Hussong's Cantina into the streets. Many hotels have strict rules about having guests and alcoholic beverages in the rooms (one look at the crowd and you can understand why). Be sure to ask for a room far from the hotel's center if you're planning to sleep rather than party.

Ensenada is the best shopping town in Baja Norte, with elegant stores carrying imports from Mexico's leading crafts centers and dozens of storefronts selling wool blankets, serapes, plaster statues, and colorful papier-mâché birds. Leather goods are popular and of good quality. The liquor stores contain the usual array of Mexican beer and liquors but also have a good selection of wines from the excellent local vineyards and wineries.

The hillsides and valleys outside Ensenada are known for their grapes and olives; many wineries have tours that can be arranged through hotels in Ensenada. The Santo Tomás Winery is located in town and has tours daily except Sunday. The Cetto and Calafia wineries are located in the Guadalupe Valley, on Hwy. 3 toward Tecate. The valley is about a 30-minute drive from Ensenada on a good paved highway that runs into the hills past cattle ranches and orchards. In San Antonio de Las Minas, about 15 minutes from Ensenada, there is the excellent gourmet Restaurante Mustafa; other than that, there's nothing to do along the road except marvel at the boulders, cliffs, and scenery. Valle Guadalupe has a few small markets and a Pemex station; Olivares Mexicanos, called the world's largest olive plantation with 120,000 trees, lies just outside the town. The Cetto and Calafia vineyards run for miles along the road toward Tecate. The drive is a pleasant half-day adventure, and the view coming back over the hills to the coast is spectacular.

Gushing Geyser

La Bufadora is an impressive blowhole in the coastal cliffs at Punta Banda, off Hwy. 1 at Maneadero, about 15 minutes south of Ensenada. The drive 12 miles west on Hwy. 23 is a slow and somewhat risky trip, but the scenery at the coast is worth the effort. The geyser here has been known to shoot as high as 75 feet; tourists gather on a concrete platform at the edge of the cliffs and take their chances with the water's spray. Small seafood restaurants, taco stands, and souvenir shacks line the road's end. Agua Caliente (hot springs), 20 miles southeast of Ensenada on Hwy. 3 has, besides its springs, a picnic ground open to the public. Parque Nacional Constitución de 1857 and Laguna Hanson are located on a dirt road off Hwy. 3.

Though you don't need a tourist card if you are staying in Ensenada for fewer than 72 hours, those traveling south of Ensenada will have to fill out tourist cards (using a birth certificate, passport, or voter's registration card for identification) and go through the checkpoint at Maneadero, a small farming community. The checkpoint is often closed; when open, a customs guard will wave you to the side of the road.

Rambling Ranchlands

The drive from here to Guerrero Negro, Baja California Sur's border town, is a solitary one, except during holidays. Hwy. 1 runs past small farming communities, huge ranches, and miles of uninterrupted chapparel. The Santo Tomás Valley, with the oldest vineyards in Baja, is about 15 minutes south of Maneadero on Hwy. 1. A rough dirt road leads west off Hwy. 1 to Puerto Santo Tomás on the coast and some private campgrounds. The Bradley's gas station near Colonet is famous for its antique glass reservoir pump. Less than 10 km south is the turnoff for the San Pedro Mártir National Park and Observatory, nearly 50 miles east on a rutted dirt road. Mike's Sky Ranch and the Meling Guest ranch, two isolated lodges, are located along this road.

San Quintin, 115 km south of Ensenada, is a busy farm town said to be the windiest spot in Baja. The fishing and hunting are good here, and the remains of a failed colonial settlement may be seen. The highway south runs through canyons, dry riverbeds, and desert filled with over 800 varieties of cactus and towering boulders. Cataviña has a gas station and a few small hotels; farther south are turnoffs for a dirt road to San Felipe and a better paved road to Bahia de Los Angeles. At the end of Baja Norte, 255 km from Ensenada, stands a 140-foot steel monument of an eagle, marking the border between the Baja states. The time changes from Pacific to mountain time as you cross the 28th parallel. Guerrero Negro, Baja Sur's northernmost town, with hotels and gas stations, is two km south. The area is most popular in the winter, when thousands of California gray whales migrate to the lagoons to give birth to their calves.

PRACTICAL INFORMATION FOR ENSENADA
AND POINTS SOUTH

 HOW TO GET THERE. Ensenada is about 60 miles south of Tijuana, on the Pacific coast. Though it is an important port city, it has only a small airstrip, called *Aeropuerto El Cipres,* for small private planes; call 6–6301. Most people who visit Ensenada drive their own cars. Tourist cards are required only if you are traveling south of Ensenada or staying longer than 72 hours.

By Car. Mexico Hwy. 1, called Ensenada Cuota (toll road), runs from the Tijuana border crossing to Ensenada along the coast; follow the Rosarito-Ensenada signs. The toll booths along the road accept U.S. and Mexican money; tolls are usually about 30 cents, and the entire one-way trip about $1.80. The road is excellent, though it has some hair-raising curves atop steep oceanside cliffs, and is best driven during daylight since the road is not lit at night. The Green Angels patrol the road in their green Jeeps and will assist with car breakdowns. (See *Facts at Your Fingertips* section.) Emergency telephones have recently been installed along the highway. The free road, called the Old Ensenada Highway, runs parallel to the toll road off and on, cutting east of the low hills along the coast. The free road doubles your traveling time and is sometimes rough.

By Bus. Ensenada can be reached by bus from Tijuana, Mexicali, and Mexico City. *Autotransportes de Baja California* and *Estrellas de Oro* travel throughout Baja, linking all the major cities. The bus station is at Av. Riveroll between Calles 10 and 11. For information, call 8–2322.

By Ship. Ensenada is a year-round port of call for Carnival Cruise Lines' *Azure Seas,* which sails from Los Angeles twice each week; for information call 800–232–4666. Crown Cruise Lines' *Viking Princess* has one-day cruises from San Diego several times a week and some overnight trips; call 800–421–0522. The *Ensenada Express* has day trips to Ensenada from San Diego; call 619–232–2109.

TELEPHONES. To call Ensenada from the United States, dial 70–667, then the local number. In Mexico, the area code for Ensenada is 667. Long distance phones are scattered throughout town; there is one near the bus station and another outside the Calmariscos restaurant. Some helpful numbers to keep handy:

Tourist Information Office, 4–0142.
Chamber of Commerce, 8–3770.
Convention and Visitors Bureau, 8–2411.
Secretary of Tourism, 6–2222.
Police, 9–1751.
Hospital, 8–2525.
Red Cross, 8–1212.

Air Evac International is an air ambulance that flies into Mexico to bring injured tourists back to the United States; the number in San Diego is 619–425–4400.

HOTELS. Ensenada has become a major resort town, with resort prices that continue to rise. The most popular hotels are concentrated in a five-block area along Av. López Mateos, the center of tourist activity. Most hotels take credit cards; some insist on advance payment. The *Tijuana and Ensenada Convention and Visitors Bureau* is connected with a San Diego office that reserves hotel rooms and distributes tourist information; the number in San Diego is 619–299–8518. *Baja Reservations,* 3939 La Salle Ave., San Diego, CA 92110, also reserves rooms; call 619–222–9099. Rates during the week are sometimes cheaper than those on weekends. Categories listed here are based on rates as follows: *Expensive,* $45 and up; *Moderate,* $25–45; *Inexpensive,* under $25.

ENSENADA

Expensive

Bahia. Av. López Mateos and Av. Riveroll; 8–2101. This long-time favorite is getting somewhat rundown. Located in the center of town, it has 64 rooms, a large parking lot, restaurant, disco, large pool, and a plain, rowdy bar facing the street, as well as car rentals, a tourist agency, and a group of shops that are some of the best in town.

El Cid. Av. López Mateos 1000; 8–2404. The decor is dark Spanish colonial; the 50 rooms are decorated with various Mexican themes, and the disco has a folklorico show every Saturday night. Pool, bar, restaurant, coffee shop, banquet rooms, convention facilities, and laundry.

Estero Beach Hotel Resort. Six miles south of town on Estero Beach, off Mexico 1; Box 86, Ensenada, B.C. 6–6225. A large beach resort with 74 units, a bar, a restaurant, shops, tennis courts, and a golf-driving range. One of the few places that is actually on the beach. Facilities for trailers and recreational vehicles.

Motel Casa del Sol. Av. López Mateos and Av. Blancarte; 8–1570. An attractive establishment with 43 units. Laundry and dry cleaning services, a baby-sitting service, a pool, parking, a good restaurant, and nice shops.

La Pinta. Av. Floresta and Blvd. Bucaneros; 6–2601; 800–472–2427 in the United States. Part of the El Presidente chain and one of 6 La Pinta Hotels on Baja. One block from the beach; 51 rooms, a restaurant, bar, disco, pool, and tennis courts.

Las Rosas. Mexico 1 north of town. Modernistic 3-story hotel on the beach built by the owners of the Estero Beach Hotel. Ocean-view rooms with large windows. A pool, spa, sauna, restaurant, bar, and racquetball courts.

San Nicolas. Av. López Mateos and Av. Guadalupe; 9–1901; 800–532–3737 in the United States. Box 4C, San Ysidro, CA, 92073. An older attractive resort with 135 units, convention facilities, a restaurant, bar, disco, and pool; 3 blocks south of downtown; quieter than some hotels in town.

Moderate

Cortés Motor Hotel. Av. López Mateos 1089; 8–2307; 800–528–1234 in the United States. Box 396, Ensenada, B.C. A Best Western motel with 62 air-conditioned rooms, a pool, garage parking, and restaurant.

Las Dunas. Calle Caracoles 169; 6–3095. Billed as a "hometel," with 28 kitchenette suites, patio, pool, cable TV. One block from the water, a few blocks south of town.

Fiesta Inn. Av. Sangines 237; 6–1361; Box 1171, Ensenada, B.C. A plain 2-story motel south of downtown; some kitchen suites.

Misión Santa Isabel. Av. López Mateos at Av. Castillo; Box 76, Ensenada, B.C.; 8–3616. A mission-style hotel with 31 rooms, a restaurant, bar, and pool.

Quintas Papagayo. Mexico 1 north of town; 8–3675. Reservations: Box 150, Ensenada. A bungalow and low-rise seaside establishment opened by the Hussong family in 1947. Options such as fireplaces, kitchens, patios, and decks increase the price. Tennis courts, a restaurant, bar, and pool.

Ramona Beach Cottages. On Mexico 1, 4 miles north of town; 8–1245. Recently renovated, with 19 rooms and cottages, some with kitchens. A pool and parking; no restaurant.

TraveLodge. Av. López Mateos at Av. Blancarte 130; 8–1601; 800–255–3050 in the United States. Box 1467, Ensenada, B.C. An American-affiliated hotel with 50 units. Service bars in rooms; some rooms have VCRs. A heated pool, cantina, and restaurant.

Villa Marina. Av. López Mateos and Av. Blancarte; 8–3351. A 60-unit motel with a restaurant, pool, and bar.

Inexpensive

America Motel. Av. López Mateos 1309; 6–1333. Plain building with 20 units and parking. Across the street from the tourist information office.

California Trailer Park and Motel. Five miles north of Ensenada on Hwy. 1; 6–2037. Reservations: Box 262, Ensenada, B.C. New motel with trailer park, concrete spaces, and hookups.

Coronado Motel. Av. López Mateos 1275; 6–1416. A bit shabby, but clean, with 22 rooms and parking.

Flamingo. Av. López Meteos 1797; 6–1666. A small, plain hotel with 27 rooms, bar, and restaurant.

Motel Presidente. Av. López Mateos and Av. Rayon; 6–1476. An older motel with 54 rooms and a swimming pool; no restaurant.

Rudi's Motel. Av. Hidalgo 450; 6–3245. Simple and clean, with 32 rooms and parking. A few blocks south of town.

LA BUFADORA

La Jolla Beach Camp. *Inexpensive.* On Punta Banda, just off the road to La Bufadora. Reservations: Alejandro Pabloff, Box 953, Ensenada, B.C. Rest rooms and showers.

Rancho la Bufadora. *Inexpensive.* Campsites 16 miles south of Ensenada on the road to La Bufadora. Reservations: Box 300, Ensenada, B.C. No hookups.

Villarino Camp. *Inexpensive.* On the road to La Bufadora. 60 recreational vehicle sites with hookups.

CATAVINA

Hotel La Pinta. *Expensive.* Off Mexico 1, 1 mile north of Rancho Santa Inés. Box 179, San Quintin, B.C.; 6–2601 in Ensenada; 800–472–2427 in the United States. An El Presidente hotel in the middle of Baja's Desert National Park. Its 28 rooms are air-conditioned. Restaurant, bar, tennis, and pool.

Cataviña Campground. *Inexpensive.* Next to Hotel La Pinta, 1 mile north of Rancho Santa Inés, off Mexico 1. Trailer and tent sites, electricity, showers, rest rooms, a gas station, and a restaurant.

SAN QUINTIN

Hotel La Pinta. *Expensive.* Box 168, San Quintin, B.C. 6–2601 in Ensenada; 800–472–2427 in the United States. Another El Presidente hotel by the beach; 60 rooms, a pool, tennis, bar, and restaurant.

Cielito Lindo Motel. *Inexpensive.* Two miles west of Mexico 1; no phone. A small establishment with 24 rooms next to a campground with 100 recreational vehicle sites, electricity, rest rooms, showers, and restaurant.

SANTO TOMÁS

El Palomar Campground. *Inexpensive.* North of town on Mexico 1; 21 trailer and tent sites with showers, rest rooms, and a gas station.

DINING OUT. Since Ensenada is a sportfishing town, fish is the primary choice for dining. The lobster, shrimp, and abalone are great, and a variety of fresh fish are prepared in French, Italian, and Mexican sauces. On the street, at the fish market, and in inexpensive restaurants, seafood cocktails, ceviche, and fish tacos are the main delights. During the winter hunting season, quail and pheasant are popular. A dinner for 1, not including drinks, tax, or tip, costing over $15 is considered here as *Expensive;* $8–$15, *Moderate;* and less than $8, *Inexpensive.* Abbreviations for credit cards are AE, American Express; MC, MasterCard; and V, Visa.

Expensive

La Cueva de los Tigres. About 2 miles south of town at Km 112 at Playa Hermosa; 6–4650. The dining room looks out on the water, especially nice at sunset. The enduring specialty, abalone in crab sauce, has won international awards. The restaurant is so popular that patrons regularly drive down from California for dinner. AE, MC, V.

El Rey Sol. Av. López Mateos 1000; 8–1733. A family-owned landmark French restaurant over 40 years old in a charming renovated hacienda-type building with stained-glass windows, wrought-iron chandeliers, and linen tablecloths. French and Mexican presentations of fresh fish, poultry, and vegetables grown at the family's farm in the Santo Tomás Valley. Excellent abalone and shellfish appetizers; pastries baked on the premises. AE, MC, V.

Valentino. Blvd. Costera 915; 4–0022. A romantic setting in a dimly lit room with candles and blue tablecloths; also patio dining. Seafood and steaks; Sunday champagne brunch. AE, MC, V.

Moderate

Carnitas Uruapan. Av. Sangines 36; 6–1044. Branch of a famous Tijuana hangout. Primarily serves *carnitas,* chunks of marinated, roast pork served with fresh tortillas, salsa, onion, tomatoes, and cilantro. Patrons share long wooden tables in this informal setting. No credit cards.

Casamar. Blvd. Lázaro Cárdenas 987; 8–1896. Popular for its wide variety of excellent seafood. Large groups, families, and couples seem equally comfortable in the main dining room, which bustles with activity. MC, V.

Casamar 2. Av. Macheros 499; 8–2540. Just off Blvd. Lázaro Cárdenas on the service road to the sportfishing piers. Seafood, Mexican specialties, and breakfast are served indoors or at outdoor tables overlooking the harbor.

Las Cazuelas. Av. Sangines and Blvd. Costera; 6–1044. A seafood and steak restaurant serving breakfast, lunch, and dinner with an adjacent disco.

Del Mar. Av. López Mateos 821; 8–2191. Romantic spot for a candlelight dinner on the lower level of one of Ensenada's most appealing shops. Seafood is the specialty. MC, V.

Enrique's. A half mile north of town on Mexico 1; 4–4061. A small, colorful restaurant with a reputation for good Mexican and American food. Closed Tuesdays.

La Gondola. Av. López Mateos 664; 8–3963. An Italian cafe by the sea; open from breakfast until midnight. MC, V.

Popeye's. On the waterfront; 8–3743. Large windows look out on the harbor from the large dining room that gets noisy when crowded; good seafood and breakfasts.

Restaurant Cosmos. Av. Macheros 7 at Blvd. Costera; no phone. A bit of everything, from steak and eggs to Mexican seafood specialties; tables on the sidewalk near the fishing pier.

Smitty Gonzalez. Av. Ryerson and López Mateos; 4–0636. A new 2-story restaurant serving good Mexican specialties; the video disco upstairs is popular.

El Toro. Blvd. Lázaro Cárdenas 999; 4–0964. The main steak house in town, across the street from the waterfront. The beef is choice and tender; flaming dishes are prepared at your table. Quiet, romantic setting. MC, V.

Tortilla Flat. Above the sportfishing terminal in the harbor; 8–2586. One of the few places with a good view of the harbor, this restaurant aims to please the tourist with seafood and Mexican specialties, tropical drinks, and a lively bar. MC, V.

Inexpensive

Cafe Colonial. Calle 2, 325; 8–3510. A clean, modest place with good Mexican food. Off-street parking. AE, MC, V.

Calmariscos. Calle 3, 474, near Av. Ruiz; 8–2940. Some of Ensenada's best seafood, including great turtle steaks, is served in this modest restaurant. Open 24 hours. V.

Ja Ja Ja. On the corner of Ruiz and López Mateos. A popular taco stand next door to Hussong's Cantina; great fish tacos.

Muy Lam. Av. Ruiz 373; 8–1321. Chinese dishes served in the heart of downtown. MC, V.

Señor Taco. Ruiz 171. A clean, inviting storefront with benches and stools along the walls; good basic Mexican food and great prices.

Via Venetto. Blvd. Lázaro Cárdenas 853; 8–2516. Ensenada's best-loved pizza is served in a dark dining room with latticework walls, stained glass lamps, and posters of Italy.

 HOW TO GET AROUND. Most of Ensenada's attractions are within five blocks of the waterfront, and it is easy to take a long walking tour of the city. A car is necessary, though, for reaching La Bufadora, the Chapultepec hills, and most beaches. Buses travel the route from Ensenada to Guerrero Negro at the border between Baja Norte and Baja Sur and down to the southernmost tip of Baja. Addresses can be somewhat confusing within the city, particularly along the waterfront, where the road is called Blvd. Costera, Gral. Lázaro Cárdenas, Alternate Hwy. 1, and Carretera Transpeninsular.

By Car. Ensenada is an easy city to navigate; most streets are marked. If you are traveling south, you can bypass downtown Ensenada on the Hwy. 1 truck route down Calle 10. To reach the hotel and waterfront area, stay with alternate

Hwy. 1 as it travels along the fishing pier and becomes Blvd. Costera, also known as Lázaro Cárdenas. Cárdenas ends at Calle Agustin Sangines, also known as Calle Delante, which leads out to Hwy. 1 traveling south. Hwy. 3 to Ojos Negros and San Felipe in the south and Guadalupe and Tecate in the north intersect Hwy. 1 at the north and south ends of the city. The parking meters along Ensenada's main streets are patrolled regularly; parking tickets sometimes come in the form of a boot on the car's tires or removed license plates. Be sure to carry some 1-peso and 5-peso coins for the meters.

Car Rentals. *Hertz, Scorpio,* and *Ensenada Rent-a-Car* (8–1896) car rental agencies all have offices along Av. Alvarado between Av. Lázaro Cárdenas and Av. López Mateos. The agencies sell Mexican car insurance. If you are planning to return your rental car elsewhere, be sure the agency has an office there.

By Bus. The main bus station is at Av. Riveroll between Calles 10 and 11; phone 8–2322. *Tres Estrellas de Oro* and *Autotransportes de Baja California* travel the entire Baja route and connect with buses to Guadalajara and Mexico City.

By Taxi. There is a central taxi stand *(sitio)* on López Mateos near the Bahia Hotel; phone 8–3475. Be sure to set the price before the taxi starts moving. Destinations within the city should cost less than $5.

TOURIST INFORMATION. The *State Tourist Commission* office is on Av. López Mateos 1305 near the hotels; phone 6–2222. The office is open Monday through Friday, 9 A.M.–7 P.M.; Saturday, 9 A.M.–1 P.M.; and Sunday, 10 A.M.–1 P.M. The office has a wide selection of brochures, and the helpful English-speaking staff can make reservations for you. The *Convention and Visitors Bureau* is at the corner of Avs. López Mateos and Espinoza; phone 8–2411; a new office is planned for the Blvd. Costera, by the waterfront.

USEFUL ADDRESSES. *Police:* Ortiz Rubio and Libertad; *Hospital:* Ave. Ruiz and Calle 11; *Post Office:* Juárez 1347.

ENGLISH-LANGUAGE MEDIA. Tourist newspapers and brochures are available at most hotels and many curio shops. The *Baja Times* and *Ensenada News and Views* both carry ads for new restaurants and stores and list special events.

SEASONAL EVENTS. The *Mardi Gras* or carnaval takes place at the end of **February,** with cockfights, parades, and fireworks. In **March,** the *Tijuana-to-Ensenada Bike Race* attracts hundreds of bicyclists and spectators from California and Baja. In **April,** the *Newport-to-Ensenada Regatta,* which has been held annually since 1930, brings hundreds of boats from the Los Angeles area to Ensenada. In **September,** the *Transpeninsular Bike Race* and the *Ensenada Festival* are held, along with a seafood fair and cook-off, at which the restaurants present their best dishes. *La Carrera,* a popular international road race from San Felipe to Ensenada, is held in **September** or **October.**

TOURS. The *Bodegas de Santo Tomás* has tours of Baja's oldest winery, located in town at 666 Av. Miramar, phone 8–3333. Tours run daily at 11 A.M., 1 P.M., and 3 P.M. Group tours should be arranged in advance. The winery is closed on Sunday.

Half-day bus tours of Ensenada and the surrounding countryside are available from *Viajes Guaycura,* López Mateos 1089; 8–3718.

El Paseo Tours, 563 Third Ave., Chula Vista, CA 92010; 619–585–7495, has overnight tours to Ensenada from San Diego that include transportation, hotels, and meals.

PARKS AND GARDENS. In Ensenada, the nicest city park is *Parque Revolución,* near the Mother's Monument at Av. Obregón and Calle 7. The park has a center bandstand, a children's playground, and plenty of comfortable benches in the shade. *El Mirador,* the lookout, is located high up in the Chapultepec hills on a rutted dirt road off Calle 2. The overall view of the city and bay is amazing; a visit to the lookout helps orient you and makes navigating the city much easier.

La Bufadora is a geyser in the ocean cliffs 30 miles south of Ensenada that has become one of the area's top attractions. To reach la Bufadora, take Hwy. 1 south to Hwy. 23, then travel another 12 km to the end of the road. Hwy. 23 is a two-lane road—part pavement, part gravel and dirt. The road passes some small beach communities and trailer parks as it winds over the steep cliffs; night driving is not recommended. The view of the ocean above La Bufadora is spectacular. Restaurants and food and curio stands line the road where it ends in a large parking lot. There is a viewing stand by the cliffs, where the water enters a narrow crevice and spurts high overhead.

Parque Nacional Constitución de 1857 is 50 miles east of Ensenada; the road is unpaved and rough for the last half of the trip, but the view of Laguna Hanson and its wild, stark surroundings is terrific.

BEACHES. The waterfront in Ensenada proper is taken up by fishing boats; the best swimming beaches are south of town. *Estero Beach* is long and clean, with mild waves. Surfers populate the beaches off Hwy. 1 north and south of Ensenada, particularly at *San Miguel, California, Tres Marias,* and *La Joya* beaches; scuba divers prefer *Punta Banda,* by La Bufadora. Lifeguards are rare, so swimmers should be careful. The tourist office in Ensenada has a map that shows safe diving and surfing beaches.

SPORTS. Hunting and **fishing** are popular sports around Ensenada, which calls itself the "Yellowtail Capital of the World." There is no racetrack in Ensenada, but those who are hooked on horseracing can place their bets and watch televised races from Tijuana's Agua Caliente Racetrack and Los Angeles's Santa Anita and Hollywood tracks at the Agua Caliente's Foreign Book on López Mateos, behind the Riviera-Pacífico building; 6–2133.

Sportfishing. Fishing boats leave the Ensenada sportfishing pier regularly. The best angling fishing takes place from April through November, with bottom fishing good in the winter. Charter vessels and party boats are available from several outfitters along Av. López Mateos, Blvd. Costera, and off the sportfishing pier. Most hotels can arrange fishing trips. Licenses are available at the tourist office or from charter companies. Some companies that organize fishing trips and rent equipment are these:

Boats Juanito y Hijos, Calle La Joya 263, arranges trips for up to 6 persons.

Club Calafia, 5580 La Jolla Blvd., 421, La Jolla, CA 92037 (706–612–1580) runs charter fishing trips out of Ensenada.

Pacific Anglers Fleet, at the sportfishing pier, arranges charters; call 4–0865.

El Royal Pacífico offers advance-sale tickets and reservations on sportfishing boats in Ensenada from their U.S. office in Mission Viejo. Write 26651 Naccome Dr., Mission Viejo, CA 92691, or call 714–859–4933.

Hunting. The hunting season for quail and other game birds runs from September through December. Hunting trips can be arranged through *Uruapan Lodge,* Gastelum 40 downtown; tel. 8–2190. The lodge package includes transportation from the border, a room, meals, hunting equipment, and licenses for $100 per day.

Golf may be played at Bajamar, an excellent 18-hole course 20 miles north of Ensenada at the Bajamar condominium and housing resort. For information, call 8–1844.

Tennis may be played at Bajamar and the Baja Tennis Club at San Benito 123; a few hotels have their own courts.

Charreadas (Mexican rodeos) are scheduled infrequently at the ring at Av. Alvarado and Calle 2; 4–0242.

HISTORIC SITES. The impressive *Riviera del Pacífico* on Blvd. Costera was built in the 1920s with money raised on both sides of the border; heavyweight fighter Jack Dempsey was one of the more famous shareholders. An enormous gambling palace, hotel, restaurant, and bar, the Riviera was a glamorous place frequented by wealthy Americans and Mexicans, particularly during Prohibition. When gambling was outlawed in Mexico and Prohibition ended in the United States, the palace lost its clientele and went through years of openings and closings. In 1977, the Tourism and Convention Bureau began refurbishing the palace and its lavish gardens. Visitors can now tour the immense ballrooms and halls, which host occasional art shows and civic events.

Riviera del Pacífico is sometimes used as convention center, but for the most part, remains empty, though it still retains its grandeur. For information, call 6–4310.

CHURCHES. The largest cathedral, *Guadalupe Catholic Church,* is located at Floresta and Juárez. The church is currently undergoing renovation; its stained glass windows are quite impressive, though the church itself is not as grand as most in major Mexican cities. Most of Mexico retains old customs, so women visitors are advised to wear a head covering in churches; a handkerchief will do.

FILM, MUSIC, DANCE, STAGE. The *Teatro de la Ciudad* on Calle Diamante holds occasional dance shows and plays. There are many Spanish-language movie theaters in town along Av. Juárez; *Cinema Gemelos* is a multicinema playing Mexican films, located on the south end of town at López Mateos and Av. Balboa.

SHOPPING. Browsing and bartering are popular Baja pastimes, and the selection on Mexican handicrafts in Ensenada is far superior to that in Tijuana and Mexicali. Most of the tourist shops are located along Av. López Mateos near the hotels and restaurants. Dozens of curio shops and arcades line the street, all selling basically the same selection of pottery, woven blankets and serapes, embroidered dresses, and onyx chess sets. Four blocks inland from López Mateos is Av. Juárez, the center of downtown for the locals. Large department stores, farmacias (drugstores), and shoe stores line the avenue.

La Rana, at López Mateos 715, has a wide selection of beach attire and surfing supplies. *Originales Baja,* López Mateos 623, sells large brass and copper birds, wood carvings, and glassware. *Artes de Quijote,* 503 López Mateos, has an impressive selection of high-quality carved wooden doors, huge terra cotta pots, wooden puzzles and games, tablecloths and napkins from Oaxaca, and large brass fish and birds. *Joyeria Princess,* a few doors down, has a good selection of gold and silver jewelry at reasonable, set prices. In the *Mitla Bazaar, Elles* and *Fila* have designer men's and women's clothing. *Mike's Leather,* at 621 López Mateos, has a nice selection of leather clothing and dyed huarachas, as do *El Escorial* and *Azteca. Fantasias del Mar,* López Mateos 821, has exotic shells, coral jewelry, and paintings. The government craft store, *Fonart,* at López Mateos 1303, next door to the tourism office, is filled with high-quality crafts from all over Mexico. Especially nice are the black pottery from Oaxaca and wooden dolls and animals from Michoacan. *La Mina de Solomon,* next to the El Rey Sol restaurant on López Mateos, carries handcrafted gold jewelry. *Artes Bitterlin,* in the same building, is a gallery carrying antiques, sculpture, painting, and Sergio Bustamante copper and brass animals.

On Av. Ruiz, *Hussong's Edificio,* next door to the infamous Hussong's Cantina, has a collection of shops selling silk-screened T-shirts, surfboards, and Ensenada bumper stickers and souvenirs. *Avila Imports,* across the street from Hussong's, sells French perfumes, Hummel statues, and crystal. *Beibylandia,* at Ruiz 232, has a wide assortment of baby clothing, furniture, and toys. *Libreria Banuelos,* at Ruiz 370, and *El Spana* at Ruiz 217, have a good selection of English-language magazines and books. *El Pegaso,* 121 Obregón, is a bit out of the way but well worth the trip. The store carries beautiful clothing, jewelry, furniture, and crafts from all over Mexico and shares its inventory with its sister store in San Miguel de Allende. The items here are a bit higher priced than at the main curio stands, but their quality is far superior. The *Astra Shopping Center* at Calle Delante and Hwy. 1 has major department stores and small handicraft shops. *Los Globos,* a large swap meet on Calle 9, is open on weekends.

 NIGHTLIFE. Ensenada is a party town for college students, surfers, and young tourists, and the bars, particularly along López Mateos and Ruiz, get rowdy at night. Most of the expensive hotels have bars and discos that are less frenetic. *Hussong's Cantina,* on Av. Ruiz, is perhaps Ensenada's most prominent landmark; no trip is complete without entering this dark, dingy, noisy, enormous saloon, in which vendors hawk rugs, roses, and polaroid photos and the constant crowd never seems to diminish. *Papas and Beer,* across the street, is newer, cleaner, and trendier, but the crowd is just as rowdy, yelling from the second-story balcony to the strollers below. *Bandito's,* in the same block, is a boisterous disco. Billiard parlors line Calle 2 between Ruiz and Gastelum; this is definitely men-only territory.

Tortilla Flats, on the harbor with a view of the fishing boats, has dining and dancing of a more mellow sort; *Carlos n' Charlie's,* on Blvd. Costera, is more family oriented, but rowdy. *Club Bananas,* nearby, is a neon video-disco bar that is popular with the college crowd, as is *Tequila Connection,* at Alvarado 12, just off Costera. The *Plaza Mexico Video Store* next door is packed in the evenings with people renting videos to play in their hotel rooms or cabins. *Smitty Gonzales,* a new restaurant and disco on Av. Reyerson, attracts devoted disco dancers. *Joy's Discoteque,* at López Mateos and Balboa, is popular with the locals, as is *Xanadu Disco* on Ejercito Nacional.

The plain bar at the *Bahia Hotel* with windows opening on to López Mateos is full day and night with weary shoppers grabbing a beer. The Bahia dining room has nightly floor shows and dancing to tropical and cha-cha music. Cover charge. *Casamar Restaurant's* small lounge features live jazz on Friday and Saturday nights. The *El Cid Hotel* has a disco where folklorico dances are held every Saturday at 7 P.M.

ROSARITO BEACH

A Suburban Resort

by
MARIBETH MELLIN

Not long ago, Rosarito Beach (or Playas de Rosarito) was a small seaside community with no tourist trade to speak of. It was, and still is, part of the municipality of Tijuana, an overlooked suburb of sorts on the way to Ensenada. Today, Rosarito has its own identity as an important resort area that is undergoing massive development. It is predicted that, within the next two years, Rosarito will be a municipality whose local government will oversee a rapidly growing population of Mexicans and transplanted Americans.

Juan Machado was the first developer of Rosarito Beach, back in 1827 when the governor of Baja California granted him 407,000 acres of Baja's coastline, called El Rosario. Machado took over the crumbling Misión del Descanso, near Cantamar, and converted it into a rambling ranch. In 1920, 14,000 of those acres were turned over to a group of investors headed by Los Angeles attorney Jacob Morris Danziger. In 1924, Danziger began advertising "El Rosario Resort and Country Club" in California newspapers. A man of generous imagination, he lured tourists to the area with claims of good roads, fishing, camping, bathing, and picnic grounds—despite the reality that the area was primitive at best, with no roads to speak of and no gas, oil, or other essential creature comforts.

Danziger rushed his project toward completion as he eyed the competition building the new Agua Caliente resort in Tijuana; his resort, he said, would be finished by 1926 and would include a casino, golf course, ballroom, and guest houses that would be available through membership in his private Shore Acres Country Club. Before long, Danziger was hit with a series of lawsuits for back pay and the like and eventually had to sell his shares in Shore Acres; at that point, the resort was but a 10-room hotel with one bathroom.

Arrival of Investors

In the early 1930s, Manuel P. Barbachano bought the hotel and surrounding acreage. This was an exciting time in Baja—gambling, horse racing, and a continuous flow of alcohol attracted thousands of glamorous Americans who were escaping from the boredom of Prohibition. The Agua Caliente Spa in Tijuana was completed; other investors built the huge Riviera del Pacífico Hotel and gambling casino in Ensenada, and the Rosarito Beach Hotel began to grow. Barbachano was instrumental in getting electricity and telephone service installed throughout northern Baja, which further encouraged tourism. The entire region became extremely popular; smaller hotels and watering holes opened up along the rough road from Tijuana to Ensenada. But the end of Prohibition in the United States and the outlawing of gambling in Mexico brought a halt to the weekly migration of Hollywood stars in search of liquor and fun. Before long, Agua Caliente and Riviero del Pacífico closed down. The Rosarito Beach Hotel, however, continued to expand.

Barbachano invested even more in his hotel, hiring a Belgian architect to design the spacious lobby, dining room, and bars. Mexican muralist Matias Santoyo covered the lobby's walls with intricate colorful murals depicting Mexico's history; another artist, whose name is now unknown, created an elaborate reproduction of the Mayan calendar on goat skins affixed to the hallway walls with tempera made of egg whites. The hotel continued to attract wealthy Americans, some of whom built vacation villas along the beach. As the roads improved, particularly after Baja's Transpeninsular Highway was completed in 1973, Rosarito Beach grew. The hotel's current owner, Hugo Torres, added vacation suites along the beach and timeshare and condo units. In 1980, the Rosarito Beach Hotel was still the only major resort in the area; a few smaller restaurants and hotels had been built outside town, but it was still possible to feel like you had discovered an unknown paradise—your personal piece of the beach. This sense of solitude and privacy has now disappeared, and Rosarito Beach has become a major resort town.

Building Boom

The 1980s have brought an amazing building boom to Rosarito. The main street, alternately known as the Old Ensenada Highway and Boulevard Benito Juárez, is packed with restaurants, bars, and shops. The new Quinta Del Mar resort, with its high-rise condos, lavish restaurants, and sprawling hotel buildings, has brought new life to the north end of town, where there used to be only a few taco stands and clusters of horses for rent. Signs for new shopping centers stand before the few remaining vacant lots. Rosarito Beach has hit the big time.

Still, it is a relaxing place to visit. Southern Californians have made Rosarito (and much of Baja Norte) practically a weekend suburb; surfers, swimmers, and sunbathers find a sense of adventure at the beach. The oceanfront seems much wilder and purer south of the border; for long stretches both north and south of Rosarito, the coastline cliffs are free of houses and highways and the horizon seems miles away above the gray-blue-green waters. Whales pass not far from shore on their winter migration; dolphins and sea lions sun on rocky points in the cliffs. Whether you travel the toll road (*Ensenada Cuota*) or the free road (called *Ensenada Libre* or the Old Ensenada Highway), the view is startling, soothing, and sensational, particularly on a clear day.

Rosarito Beach is the main stopover between Tijuana and Ensenada; its early development presaged its current dominance of the area. The beach is one of the longest in northern Baja—an uninterrupted stretch of sand from the power plant at the far north end of town to below the Rosarito Beach Hotel, about five miles south. This stretch is perfect for horseback riding, jogging, and strolling from sunrise to sunset or under a full moon.

Vacation Developments

The old road becomes Blvd. Benito Juárez as you enter town; as Rosarito has grown, the main drag has become a super sideshow of sorts, with hotels, restaurants, stores, taco stands, horse fields, open-air markets, and plenty of people to watch. Rosarito has always attracted a varied crowd. Today's group is an assemblage of prosperous young Californians building white villas in vacation developments, retired Americans and Canadians homesteading in trailer parks, and travelers from everywhere and of every age.

Some say the region has become "yuppiefied," but the members of the thriving tourism board seem happy. So do the visitors, who find a combination of hedonism and health in Rosarito.

One of the area's most popular attractions is its seafood; no visit is complete without a meal of lobster, shrimp, or abalone. Prohibition may have ended long ago in the United States, but the visiting Americans act as if they've been dry for months—margaritas and beer are the favorite thirst quenchers. People let down their hair and their inhibitions here (to a degree closely guarded by the local constables).

A typical Rosarito day might begin with a breakfast of eggs, refried beans, and tortillas, followed by a horse ride down the beach. Lying in the sun or strolling through the shops takes care of midday. Siestas are imperative, whether they're spent back on the beach, by the pool, or at a waterfront bar. After more shopping, strolling, or sleeping, it's time for dinner—a major event for most visitors. Rosarito's developers are working on building enough hotel rooms to meet the demand; its restaurant owners have acted more quickly. There are at least 50 restaurants in the Rosarito area. Most have similar menus—seafood, steak, and Mexican basics—but each has its own style of cooking, clientele, and ambience. There is no lack of food here.

Favorite Side Trips

Those who've traveled the area often have favorite side trips from town. The most popular, according to the sheer number of visitors, is Puerto Nuevo, or Newport. A few years ago, the only way to know you'd reached this fishing community was by the huge painting of a 7-Up bottle on the side of a building. You'd drive down the rutted dirt road to a row of restaurants—some just a big room in front of a family's kitchen. There you'd be served the classic Puerto Nuevo meal—grilled lobster, refried beans, rice, homemade tortillas, butter, salsa, and lime. The meal became a legend; now there are at least 25 restaurants in rows spread over a dirt field on the top of a cliff. The place is packed on weekends, all day long, though the meal has few variations. And now there are T-shirts for sale.

Those seeking a bit less frenetic spot stop at La Fonda, Popotla, Calafia, or Bajamar, all on the road to Ensenada. The Halfway House is popular with hang gliders, who fly off the high sand dunes nearby, over the scores of dune buggies. And at busy times, it seems nearly every clifftop clearing has at least one car parked there, its passengers enjoying the view.

PRACTICAL INFORMATION FOR

ROSARITO BEACH

HOW TO GET THERE. Rosarito Beach is 18 miles south of Tijuana on the coast. There is no airport or bus terminal, but **buses** traveling between Tijuana and the southern tip of Baja stop on Blvd. Juárez in Tijuana. **Taxis,** called *rutas,* will drive you from downtown Tijuana at Calle Madero and Calle 3 to Rosarito. The drivers usually won't leave until they have four passengers in the back seat. The fare is low—under $5.

The easiest way to get to Rosarito Beach is by **car;** be sure to get Mexican auto insurance before you cross the border. There are insurance stands and drive-throughs at the last two exits on I–5 before the border. Once you cross the border, follow the signs for Ensenada Cuota, the toll road south, which runs along the coast. Take the Rosarito exit, which leads to what is alternately called the Old Ensenada Highway, Ensenada Libre, and Blvd. Juárez in Rosarito.

TELEPHONES. To call Rosarito from the United States, dial 70, then area code 661 and the number. Emergency calls: *Police,* 134; *Fire,* 136; *Red Cross* 132.

HOTELS. Although Rosarito is going through a building boom with a lot of new hotels and motels under construction, there is still a shortage of rooms. Reservations are a must on holiday weekends; the town gets filled up on Friday nights. Two businesses in San Diego can reserve rooms for you in Rosarito (many hotels require a two-night stay for a confirmed reservation). *International Marketing and Promotions* (IMPA) acts as an agent for Baja's Tourist and Convention Bureaus; for Rosarito information and reservations write or call IMPA, 7860 Mission Center Court, 202, San Diego, CA 92108; 619–298–4105, or 800–522–1516 in California. *Baja Reservations,* 3939 La Salle Ave., San Diego, CA 92110 (619–222–9099), also handles Rosarito reservations and rentals. The rates in Rosarito have climbed considerably and are usually $50 and up for an *Expensive* double room, $35–$50 for *Moderate,* and $25 and less for *Inexpensive.*

Expensive

Quinta del Mar. Blvd. Juárez 25500; 2–1145, or 800–228–7003 in California. Reservations: Box 4243, San Ysidro, CA 92073. A new resort complex with some moderately priced rooms and some expensive townhouses near the beach and high-rise condo rentals with ocean views. The resort complex includes rooms with and without TV, 3 restaurants and bars; a pool and whirlpool; steam baths; tennis, basketball, and volleyball courts; a beauty shop, children's playground, and access to the beach. The high-rise condo building has a rooftop Jacuzzi and tennis court.

Rosarito Beach Hotel. Blvd. Juárez at the south end of town; 2–1106; Box 145, San Ysidro, CA 92073. A resort dating back to the Prohibition era; the main building is charming, with its huge ballrooms, tiled baths, and glassed-in pool deck overlooking a long beach. The rooms and suites in the newer buildings are not nearly as enchanting as those in the old resort building. The good restaurant serves a lavish Sunday brunch and powerful margaritas. Nice beach, tennis courts, pool, and a new health club with racquetball courts and running track.

Moderate

Baja del Sol. Old Ensenada Highway, Km 27; 2–1350. Small hotel with pool, restaurant, and bar.

Rene's Motel and Trailer Park. Blvd. Juárez south of town; 2–1020; Box 1169, San Ysidro, CA 92073. One of the oldest motels and restaurants in the area; 42 rooms in cottages leading to the beach, pool, restaurant, and bar.

Inexpensive

Km 26 RV and Trailer Park. On the beach; 619–329–1638 in San Diego, CA. Beachfront hookups and showers.

Motel Colonial. Calle Primero de Mayo; 2–1575. A small motel that's a bit rundown, but one of the few actually on the beach.

Motel Don Luis. Blvd. Juárez; 2–1166. A two-story motel on the way into town, with rooms, suites, and apartments, and El Jardin restaurant.

Motel Quinta Chica. Blvd. Juárez; 2–1301 or 800–228–7003. New modern motel with 90 rooms, TV. Restaurant and bar across the street.

La Playa Trailer Park. Blvd. Juárez; 2–1333; Box 611, Rosarito, Baja California Sur, MX. Beachfront spaces for recreational vehicles with hookups.

SOUTH OF ROSARITO

Calafia Cliffs. *Expensive.* Km 35.5, Old Ensenada Highway; 2–1581; 5580 La Jolla Blvd., Ste. 421, La Jolla, CA 92037. Furnished weekend and long-term mobile home rentals set down from the road on the ocean cliffs.

La Paloma. *Expensive.* Km 28 on the Old Ensenada Highway; 619–298–4105 in San Diego, CA. 7860 Mission Center Court, 202, San Diego, CA 92108. Resort condo on the ocean with tourist rentals.

Plaza del Mar. *Expensive.* Km 58 on the Old Ensenada Highway; take La Misión exit from the toll road and go north 1 mile; 706–685–9152. Box 4520, San Ysidro, CA 92073. A hotel, spa, and oceanfront resort community set behind an archaeological garden. Large rooms, some with ocean views, and a restaurant; bar with live music on weekend nights, heated pool, sauna, game room, and volleyball, shuffleboard, and tennis courts.

La Fonda. Km 59 on Old Ensenada Highway; Box 268, San Ysidro, CA 92073. An older hotel on the ocean with 18 rooms and 2 kitchen apartments; a popular restaurant and bar.

Baja Seasons. *Inexpensive.* Km 72 on Old Ensenada Highway; 800–982–BAJA. A new trailer camp with hookups and an ocean view.

Costa Del Sol Trailer Park. *Inexpensive.* Km 30.8 on Old Ensenada Highway. A few hookups for travelers, but most spaces are taken by long-term guests.

Popotla RV Park. *Inexpensive.* Km 33 on Old Ensenada Highway; 2–1504. Forty-five spaces with hookups.

DINING OUT. There may be a shortage of hotel rooms in Rosarito, but the restaurants are abundant. New places open constantly, and, although the competition is heavy, nearly all the places have the same items on their menus—lobster, shrimp, fresh fish and steak—at nearly the same prices. Lobster dinners usually cost about $12 and shrimp or steak dinners, about $7.50. The restaurants compete more heavily with their drink prices; many offer free margaritas or a bottle of wine with dinner. In this listing, the price for an *Expensive* dinner for 1, without drinks and tip, is about $15; *Moderate* is about $10; *Inexpensive* is about $6. Credit card abbreviations are: AE, American Express; MC, MasterCard; V, Visa.

Expensive

Azteca. Rosarito Beach Hotel, Blvd. Juárez; 2–1106. A busy dining room with a view of the hotel's pool and beach area; lavish Sunday brunch; Mexican food and seafood. AE, MC, V.

La Masia. Quinta del Mar Hotel, Blvd. Juárez 25500; 2–1300. An elegant restaurant with gourmet international cuisine. AE, MC, V.

La Misión. Blvd. Juárez 182; 2–0202. A lovely quiet restaurant with adobe walls, high-beamed ceilings, and tables spaced far apart. Gourmet international seafood and steaks; live Latin American folk music on weekends. MC, V.

New George's. Costa Azul 75; 2–1608. Patio dining with an ocean view. Specialties include quail, rabbit in wine-raisin sauce, steak and seafood, and tropical drinks. MC, V.

Los Pelicanos. At the end of Calle Ebano; no phone. One of the few restaurants on the beach, with huge windows and a great sunset view. Steaks and seafood. The bar upstairs also has a good view and great margaritas. Outdoor *palapas* are available for dining and drinking in the summer. MC, V.

Moderate

La Fachada. Blvd. Juárez; 2–1785. Breakfast, lunch, and dinner; steaks and seafood. MC, V.

La Flor de Michoacan. Blvd. Juárez 146; no phone. *Carnitas,* Michoacan style, with tortillas, guacamole, and salsa. Tacos, tortas, and tostadas. Orders to go.

El Jardin. Blvd. Juárez 111; 2–1166. Continental and International dishes, children's menu, seafood and poultry. MC, V.

El Nido. Blvd. Juárez 67; 2–1430. A dark, woodsy place with steaks grilled over mesquite wood; an open fireplace in the center of the dining room. MC, V.

El Oasis. Blvd. Juárez 4358; 2–1942. Traditional homemade Mexican food, steaks, and seafood. Tropical music in the dance hall, an ocean view, and banquet facilities. Open 24 hours.

Ortega's. Blvd. Juárez 200; 2–0022. The newest member of the Ortega's chain, founded in Puerto Nuevo in 1945. Breakfast, lunch, and dinner with seafood and continental specialties. Large Sunday brunch for about $6.

Palacio Real. Blvd. Juárez 984; 2–1412. Chinese food and seafood.

Pizzas Venecia. Km 21.5 on Old Ensenada Highway; no phone. Italian food, including pizza, spaghetti, ravioli. Closed Wednesdays.

El Rancho Restaurant and Bar. Km 25 on Old Ensenada Highway. Rosarito Beach; 2–1717. A large, airy place, popular for its traditional Mexican food and great breakfasts. Patio dining and folklorico dancing on weekend afternoons. MC, V.

Rene's. Blvd. Juárez; 2–1020. One of the oldest restaurants in Rosarito, operating since 1924. Breakfast, lunch, and dinner specials, including *chorizo* (Mexican sausage), quail, frogs' legs, and lobster. Ocean view from dining room, lively bar, mariachi music. MC, V.

Restaurant Nickolas. Blvd. Juárez; 2–1565. A small place with good thin-crust pizza, Italian dishes, wine and beer, and a player piano.

Rosarito Village Cafe. Blvd. Juárez 777; no phone. Mexican restaurant and take out; lively bar with cheap margaritas and loud mariachis, next door to the Rosarito Beach Hotel; a popular watering hole.

Vince's Lobster Trap. Blvd. Juárez 39; no phone. Seafood restaurant, fish market, and deli. Popular with the locals.

Viva Gonzalez. Blvd. Juárez 85; no phone. Steaks, lobster, and Mexican food. Upper-level video music and bar.

Inexpensive

El Capitán. Blvd. Juárez across from the polo field; no phone. A small *palapa* restaurant a few feet off the road, with tables scattered about in the overgrown weeds. Great seafood cocktails and simple fish dinners.

Carnitas El Cachanilla. Km 20 on Old Ensenada Highway; 2–0250. Good *carnitas* with homemade tortillas and great *menudo* (tripe soup).

Pollos Los Dorados de Villa. Blvd. Juárez 350; no phone. Broiled, barbecued, roasted, and baked chicken and good breakfasts in a newly renovated restaurant with outdoor *palapas*.

SOUTH OF ROSARITO BEACH

Expensive

Cava Calafia. Km 35.5 on Old Ensenada Highway; 2–1581. Private haute cuisine dining available by reservation only.

La Fonda. Km 59 on Old Ensenada Highway; no phone. A good spot to stop on the way to or from Ensenada. La Fonda specializes in seafood but also serves good Mexican food and beef. The bar is usually crowded and the patrons boisterous. There's a nice outside patio overlooking the ocean.

Moderate

D'Carlos Restaurant/Bar. Km 47 on Old Ensenada Highway; 4–1114. Seafood, steaks, quail, chicken, and burgers.

Don Pacho Seafood. Km 40 on Old Ensenada Highway; no phone. Seafood and lunch specials.

Francisco's Steak and Seafood. Km 35.5 at Calafia; 2–1581. A nicely decorated restaurant overlooking the ocean, serving seafood, Mexican dishes, and steak. The large bar has numerous outdoor patios scattered along the cliffs. Catering to group events. MC, V.

Puerto Nuevo, also known as Newport. Km 44 on Old Ensenada Highway. Puerto Nuevo is a village of restaurants, easily 25 or 30, that serve the same thing—grilled lobster or shrimp, Spanish rice, refried beans, homemade tortillas, melted butter, lime, and hot sauce. Some restaurants have full bars; some serve only wine and beer. The atmosphere of individual places ranges from rowdy to family dining, aided by roaming mariachi bands, curio and flower sellers, and photographers. **Ortega's,** with at least 3 branches in Puerto Nuevo and 2 in Rosarito, is the wildest, most crowded place; **Ponderosa** is smaller and quieter, run by a gracious family; **Costa Brava** is a newer, more elegant place, with tablecloths and an ocean view. Lobsters are priced for small, medium, and large; the medium is usually about $10.

Restaurant/Bar Popotla. Km 33 on Old Ensenada Highway; 2–1504. Sunday champagne brunch, special shrimp stuffed trout and good Spanish *flan.* Sunken fireplace in the dining room, dance floor in the bar, ocean view.

HOW TO GET AROUND. You can tour most of Rosarito proper **on foot,** which is a good idea on weekends, when Blvd. Juárez has bumper-to-bumper traffic. To reach Puerto Nuevo and other points south, continue on Blvd. Juárez, also called Old Ensenada Highway and Ensenada Libre, through town and south. Few roads lead off the old highway; most points of interest are right on the road. **Taxis** travel this stretch regularly; settle the fare before departing. **Buses** from Tijuana and Ensenada stop across the street from the Rosarito Beach Hotel; if you wish to stop at other beach areas along the way be sure to take a local rather than an express bus.

TOURIST INFORMATION. There is a tourist information office on Blvd. Juárez just south of La Quinta; 2–0396 or 2–1005. Three banks—Banco Serafin, Multibanco, and Banamex—exchange dollars for pesos and are open only from Monday through Friday, 9:30 A.M.–1:30 P.M. Money exchange booths along Blvd. Juárez will also exchange dollars for pesos and are open on weekends.

ENGLISH-LANGUAGE MEDIA. A variety of free newspapers are available in the hotels and shops. The best are *Ensenada News and Views* and *Baja Times*. The Convention and Tourist Bureau publishes *The Baja Shopper*, filled with ads for new shops and restaurants.

SEASONAL EVENTS. The *Rosarito Spring Fair* runs from the end of **March** into May, with special events such as dances, volleyball and softball tournaments, and seafood fairs scheduled every weekend. The *Rosarito to Ensenada Bicycle Race* takes place in **April;** the *Motorcycle Gran Prix* is held in **May.**

TOURS. Motorcoach tours of the Rosarito Beach area can be arranged by *Baja Adventures,* 16000 Ventura Blvd., Ste. 200, Encino, CA, 91436; 818–906–BAJA; toll free in CA, 800–345–BAJA; toll free outside CA, 800–543–BAJA. Tours leave alternate weekends year round from the Amtrak Station in San Diego. Write or call for brochures and information.

SPECIAL-INTEREST SIGHTSEEING. Most sightseeing involves driving down the coast and stopping off at an empty beach. The *Plaza del Mar,* Km 58 on Old Ensenada Highway (no phone), is an archaeological garden with replicas of pre-Columbian pyramids and an exhibit of stone art; open to the public at no charge. By far the most popular side trip is *Puerto Nuevo,* also called Newport, Km 44 on the Old Ensenada Highway. What was once a small fishing village with a few shacks serving as seafood restaurants is now a full-blown restaurant row with over 25 restaurants all serving lobster and shrimp "Puerto Nuevo style" with beans, rice, and homemade tortillas. The entire area is packed on weekends, although some places, like Ortega's, draw bigger crowds. New to the area is a row of shops with some nice Mexican crafts. The houses and restaurants are on dirt roads that get rutted and muddy in the rain; park close to the highway and walk around until you find a place that looks good.

PARKS. Rodriguez Park, on the beach at the end of Calle Rene Campoy, has barbeque pits, picnic tables, and a nice grassy lawn.

BEACHES. Rosarito has beautiful beaches, with long sandy stretches for walking, running, or horseback riding and good waves for swimming and body surfing. Horses are available for rent on the beach and along the main street; early morning rides on the beach are popular. During peak seasons, roaming vendors sell crafts and drinks. There are no lifeguards, so swim at your own risk.

The waves are said to be particularly good for **surfing** at Popotla, Km 33, Calafia, Km 35.5, and Costa Baja, Km 36 on the Old Ensenada Highway.

 PARTICIPANT SPORTS. Fishing. There is a small fishing pier at Km 33 on the Old Ensenada Highway and surfcasting is allowed on the beach. There is no place in Rosarito to get fishing licenses, but the tourism officials say they are not necessary if you fish from the shore.

Golf. Played at Bajamar, an excellent 18-hole course 20 miles north of Ensenada at a vacation home resort. **Tennis** is also here.

Hang Gliding. The large sand dunes just south of Cantamar, at Km 54 on the Old Ensenada Highway, are a popular spot for hang gliders from California. It may be possible to get a few lessons during the informal classes held there.

Horseback Riding. Horses can be rented from stands on the north end of Blvd. Juárez and sometimes on the beach. Check the horses carefully; some are thin and pathetic. Rates average around $2 per hour.

 SPECTATOR SPORTS. Charreadas (Mexican rodeos) are held infrequently at the *Lienzo Tapatio Charro Ring* on the south end of town and the new *Ejido Mazatlan Charro Ring* on the east side of the toll road. At press time, a new *polo field* was under construction in the middle of town; the polo club will be private but the meets may be open to the public.

 HISTORIC SITES. Ruins of the *Misión el Descanso,* founded in the late 1700s by Dominican missionaries, can be seen behind a new chapel. The ruins are in poor condition, consisting mainly of clumps of stone and adobe. To reach the mission, take the Old Ensenada Highway south about 12 miles to the sand dunes just past Cantamar; turn left on the dirt road going under the toll road. The mission is a quarter-mile up the dirt road on the left.

 SHOPPING. The two major resort hotels have shopping arcades on the premises, with laundromats, taco stands, and some nice crafts stores. The *Calimax* grocery store on Blvd. Juárez is a good place to stock up on necessities, and there are plenty of liquor and beer stores all over town.

At the shopping arcade near La Quinta Hotel, La Casa del Arte has wicker and willow furniture, large woven rugs, and carved wood furniture. *Tienda Gonzalez* carries nice wool serapes and rugs. *Muebles Rangel* has carpeting and wicker furniture; *Oradia Imports* specializes in French perfumes. The *7–11* liquor store has styrofoam ice chests, ice, bottled water, and kites—all essential beach supplies. *Taxco Curios* has a large selection of silver jewelry. The last shop in the row, *Interios Los Rios,* has exquisite custom furniture, unusual pottery from Michoacan, and a delightful selection of ceramic "Tree of Life" candela-bra.

Farther south on Blvd. Juárez, midway between La Quinta and the Rosarito Beach Hotel, is the gigantic weekend *Tiangus,* a swap meet with a dazzling array of crafts priced inexpensively. Although bartering is frowned on in the shops, it is expected here. The nearby *Touch Boutique* has willow chairs with leather trim and some unusual tableware.

Closer to the Rosarito Beach Hotel, still on Blvd. Juárez, is the *Pandificadora Bohemia,* a bakery with excellent cookies, cakes, and *bolillos,* or hard rolls. *Gallegos Stained Glass* has beautiful Tiffany lamps and stained- and beveled-glass pieces and takes custom orders.

Just outside town on the Old Ensenada Highway heading south are three large pottery yards—*Maya, Cielito Lindo,* and *Los Hermanos*—all with rows and rows of clay pots, fountains, and fireplaces. Puerto Nuevo has a few good curio shops with silk-screened T-shirts, shell art, and hanging papiêr-maché birds and animals.

 NIGHTLIFE AND BARS. The many restaurants in Rosarito Beach try to keep their customers entertained at night with live music, piano bars, or folklorico dance shows. Driving is a bit hazardous at night, particularly when one has been drinking, so it's best to keep your car at the hotel and walk around. Listed here are some of the livelier places.

Bar La Quinta. Quinta Del Mar Hotel; 2–0016. Live music Wednesday through Sunday nights and recorded disco music on other nights; large dance floor.

Beachcomber Bar and Salon Mexicano. Rosarito Beach Hotel; 2–1106. The Beachcomber overlooks the ocean and has live piano music. The disco has a live band and dancing.

Francisco's. Calafia, Km 35.5 on the Old Ensenada Highway; 2–1581. Live music and dancing Friday through Sunday afternoons and evenings.

Hosteria Derby. Blvd. Juárez 890; 2–1422. Live guitar music nightly.

El Oasis. Blvd. Juárez 4358; 2–1942. A piano bar, with romantic music and a view of the ocean. Open 24 hours.

The Place. Blvd. Juárez 16; no phone. A small nightclub with live jazz and disco bands on weekend nights.

Rene's. Blvd. Juárez south of town; 2–1061. A rowdy place with a live dance band, mariachis, and wide-screen satellite TV.

Popotla. Km 33 on Old Ensenada Highway; 2–1504. Has live music and dancing Friday through Sunday.

BAJA SUR

LORETO

Baja's First Capital

by
JIM BUDD

The original capital of the Californias, Loreto now aspires to be simply a "capital" resort area. A start has been made, but it still has a long way to go.

In the late 1970s, when Mexico was oil rich, Fonatur, the Mexican Government agency charged with creating master-plan resorts, tapped the Loreto area for development. Much happened. Streets were paved in the dusty little village and nearly 2,000 acres were urbanized for future expansion. Telephone service was brought in, along with electricity, potable water, and sewage systems. The little town of 7,000 got an international airport. One big luxury hotel was built, as was a

97

championship tennis center, where John McEnroe was signed as touring pro.

Then everything came to a halt. No new hotels have opened since 1980. The Loreto Tennis Tournament, where McEnroe puts in an appearance, moved to Ixtapa. Although U.S. Vice-president George Bush spent his 1986 Christmas holidays in Loreto, he did so because he wanted to hold an unpublicized meeting with Mexican President Miguel de la Madrid. Loreto was the place to do it.

Escapists' Destination

In brief, Loreto is a good place to escape the crowds and relax, then do nothing for a while and relax some more.

In between, there may be some time for fishing. Long before Fonatur arrived, Loreto was a favorite getaway for a few knowing American sports enthusiasts. Their fears that it would be spoiled have thus far been unfounded. Loreto is pretty much the way it was a decade or two ago, except that people can get there more easily now.

Located on the Sea of Cortés, some 600-miles south of the California border, Loreto's setting is truly spectacular. The gold and green hills of the Sierra Gigante seem to tumble into the cobalt sea. Rain is rare. According to the local promotors, the skies are clear 360 days of the year. There are not even any bugs—or at least there are few—to plague vacationers. The dry, desert climate is not one in which insects thrive.

Understandable it is, then, that Loreto became the site of the first California mission. Padre Eusebio Kino, one of the pioneering friars, apparently selected the area in 1683 with Padre Juan Salvatierra, starting work on the buildings in 1697. It was from Loreto that Junipero Serra set out in 1769 to found more missions in the land then known as Alta California.

Missions Abandoned

Mexico won its independence from Spain in 1821, and the missions gradually were abandoned. The priests who often were from the mother country were ordered to return home. Loreto had been the administrative as well as religious center of the Californias, but, with the withering of the mission and a hurricane that virtually destroyed the settlement in 1829, the capital was moved to La Paz.

For the next century plus a few decades, the village languished. The U.S. fishermen who rediscovered the town were a hearty breed, who flew down in their own aircraft and were content to go out after marlin and sailfish in open launches. Loreto's several small hotels were built to serve this rough-and-ready set; most of them date back to the time when no highway came down this far and there was no airport worthy of the name.

Fonatur is a more recent arrival. Its projects take in not only the village, but some 15 miles of coastline. An area known as Nopolo is slated to be the address of swank hotels, while Puerto Escondido is to be the site of a major marina plus an already-built recreational vehicle and trailer park. The little town is destined to be a bedroom community for all the people who will work at the hotels, shops, and restaurants that have yet to be built. The infrastructure has been completed, and Loreto sits waiting.

EXPLORING LORETO

One could allocate 15 minutes for a tour of downtown Loreto and still have time left over. The church, Our Lady of Loreto, the mother of the California missions, is the only sight to see. A museum dedicated to missionary life adjoins the church. There are a couple of small shops and restaurants plus one hotel within walking distance. The town is on the waterfront, but the beach is a bit rocky.

Nopolo, where the luxury resorts are scheduled to go up, is about five miles south of town. Already out this way is the Hotel El Presidente, a five-star establishment complete with Hobie Cats and sailboats on its beach, a coffee shop, a specialty restaurant, a lobby bar, and a lively discotheque. Across the way is the nine-court tennis complex that is eventually scheduled to more than double in size. An 18-hole golf course designed by Desmond Muirhead is to be constructed just beyond the tennis complex.

According to Fonatur's plans, there will be 5,700 hotel rooms in the Nopolo area, along with perhaps 1,000 private homes and condo units within 10 years. Whether this actually will come to pass depends on the willingness of private investors.

More progress has been made ten miles down the road in Puerto Escondido, where the marina in the well-protected harbor already contains 100 boat slips. Ashore, the big recreational vehicle park is one of the largest and best in Mexico. Facilities for motorists and sailors alike include a snack shop, bar and restaurant, stores, showers, a swimming pool, laundry, and tennis courts.

Picnic trips to nearby Coronado Island may be arranged in Loreto proper, at Nopolo, or in Puerto Escondido. The island, along with its neighbors, is inhabited only by sea lions. Snorkeling and scuba diving are excellent out this way.

The second of the California missions, San Javier, is 22 miles from Loreto. It is, in many ways, more imposing than the first. Completed in 1757, it was built along Moorish lines, soaring high above the valley floor. Tours can be arranged to San Javier that also take in Piedras Pintas (the painted rocks), where the work of some unknown prehistoric artist is on display.

A longer excursion involves driving some 80 miles up the coast to Mulegé (moo-leh-HAY). Like Loreto, Mulegé is an old mission that was discovered by U.S. sports fishermen in the days when the only way to arrive was aboard a private plane. Many fishermen still fly in. The 32-room Hotel La Serenedad has a 4,000-foot landing strip outside its front door. The drive to Mulegé and back, with the cobalt sea on one side and the craggy hills of the Sierra Gigante on the other, is truly spectacular.

PRACTICAL INFORMATION FOR LORETO

HOW TO GET THERE. By air. You can fly, either in your own plane or aboard *Aeroméxico,* which comes in daily except Tuesdays from Los Angeles. The airline also operates direct flights from Mexico City via Guadalajara.

By Car. Loreto is 750 miles south of the California border via Mexico Hwy. 1; La Pinta Hotel at Cataviña is a good spot to stay overnight. Early starts are recommended to avoid nighttime driving. *Tres Estrellas de Oro* provides bus service along this route.

TELEPHONES. To reach Loreto from the United States, dial 01152–683 and then the local number. The number for the *Tourist Office* is 3–0344, and the *police* (who may not speak English), 3–0035. The nearest U.S. consular agent is in Mulegé; his number is (685) 1–0011.

HOTELS. The choices are good, but limited. With one exception, the hotels are out of town and isolated. A double at an *Expensive* hotel will cost above $50; Moderate, $40–$50; Inexpensive, less than $40.

El Presidente. *Expensive.* Nopolo Beach; 3–0700. A 250-room modern establishment. Across from the tennis center, it features all water sports, including fishing and sailing. Amenities include a tour desk, coffee shop, specialty restaurant, lobby bar with entertainment, and disco.

Misión. *Moderate.* López Mateos Blvd., in town; 3–0048. An old favorite, with 54 rooms, a small pool, and a friendly bar. The beach across the street is stony, but most guests come to fish; arrangements for fishing may be made at the hotel.

Oasis. *Moderate.* Loreto Beach (U.S. phone 714–534–8630). One of the original fishing camps and a favorite with those who want to spend as much time as possible on the water. The hotel has its own fleet of skiffs.

La Pinta. *Moderate.* Blvd. Misión de Loreto; 3–0025. Part of a chain of Baja California hotels, this 48-room property is a much-remodeled fishing camp on the beach. It has its own fleet of launches, a pool, and 2 tennis courts.

Serenidad. *Inexpensive.* In Mulegé; 1–0011. Some 80 miles north of Loreto but, in the opinion of many, worth the trip. The 32 rooms have fireplaces (nights can get chilly), and the Saturday barbecue is a Baja institution.

DINING OUT. César's, on the plaza in Loreto and **Tripuí** at the recreational vehicle park in Puerto Escondido, are the best places outside the hotels. Both are *Moderate* and both serve Mexican food.

 HOW TO GET AROUND. Taxis are in good supply and fares are inexpensive. It might be wise, however, to establish the fare before you get in. There is a **car rental** agency at the airport and in the Hotel El Presidente, but only a few vehicles (all with standard shift) are available.

 TOURS. Sightseeing in the area means dropping by the little *Museum of Missions* at Our Lady of Loreto on the plaza late in the morning, popping over to the Hotel El Presidente for a bit of refreshment, then continuing on to the recreational-vehicle park for lunch (the restaurant is quite good). Many variations on this theme are possible, but you get the idea. Use taxis for transportation.

Picnic cruises to *Coronado Island,* excursions into the mountains to visit the *San Javier Mission* and view prehistoric rock paintings, and day trips to Mulegé can be arranged through hotels. If you prefer, you may call the local tour operator, *Las Palmas,* at 3–0700.

SPECIAL EVENTS. The first week of **September** is *Fiesta Week* in both Loreto and Mulegé. The *Loreto Tennis Festival,* which stars John McEnroe, is scheduled for **December** but may be moved to some other venue.

 BEACHES. All Loreto-area hotels are on the waterfront, but the beaches are disappointing, being more stones than sand. *Puerto Escondido,* about 15 miles below Loreto proper, is probably the best place to swim in the sea. The setting everywhere is spectacular: the craggy hills tumble into the gentle surf in such a way that Fonatur promotes Loreto as the place "where even the mountains swim."

PARTICIPANT SPORTS. Fishing is what put Loreto on the map, as far as many Americans are concerned. Roosterfish, yellowtail, and mackerel are caught during the winter, while marlin, sailfish, and amberjack lie in wait during the summer. Pompano and snapper bite throughout the year. Sports people should bring tackle with them because the tackle that is available locally is likely to be primitive and worn. All Loreto-area hotels can arrange fishing and many own their own skiffs; no cabin cruisers are available. In addition to the hotels, *Alfredo's Sportsfishing* (tel. 3–0016) takes anglers out and has good guides.

Scuba specialists are *Loreto Divers* (tel. 3–0029). The coral reefs off Coronado and Carmen islands are an undersea adventure.

Sailing is at its best off the beach by the Hotel El Presidente on Nopalo Bay. Hobie Cats and similar craft may be rented.

Tennis is at its best in Baja at the *Loreto Tennis Center* adjoining the Hotel El Presidente in Nopolo, five miles south of Loreto proper. The center, where John McEnroe is touring pro, is operated by All American Sports; it has nine illuminated courts, and expert instructors.

HISTORICAL SITES AND MUSEUMS. The Church of Our Lady of Loreto, begun in 1697, was the first link in a chain of missions that eventually stretched as far north as Sonoma, CA. The adjacent museum contains relics from the missionary period.

San Javier Mission, 22 miles into the mountains from Loreto, was the second mission. Because of its Moorish architecture, it is considered more imposing.

Piedras Pintas, which means "painted rocks," near San Javier, is one of the few places where it is easy to view the prehistoric paintings found in remote areas throughout Baja California. These are estimated to be 2,000 years old.

SHOPPING. There are few opportunities for browsing and buying in Loreto. *Kino's* and *La Choya,* near each other on the waterfront, handle a nice assortment of handicrafts from all over Mexico, including sweaters and serapes. Resort wear and ceramics are also available. A smaller selection is to be found in the shop at the *Hotel El Presidente,* which also stocks reading material in English.

NIGHTLIFE. After-dark entertainment is pretty much limited to the lobby bar and disco at the Hotel El Presidente; this is also the only place with TVs in the rooms and a satellite dish to pick up U.S. programs. The bars at the other hotels usually attract a congenial crowd, but these fisherfolk turn in early.

LA PAZ

Baja Sur's Administrative Center

by
JIM BUDD

Capital of Baja California Sur, La Paz has a reputation as "bargain city." With some 150,000 inhabitants, it is the only community of any size on the peninsula below Ensenada. Those who enjoy a bit of bustle like that. But the big attraction is low prices. At press time, double rooms at the best hotels were $40, and that is only the beginning.

La Paz owes what little prosperity it enjoys to Mexican buyers from the mainland who come to do a bit of duty-free shopping. These price-conscious folk are not interested in spending a bundle on a fancy room or feasting on gourmet delicacies.

Much the same can be said for Americans who find their way to La Paz. Most of them are sports fishermen who want a good boat and crew at a reasonable price, a congenial spot to quaff a few beers, and a clean place to sleep. They find it all in La Paz.

This is not to say that the hotels are flophouses or the restaurants, soup kitchens. Back in the 1970s, with the opening of the Transpeninsular Highway, many speculators were betting that La Paz was going to turn into another Acapulco, and some nice hotels went up. The expected crowds never came (The Capes get most of the luxury trade), and price lines had to be held for the hotels to survive.

Founded by Cortés

La Paz has a history of struggling to survive. The first settlement in these parts was founded by Hernán Cortés in 1535, but within a couple of years it vanished. Every so often, new attempts were made, for the bay was rich with oyster beds and pearls. The trouble was that once anyone had a bag full of pearls, he would leave and head to a place where he could enjoy his new wealth. Not only was the desert setting unappealing to the Spaniards, but the local Indians were a constant menace.

Finally, in 1720, the Jesuits were sent to pacify the tribes. They did so in an unexpected manner, bringing with them diseases that gradually wiped out the natives. Within 30 years, there were no Indians left to minister to, and the mission was abandoned.

Present-day La Paz dates back to 1811 when a permanent settlement finally was established. In those days, the rest of Mexico was being torn apart by the struggle for independence, and the Baja hamlet was a quiet refuge that lived up to its name (La Paz means "peace"). Permanent existence was guaranteed in 1829 when, after Loreto was leveled by a hurricane, La Paz became the capital of the Californias.

That distinction all but cost the settlement its name. In 1847, during the Mexican War, American troops invaded and managed to occupy La Paz only after bloody fighting. The troops were happy to leave once peace was restored and strongly advised Washington not to press Mexico into ceding what appeared to be an empty and worthless peninsula.

In 1853, a fresh band of Americans under William Walker seized the city. Walker proclaimed himself president of an independent republic, although apparently his real aim was to bring Baja into the American union as a slave state. Whatever he was up to, Walker's plans failed; Mexican authorities soon had him running.

For the next century, La Paz went back to pearl diving and long siestas. Then, just as things were starting to look good, some disease killed all the oysters. After that, with a wink from federal authorities, what was then a territorial capital turned to smuggling to get by.

Foreign Goods Plentiful

Normally, Mexico imposes stiff duties on imports and requires special licenses—almost impossible to obtain—to bring in many products. The idea is to encourage domestic industry, but it also encourages dealing in contraband. The main reason many Mexicans travel abroad is to shop. By making La Paz and the rest of the peninsula a duty-free zone, the federal government encouraged many people to do their illicit buying within the country's borders. Perhaps the most curious thing about La Paz is its many hole-in-the-wall stores that are jammed with electronics from the Orient, French perfumes, Czech crystal, Danish butter, and Chinese shoes.

The airport that brought the shoppers in also turned out to be a fine gateway for sports fishermen. In the 1950s, Southern Baja was winning fame as one of the best places in the world to hook a billfish. The super-rich were buzzing down to hideaway camps aboard their private planes. The merely comfortable followed that trail on scheduled flights to La Paz.

But La Paz is not primarily a resort town. It is more a commercial and administrative center (Southern Baja became a state in 1974), although in no way can it be called hectic. The atmosphere is more that of some outpost of a colonial empire. For the tourist, this is all to the good. There is more to do than just fish. Lingering over a beer for an hour or two at a sidewalk cafe while watching the pelicans dive is part of the routine. The shops are fun. At night, along with disco hopping, there are cinemas to enjoy.

EXPLORING LA PAZ

Running down the east coast of Baja California, Mexico Hwy. 1, makes a gentle, hardly noticeable U turn as it nears La Paz, so that the city looks north when you expect it to look east. This may not seem important, but at dawn and dusk, the sun seems to be on the wrong side of the sky.

The highway, once it reaches town, becomes Paseo Alvaro Obregón, which everyone calls simply El Maelcón. This is pretty much the main street, with a couple of hotels, airline offices, restaurants, curio shops, and sidewalk cafes. The local tourism office is on the beach side of the road, across from 16 de Septiembre.

A street named Agustín Arreola, which runs inland from the Perla Hotel on the Malecón, leads to the commercial heart of the city, where there are a couple of big department stores with attractive imports and any number of jumbly little shops in a maze of lanes and avenues that must have been laid out during a bad dream. The old territorial capitol faces one side and the cathedral, Our Lady of Peace (for whom La Paz was named), faces the other. The plaza is peaceful—a quiet little park 3 blocks from the waterfront.

Three blocks farther in is the Museum of Anthropology, a bit out of the way, but worth the effort. On Cinco de Mayo at Altamirano, the museum gives a good overall picture of life in Southern Baja to the present. On display are old maps, relics from the missions, artifacts and outfits used by 19th century cowboys, and contemporary handicrafts fashioned from cork, palm fiber, and leather.

Although there is a beach of sorts on the seaward side of the Malecón, better swimming beaches can be found above and below the city. A couple of good hotels are located in each direction, but the best beaches, a few miles below La Paz, have no hotels. Coromuel is the closest to town; Pichilingue, where the ferry from Mazatlán puts in, has restaurants and restrooms.

Boats go out to Balandra and to Cerralvo Islands. Both have lovely beaches and facilities for water sports. Bringing along a box lunch is a good idea.

Visitors staying in La Paz may want to rent a car or take a bus to San José del Cabo (see section on *The Capes*), which is about a four-hour drive. A shorter trip may be made by rental car or taxi to El Triunfo, once a bustling silver-mining center but now little more than a ghost town. Here, local artisans weave wonderful baskets from palm leaves.

Most people who come to La Paz, however, do so for the fishing. Although hotels can make the arrangements, many sports people prefer to do their own negotiating with outfitters. Striped marlin, roosterfish, tuna, bonito, and yellowtail can be caught throughout the year and black marlin and sailfish, from June through November.

PRACTICAL INFORMATION FOR LA PAZ

HOW TO GET THERE. By Car. La Paz is about a 920-mile drive down Mexico 1, the Transpeninsula Highway. Overnight stops should be planned at Cataviña and either Mulegé or Loreto; driving after dark is to be avoided. *Tres Estrellas de Oro* provides bus service along this route.

By Air. *Aeroméxico* flies in daily from Los Angeles and six times a week from Tucson. Both *Aeroméxico* and *Mexicana* serve La Paz daily from Tijuana, which is just across the border from San Diego. *Aerocalifornia* flies in from The Capes.

By Sea. Ferries to and from Mazatlán make overnight sailings six days a week. Sleeping accommodations are available at a low cost, but there is little luxury aboard. Tickets must be purchased on the day of departure.

TELEPHONES. To call La Paz from the United States, dial 01152–682 and then the local number. When calling the United States, remember that collect calls are much less expensive. The number for the Tourist Office is 2–1190; police, 2–0781; and hospital, 2–111. (Police and hospital personnel may not speak English).

HOTELS. La Paz has beachfront hotels above and below town plus a variety of places to stay in the city. In this listing, categories are determined by price. The *Deluxe* hotels charge about $50 for a double; expect to pay $40 in a *First Class* establishment, $30 at a *Moderate* place, and $20 at one that is *Inexpensive.*

Deluxe

Las Arenas. Mexico 1, about an hour south of town; no phone (in California call 800–423–4785). Off by itself, all suites, a nice beach, and great fishing.

Ramada Gran Baja. Calle Rangel; 2–3900. A concrete high-rise hotel, with 250 rooms overlooking the beach. Fishing, sailing, and other water sports, as well as tennis and miniature golf. Nightly entertainment.

First Class

Los Arcos. Alvaro Obregón 498; 2–7444. Best of the downtown hotels, across the street from the beach, with 182 rooms (some in bungalows) and attractive pools. A favorite with fisherfolk.

Palmira. Pichilingue Rd.; 2–4000. West of town and close to a nice beach. Pool, tennis court, restaurant, bar, and disco.

La Perla. Alvaro Obregón 150; 2–0777. On the waterfront downtown, best known for its popular sidewalk cafe and busy nightclub.

Presidente. Pichilinque Rd.; 2–6544. By the beach, with 109 rooms, a swimming pool, restaurant, and bar. Run by one of Mexico's largest chains.

Moderate

Gardenias. Aquiles Serdán Norte 520; 2–3088. A commercial hotel in town.

Misiónes de La Paz. On an island and reached by boat (no charge); 6–8220. Well managed and wonderful for escapists. There are only 25 rooms; pool, beach, good restaurant, and evening entertainment.

La Posada. Reforma and Plaza Sur; 2–4401. A modest 25-room hotel on the beach just above town, attracting guests who could pay much more but simply love this place.

Inexpensive

Calafia. Mexico 1, east of town; 2–5811. Restaurant, air-conditioned rooms, pool. The beach is nearby.

Lori. Bravo at Madero; 2–1819. Two blocks from the waterfront, with clean, air-conditioned rooms and a restaurant.

Marcasey. Ignacio Ramirez 2016; 2–4484. Small, with suites that include kitchenettes; dining room and tour desk on the premises.

 DINING OUT. One of the nice things about La Paz is its many restaurants (relatively speaking). Steaks and seafood are the main items on most menus, but pizzas, burgers, and chow mein are not hard to come by. In this listing, expect to pay $15 for a meal in an *Expensive* place, $10 in a *Moderate* establishment, and perhaps $5 in one that is *Inexpensive.* Tips (10% to 15%) and drinks are extra; remember that even in this duty-free zone, imported liquor is expensive. Only Visa (V) and MasterCard (MC) are accepted outside the hotels but cash is preferred.

El Molino. *Expensive.* Alvaro Obregón and Legaspi; 2–6191. An attractive waterfront cafe with a nice seaside view, serving steaks, seafood, and salads.

La Venta. *Expensive.* Colima at Ramirez; 2–6885. Perhaps the most elegant restaurant in La Paz, specializing in steaks and seafood served in a garden patio. Piano music at night. MC, V.

La Arboleda. *Moderate.* Revolución at Ocampo; 2–0622. Pleasant, with tables indoors and in the patio; Mexican dishes are the specialty, and there is evening entertainment. MC, V.

El Caracol Loco. *Moderate.* At the marina just above town; 2–8404. Its name means "crazy snail"; this restaurant is something of a poor tourists' yacht club serving Mexican food and beer. MC, V.

El Moro. *Moderate.* Pichilingue Highway (Mexico 1 below town); no phone. From the name and decor, one might expect Moorish fare, but the food is Italian. MC, V.

Samalu. *Moderate.* Rangel between Colima and Jalisco; 2–2481. Mexican food and seafood. A good place for lunch. MC, V.

La Terraza. *Moderate.* Alvaro Obregón 1570; 2–0777. A sidewalk cafe that is a local institution. MC, V.

California Burger. *Inexpensive.* Revolución at Pineda; 2–4782. A bit of the United States in La Paz, serving beer as well as malts.

La Fabula. *Inexpensive.* Alvaro Obregón between Cinco de Mayo and Independencia; no phone. The imaginative local pizza parlor everybody tries at least once.

Nuevo Pekin. *Inexpensive.* Alvaro Obregón at Victoria; 2–9430. The most attractive of the many Chinese restaurants in La Paz.

HOW TO GET AROUND. Volkswagen **minibuses** provide transportation from the airport at a flat rate, with tickets sold in the terminal. Those staying at one of the beachfront hotels will need to take a **taxi** into town, where everything is within walking distance; cabs are plentiful. **Rental cars** are available at the airport and in town; rates start at about $50 a day (including insurance and taxes) for a standard-shift subcompact. Bigger air-conditioned vehicles cost considerably more when they are available.

TOURIST INFORMATION. La Paz, being the state capital, boasts the only tourist office in the state. It is located on the Malecón (Alvaro Obregón) at the foot of 16 de Septiembre and can be quite helpful; phone 2–1190.

USEFUL ADDRESSES. *Aeroméxico* is at Alvaro Obregón and Hidalgo; *Mexicana,* at Alvaro Obregón 340; and *Aerocalifornia,* at Alvaro Obregón 240 (Alvaro Obregón is the Malecón running along the waterfront). The *police station* (2–0781) is at Constitución and Altamirano, the main *hospital* (2–1111) is at Salvatierra and Bravo, and the *postoffice* is at Constitutión and Revolución.

TOURS. *Viajes Coromuel* (2–8006) features city sightseeing for about $5, half-day outings that include a swim at Pichilingue Beach for $10, and an all-day excursion to The Capes, lunch included, for $32. The *Tio Eduardo* (2–3654) leaves daily from a downtown dock for a luncheon cruise to Espírito Santo Island and returns at about 5:30; the price is about $26. During the winter months, *Viajes Cardon* (2–2958) runs a 12-hour whale-watching cruise with breakfast and lunch for $32.

SPORTS. Fishing is the big attraction in La Paz. Striped marlin, roosterfish, tuna, bonito, and yellowtail can be hooked throughout the year. Black marlin and sailfish are found from June through November. Both skiffs and well-equipped cabin cruisers up to 32 feet may be chartered. Hotels can make arrangements, or sports people may contact either *Jack Valdez* at 2–0038 or *Hugo Fisher* at 2–4011.

Scuba specialists are *Baja Diving Service* at Independencia 107; tel. 2–0719. They make trips to five areas, organize night dives, and even set up snorkeling excursions.

Tennis is available at several hotels (see listing above).

BEACHES. The seashore everywhere in Mexico is federal property. Since there are no private beaches, hotels have no authority over their waterfronts. There usually are no lifeguards, so swimmers need to be cautious. The beach by the Malecón in downtown La Paz is not attractive, but several others in the area are appealing.

Coromuel, just a couple of miles below the city, has a restaurant, rest rooms, and shaded chairs for rent.

Pichilingue, a bit farther out, is nice and has all facilities, but the view is marred by the ferry terminal and industrial installations.

Balandra, El Tecolote, and *El Coyote* are reached by a dirt road that starts at Pichilingue. All three beaches are beautiful and popular with campers.

Punta Arenas is about 30 miles south of La Paz and one of the nicest beaches in the area. There is a good resort hotel out this way, its bar and restaurant open to the public. Fishing is good, and both boats and equipment may be rented.

Cerralvo Island, reached by boat from Punta Arenas, has wonderful beaches and a Robinson Crusoe feeling to it.

Espírito Santo Island, reached by boat from La Paz (there are daily picnic cruises), is a good place for both camping and surf fishing.

MUSEUMS. *The Museum of Anthropology* (2–1190), at Cinco de Mayo and Altamirano, is an excellent introduction to Southern Baja. Exhibits include old maps, relics from the missionary era, the outfits worn and equipment used by local cowboys, and a display of handicrafts still produced in the state.

The Library of the Californias, at Cinco de Mayo and Madero (no phone), although not really a museum, displays maps and engravings of the past and chronicles the settlement of the Californias up to the Oregon line.

SHOPPING. Being a duty-free area (as is all of Baja California), La Paz specializes in imports that are either expensive or unavailable in the rest of Mexico. People from the mainland come over by plane or ferry to get what they cannot buy at home; travelers heading to the mainland must first pass through customs. Whether these imports will appeal to foreign tourists depends on the individual (neither liquor nor tobacco is exempt from duties), but it can be fun to look. *La Perla,* a big barn of a place at Mutualismo 39, claims to be the biggest department store south of Tijuana, although *Dorian's* on 16 de Septiembre, seems to stock goods of better quality. Nearby, on Callejón 21 de Agosto, the *Plaza Oriental* is a shopping complex that peddles treasures from Asia, Europe, and the United States. Men may wish to peek in at *El Trébol* on Independencia 309 and to look for bargains. Along Alvaro Obregón on the waterfront (Malecón), several shops sell Mexican handicrafts; of these, *La Carreta Delfin* is among the best. *The Weaver,* on Alvaro Obregón between Jalisco and Nayarit, is where Fortunato Silva creates his fabrics.

NIGHTLIFE. Although not exactly wild after dark, La Paz offers more in the way of entertainment than other Southern Baja destinations. Mariachis play at *La Terraza,* the sidewalk cafe by the Hotel La Perla. Inside there is a complete nightclub, *La Cabaña.* Down the street is the *Okay Maguey* disco. *La Ronda,* at the corner of Abasolo and Colima, has both live and recorded music. *Soko's,* at Alvaro Obregón and 16 de Septiembre, bills itself as a drive-in disco, where couples can dine, dance, and, if in the mood, shop for handicrafts.

THE CAPES

A Paradise for Game Fishing

by
JIM BUDD

At the tip of the Baja Peninsula are the unidentical twin towns of Cabo San Lucas and San José del Cabo, 20 miles apart but known jointly as Los Cabos—The Capes.

Fishing put this area on most travel maps. Calm seas and sheltered bays make it one of the finest places in the world to go after the big ones. The mouth of the Sea of Cortés is said to be a natural fish trap swirling with monsters of the deep. In the 1950s, for those who had the cash, no price was too high to pay to hook one of these brutes. Some of the finest hotels were built before there was a scheduled air service.

Sports people flew in their own craft. Some arrived by yacht. Some still do.

Of late, The Capes are being discovered by others as well. At few places is the seascape as dramatic as it is here, where craggy rock arches carved by nature mark the land's end. There is a special blueness to the water where the gulf and ocean meet and a dry crispness to the air in a world where only cactus grows. A wonderful day may be spent sitting on the sands and watching the whales at play.

Cabo San Lucas, Mile 1 (or, more correctly, Km 1) on Mexico 1, is the most exclusive resort town in all Baja. Although it is no longer strictly a millionaires' sandbox now that 727s and DC9s fly in from everywhere, there is a feeling of money here. Thatched-roof restaurants serve lobster dinners, and romantic trios serenade the hungry. Hotels range from first class to super deluxe, so that travelers who are watching their pesos may need to seek some other town in which to stay. The marina is filled with splendid yachts and the trailer camps house recreational vehicles that seem like palaces on wheels.

Before the highway was completed and commercial jets began to arrive, Cabo San Lucas was little more than a pair of dusty streets and a general store. When two cafes opened near each other, the neighborhood came to be known as restaurant row. None of the hotels has been built within walking distance of the others.

Hamlet Image Wanes

Still, what scarcely ranked as a hamlet has grown into a little town. Cruise ships—during the winter several put in each week—have wrought quite a change. An open-air handicrafts market, along with several shops, tempts buyers, and there is a growing number of good restaurants. Fonatur, the Mexican government resort-development agency, has been busy improving the marina facilities in Cabo San Lucas and sprucing up the waterfront.

Fonatur's big project in these parts, however, is in San José del Cabo. Three hotels are now open on the beach, and a number of condominium complexes are going up. The first 9 holes of what eventually will be an 18-hole golf course on the beach are ready, and the commercial and cultural center is in operation. Already there is a good choice of restaurants in San José, and the night life equals that of San Lucas.

The San José resort area is a mile or two outside the little town. A community of 15,000, it is the only settlement of any size south of La Paz. In many ways, it is more orderly than Cabo San Lucas. There is an attractive main street, complete with a town hall, church, plaza, and several stores and restaurants. The airlines have offices there, there are a couple of banks, and this is the place to catch a bus bound for Tijuana.

EXPLORING THE CAPES

If you arrive by jet, bus, or car, San José del Cabo is the first of the twin towns you will encounter. The international airport is less than a ten-minute drive (but it is about a half-hour drive to Cabo San Lucas).

A settlement that dates back more than 250 years, San José del Cabo is awakening from centuries of slumber. Once-musty stores have become almost lively emporiums, and half a dozen restaurants dot Avenida Mijares, the main street (and the only downtown boulevard to bear a name). The landmarks are the town hall, the local church, and an attractive plaza.

Spurring all this activity is Fonatur, which owns some 4,000 acres near the beach, where three hotels already have opened and several condominium complexes are under construction. A new golf course is in this area, along with a tennis complex featuring 9 illuminated courts and an attractive clubhouse. The Commercial and Cultural Center, which contains a small shopping mall, is close by.

San José del Cabo attracts mainly sunseekers, who arrive on charter flights. Oddly, the three hotels have been built along a stretch where the surf often makes swimming dangerous, although the beach itself is wide and inviting.

Both deep-sea and shoal fishing may be arranged at the hotels in San José del Cabo. The estuary near the hotel is a wonderful place for angling or simply exploring aboard a paddleboat. There are scuba diving expeditions, luncheon tours to view a colony of sea lions, and sunset dinner cruises. During the evening, the hotels have live music and one of them boasts a modern disco.

For all that, San José del Cabo tends to be quiet. The restless are inclined to feel there is not much to do.

Upscale Cabo San Lucas, 23 miles from San José, is cluttered in a charming sort of way and is a good deal more social. Everything in Cabo San Lucas seems to center on fishing and boats—vessels that are either chartered or owned. Restaurants advertise that they will cook what one has caught, and dinner conversations focus on brutes that were hooked and those that got away.

Many of the resort hotels are still several miles from the little town. Those in town are far enough out that either taxis or rental cars are needed to get around. Many visitors arrive in recreational vehicles, remaining for weeks or even months. Those with yachts have been known to stay for an entire season, docking their boats and flying out and back when business calls. Every day or two during the winter months, Cabo San Lucas fills up for a few hours with passengers from cruise ships.

Along with fishing, those who stay for a while in Cabo San Lucas often go to the many beaches, sail, scuba, Windsurf, and perhaps even hunt. There are few sights to see other than the natural arches in the rocks that marks the tip of the peninsula (seen from tour boats); the lighthouses at Cabo Falso (False Cape), where the view is spectacular and riding horses may be rented; Todos Santos, 50 miles up an unpaved highway on Baja's Pacific coast; and San José del Cabo and La Paz. Thus, aside from fishing, most vacationers in Cabo San Lucas simply stay put. The clear desert air is invigorating and the sharp blue sea is beautiful. Just being there makes many people happy to be alive.

PRACTICAL INFORMATION FOR THE CAPES

HOW TO GET THERE. By Car. At least 26 driving hours will be needed to cover the 1,060 miles of Mexico 1 from the border to The Capes. Overnight stops should be planned at Cataviña and Loreto, since driving after dark is to be avoided. *Tres Estrellas de Oro* provides bus service along this route.

By Air. *Aeroméxico, Mexicana,* and *PSA* fly in from Los Angeles; *Mexicana* provides nonstop service from Denver and one-stop service from San Francisco; *Aeroméxico* zips down nonstop from San Diego (Tijuana Airport), and *Aerocalifornia* links La Paz with Los Cabos.

By Sea. Cabo San Lucas is visited once a week throughout the year by Carnival Cruise Lines' *Tropicale* and from November through March by Sitmar Cruises' *Fairsea* and *Fairsky.* Princess Cruises' vessels call January through March, and Admiral Cruises' *Stardancer* makes weekly sailings during the winter. The *Coromuel,* a ferry, makes overnight crossings between Cabo San Lucas and Puerto Vallarta twice a week. Sleeping accommodations are available at low fares, but there is little luxury aboard this vessel, which also transports cars and trucks; tickets must be purchased at the ferry terminal on the day of departure.

TELEPHONES. To call Los Cabos from the United States, first dial 01152 and then the area code (684) and the local number. At press time, telephone communications in the region were poor, although improvements were promised. Many hotels, including some of the best, had no telephone service.

Emergencies are best handled through hotels or tourist offices, where English-speaking personnel usually can be found. The number for the **Tourist**

Office in San José del Cabo is 2–0233 and in Cabo San Lucas, 3–0494. For **police** in San José del Cabo, call 2–0361; in Cabo San Lucas, 3–0057. In San José del Cabo, the **hospital** phone is 2–0316; in Cabo San Lucas, 3–0102.

When calling the United States or elsewhere out of Mexico, remember that, because of Mexican taxes, collect calls are much less expensive.

HOTELS. In Cabo San Lucas, the resort properties are fairly spread out, and many of them are not too new. Those in San José del Cabo are close together and less than 10 years old. Note that some properties have no telephone. Some hotels add a service charge in lieu of tips. Expect to pay $100 for a double at a *Super Deluxe* resort, $85 at a *Deluxe* establishment, $60 for a *First Class* room, $40 in a *Moderate* hotel, and $25 in an *Inexpensive* place.

Super Deluxe

Cabo San Lucas. Hwy. 1, about 7 miles from Cabo San Lucas; no phone in hotel (for reservations call, in the United States, 213–205–0055). Spread out over a 2,500-acre beachfront estate with several categories of rooms, suites, and villas. Fishing, hunting, horseback riding, tennis, trap shooting, and an outstanding kitchen.

Hacienda. On the beach in Cabo San Lucas; 3–0122. A wide variety of accommodations on perhaps the best beach in the area. Fishing, hunting, horseback riding, sailing, tennis, water skiing, and scuba. The restaurant boasts the largest menu on The Capes.

Palmilla. Near San José del Cabo; no phone in the hotel (in the United States, call 619–576–1282). Small and posh, with 70 rooms and suites, a private airstrip, and its own fishing fleet. Two lighted tennis courts, a large pool, and lots of beach. American plan only, which comes to about $170 per day for 2. No credit cards.

Twin Dolphin. Outside Cabo San Lucas; no phone in hotel (in the United States, call 213–386–3940). One of the newer hotels in the Cabo area, small and exclusive, with 58 sea-view rooms, a pool, beach, 18-hole putting green, 2 tennis courts, and its own fishing fleet.

Deluxe

El Presidente. On the beach in San José del Cabo; 2–0038. Nicest hotel in San José, managed by a large Mexican chain; 250 rooms, deep-sea fishing, 2 lighted tennis courts, golf nearby, boating, scuba diving, 3 restaurants, and a disco.

First Class

Calinda Cabo Baja. Near Cabo San Lucas; 3–0044. Designed along the lines of a Pueblo village, with 125 rooms, 3 pools, illuminated tennis courts, and 2 restaurants. Getting to the beach is a hike.

Finisterra. In Cabo San Lucas; 3–0000. An older hotel, somewhat gloomy, with 80 rooms overlooking both the Pacific and the Sea of Cortés.

Solmar. In Cabo San Lucas; 3–0023. On the beach at the tip of the peninsula, with 65 rooms and its own fishing fleet. Charming, friendly, and well managed.

Moderate

Aquamarina Comfort Inn. On the beach at San José del Cabo; 2–0239. One of Calinda/Quality Inns' no-frills hotels, but quite nice and well managed, with 100 rooms, a lobby bar, restaurant, tour desk, and golf nearby.

Castel Cabo. On the beach at San José del Cabo; 2–0155. Pleasant but not luxurious, with 150 rooms, a beach, pool, tennis courts, and golf nearby. Fishing and tours arranged.

Mar de Cortes. In the center of Cabo San Lucas, with 72 rooms, a small pool (no beach), restaurant, and bar. A favorite of those who come to fish.

Inexpensive

Albergue. In the heart of Cabo San Lucas. A 200-bed youth hostel.

Nuevo Sol. On the beach at San José del Cabo. Spartan but a favorite with international backpackers.

 DINING OUT. Leaving a hotel to go out to dinner in The Capes almost always involves taking a taxi and is something of an event. In Cabo San Lucas, the eateries are not close to each other, but in San José del Cabo, many are in town, allowing the hungry to stroll around and see which spot appeals most. Prices outside hotels are lower than in them. Allow $20 for a meal in an *Expensive* place; $15, in a *Moderate* establishment; and under $10, in one that is *Inexpensive.* A service charge sometimes is included in the tab; if not, allow 10% to 15%. MasterCard (MC) and Visa (V) are accepted, where indicated, but restaurants prefer dollars, pesos, or traveler's checks.

SAN JOSÉ DEL CABO

Damiana. *Expensive.* Downtown; 2–0499. Something of a Mexican hacienda, serving elegant regional cuisine indoors or around the patio. MC, V.

L'ecuyer du Rey. *Expensive.* Downtown; 2–0374. A remarkably good French-run French restaurant open only for dinner.

Las Palmas. *Expensive.* On the waterfront. A thatched, open-air seafood restaurant that is one of the most fashionable spots for lunch. MC, V.

Andre Mar. *Moderate.* Downtown; 2–0374. An international restaurant open for breakfast, lunch, and dinner. MC, V.

Balandra. *Moderate.* Downtown; 2–0140. A lobster house open for lunch and dinner. Fishermen can have their catch prepared here. MC, V.

Amigo's Pizza. *Inexpensive.* Commercial and Cultural Center, hotel zone. Pizzas, hamburgers, beer, music, and color TV.

Los Toritos. *Inexpensive.* Commercial and Cultural Center, hotel zone. Tortas, tacos, enchiladas, and beer in nice surroundings.

Las Tortugas. *Inexpensive.* A downtown beer garden serving steaks, seafood, and snacks.

CABO SAN LUCAS

Alfonso's. *Expensive.* On Rafa's Beach, with a bar fashioned out of a wreck of a sailboat. Steaks and chicken, along with seafood. MC, V.

Candido's. *Expensive.* 3–0666. Open for dinner only; reservations are suggested. Something of a country-club setting, refined gathering place for sports fishermen and their spouses. MC, V.

El Delfin. *Expensive.* Luxury beneath a thatched hut. Large drinks and good seafood are the specialties. MC, V.

Giggling Marlin. *Expensive.* 3–1982. Noisy but lots of fun. The place where sports fishermen congregate after a good day. MC, V.

La Balandra. *Moderate.* 3–0012. Oldest restaurant in town, this Spanish seafood restaurant is on a street known as "restaurant row," although there are few restaurants here now. MC, V.

La Fogata. *Moderate.* Downtown; 2–0480. Steaks, seafood, and Mexican fare dominate the menu. MC, V.

Galeon. *Moderate.* 3–0443. Across from the marina, this steak and seafood house is open for breakfast and has a delightful view. MC, V.

El Rey Sol. *Moderate.* Across from the marina. Open for breakfast and throughout the day. This is a seafood house, its name not withstanding.

Patty's. *Moderate.* A spot that is geared to American tastes. Chicken, pork, steaks, barbecue, and seafood are on the menu.

Petisa. *Moderate.* A favorite spot for a sandwich or pizza. Desserts are the house specialty.

Taqueria San Lucas. *Inexpensive.* Open for breakfast and lunch only, this is a favorite hangout for the young at heart.

 HOW TO GET AROUND. Volkswagen **minibuses** provide collective transportation to and from the airport, charging about $2 for the San José del Cabo run and $4 into or out of Cabo San Lucas. **Taxis** are plentiful and inexpensive in the area. Tour operators provide **vans** to take clients fishing or on boat trips. **Rental cars** are especially useful, but they usually are standard-shift open Jeeps that are not always kept in the best repair. Prices run about $50 a day, including taxes and insurance. *Hertz, Avis, Budget,* and others have stands at the airport and in hotels.

TOURIST INFORMATION. The best sources of information are hotel travel desks. The *Cabo San Lucas Chamber of Commerce* maintains a booth by the marina, but it is not always staffed.

TOURS. Boat trips out to the natural arches in the rocks where the Pacific meets the Sea of Cortés, cost about $5 from the Cabo San Lucas Marina dock or $10 from most hotels, with transportation to the dock included. Luncheon junkets to the sea lion colony run about $18 and sunset dinner cruises, about $25.

BEACHES. The hotels in San José del Cabo are on a lovely stretch of sand; the only problem is that the surf often is too rough for swimming and there are no lifeguards. Down the coast toward Cabo San Lucas are several inviting coves where the waters are more gentle. *Caleta Linda* is a favorite for snorkeling, while *Costa Azul* is rated tops for surfing. *Cemetery Beach,* on the outskirts of Cabo San Lucas, is popular with campers.

In Cabo San Lucas, *Playa Medano,* also known as *Rafa's Beach,* is billed by the Hotel Hacienda, which stands there, as the only safe swimming beach in the area. *Playa Solmar,* on the Pacific, is reached by marching through the lobby of the Solmar Hotel. (No one seems to mind; beaches in Mexico are federal property and open to everyone.) This beach is a lovely spot for sunning and wading, but swimming can be dangerous. *Playa de Amor,* or Lovers' Beach, probably so-named because it is difficult to get to, is best reached by skiffs called *pangas.* Separated from Solmar Beach by towering cliffs, Lovers' Beach is washed by both the sea and the ocean. Snorkeling is good here, but the waters can be tricky; your best bet is to hire a boatman to keep watch.

Several lovely beaches are along the Pacific side of the peninsula north of Cabo San Lucas. They are reached by the nearly impassable, unpaved Hwy. 19 and hence usually are empty. *San Cristobal* is one of the nicest stretches of sand out this way. Swimming at these Pacific beaches is suicidal, but they make lovely picnic spots.

SPORTS. Fishing is the big sport along The Capes, with local boosters claiming 40,000 marlin hooked annually in the nearby waters. Billfish can be caught throughout the year, as can roosterfish, wahoo, tuna, and many other species. Sportsfolk can choose between skiffs (known locally as *pangas*), which carry 3 anglers and cost about $120 a day, to cruisers, which hold 4 or 5 people in addition to the crew (charter rates start at $275). Travel desks at all hotels can make arrangements for fishing trips (many hotels have their own fleets), or skippers may be contacted directly at the marina in Cabo San Lucas. For variety, there is light tackle fishing in the estuary near the San José del Cabo hotel zone, and surf fishing is good from several beaches.

Hunting for white wing dove, duck, and quail is becoming increasingly popular around The Capes. The season runs from Sept. 15 to Feb. 15. Hotels can obtain licenses, guides, and rental guns (importing firearms into Mexico involves considerable red tape).

Scuba diving expeditions are handled by *Cabo Acuadeportes* (tel. 3–0662) and *Amigos del Mar* (3–0538), both in Cabo San Lucas. The waters off Cabo San Lucas are undersea national parks, where spear-fishing and even shell collecting are prohibited. One-tank dive trips cost about $30 and two-tank trips cost $50.

Sailing, including **Windsurfing** and **paraflying,** can be set up at most hotels. *Victor's Aquatics* (tel. 2–0155), in the hotel zone at San José del Cabo, and *John Fox* (3–0122), who operates from the beach by the Hacienda Hotel in Cabo San Lucas, have some of the best equipment.

Golf is the newest sport in the area, with the first 9 holes of an 18-hole course open in San José del Cabo. This Fonatur operation also has 9 illuminated tennis courts and an attractive club house.

Riding horses can be done both in San José del Cabo and Cabo San Lucas. Check at your hotel for details.

SHOPPING. The Capes, almost devoid of shops until a few years ago, now have them popping up all over. Downtown San José del Cabo is an interesting place to browse, although the merchandise is not especially exciting; most items are Mexican curios, T-shirts, and imported toys (such imports are not available on the mainland). At press time, most of the stores in the *Centro Comercial* in the hotel zone were empty. In Cabo San Lucas, it is fun to wander through the *Tianguis,* a waterfront market set up to sell souvenirs to cruise ship passengers. Many of the nicer shops are in the hotels. The *Mexican Village* at the Hacienda Hotel is actually a little shopping complex with several boutiques. *La Paloma* claims to be the original boutique in town and stocks an excellent selection of handicrafts. A close rival is *Su Casa,* next to *Ronnie's T-Shirts.* Other attractive shops and a supermarket are to be found in the little plaza. There is no point in giving addresses here, since streets in Cabo San Lucas bear no names.

NIGHTLIFE. With fishing boats setting out before dawn, The Capes never were big for after-dark activities, but gradually this situation is changing. Several hotels have entertainment in their lobby bars, and the *Palmilla* puts on a fiesta every Friday night. *Añuiti,* in the San José del Cabo hotel zone, comes close to being a sophisticated supper club, with its dine-and-dance atmosphere. At the Hotel El Presidente, the *VideoDisco* is the best-equipped establishment of its kind on the peninsula. Its rival in Cabo San Lucas is the *Oasis Disco.* A trifle quieter is *Estela's,* a bar with live music that will not deafen customers as they munch a midnight snack or ponder a move at backgammon.

ACROSS THE SEA OF CORTÉS

PUERTO VALLARTA

A Favored International Resort

by
JIM BUDD

One of the most popular of Mexico's international resorts, Puerto Vallarta has shot into the big time nearly as fast as Cancún, across the country on the Caribbean coast. Barely a generation ago, Vallarta was an isolated fishing village that perhaps 10,000 people made their home. Today, at least 130,000 people live there, but, for all its growth, the community has retained much of the charm of yesteryear.

Puerto Vallarta is the Mexico of the picture postcards. Cobbled streets lead past whitewashed houses; bougainvillea drips from red-tiled roofs. Burro trains still clomp down from the hillsides, and fishermen return in their long boats each afternoon to dry their nets and sell their catch on the beach.

There have, of course, been some changes. The *malecón* or seaside avenue (officially named Díaz Ordáz) is now lined with bars, restaurants, and boutiques, and the once-empty side streets are jammed with traffic. Yet there is nothing garish about the village. The posh resort hotels lie along the beaches north and south of town, none of them too close to the others.

Climate Near Perfection

Located at the head of the 28-mile-wide Bahia de Banderas (Bay of Flags), Puerto Vallarta is on the same latitude as Hawaii and is blessed with a similar near-perfect climate. Parrots squawk for attention amid banana, papaya, and mango trees in the hillside jungles. Frigate birds survey the waterfront from on high, while pelicans glide over the beaches.

Wonderful weather, along with storybook charm, is what brings the crowds to Puerto Vallarta. Winter is the high season, but the area is really a year-round vacationland, for the summer rains seldom last more than a couple of hours and they make the countryside lush with greenery.

The countryside is another of Puerto Vallarta's fascinations. The town is on the edge of a mighty mountain range that crosses Mexico at about the 19th parallel. The western limit of this chain is Cabo Corrientes on the southern tip of the bay. The bay itself is dotted with fishing hamlets—villages seemingly lifted from the South Seas—many of them reachable only by boat. Puerto Vallarta itself has had highways for less than 20 years, but Guadalajara is now only a 6-hour drive away, while Mexico 200 heads up from Manzanillo, Acapulco, and the Guatemala border to cross the Ameca River just above the airport, enter Nayarit and the mountain time zone, and on toward Arizona.

Founding Uncertain

Little is known about the history of Puerto Vallarta. There is an apocryphal account of how a nephew of Hernán Cortés led the first group of Europeans into the area. Whether he actually reached the coast is not certain. Some say, however, that it was he who gave Banderas Bay its name; the Indians who met him are said to have carried many flags and made an impression. But no reliable historical text vouches for this story.

Indeed, no historical texts confirm any but recent information about this area. There are tales of pirates infesting the shores of Banderas Bay,

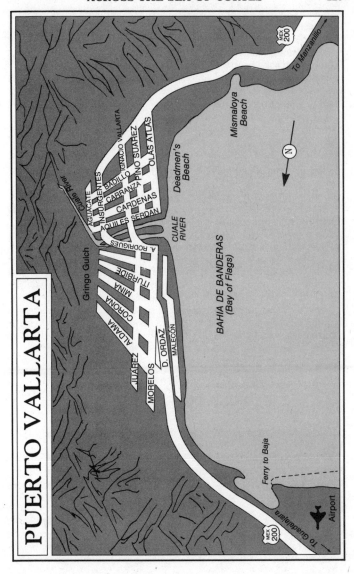

PUERTO VALLARTA

To Manzanillo

Mismaloya Beach

N

Deadmen's Beach

Cuale River

Gringo Gulch

AGUACATE
INSURGENTES
BADILLO
IGNACIO VALLARTA
PINO SUAREZ
OLAS ATLAS
CABRANZA
CARDENAS
AQUILES SERDAN
A. RODRIGUES

ALDAMA
CORONA
MINA
ITURBIDE
JUAREZ
MORELOS
D. ORDAZ
MALECÓN

BAHIA DE BANDERAS
(Bay of Flags)

Ferry to Baja

To Guadalajara

Airport

waiting to pounce on the galleons from the Orient, but no one troubled to record whether any attacks were ever made. It was only in 1918 that Puerto Vallarta first appeared on maps; it was then an obscure and isolated fishing village christened by a chartmaker to honor a heroic Jalisco governor (Puerto Vallarta is in the State of Jalisco).

By the late 1950s, a few Americans had discovered Puerto Vallarta and settled there in semipermanent residence. Mexicana Airlines flew in a DC 3 a few times each week, and there were those who predicted that the village one day would be as well known as Acapulco.

Film Brings Tourists

John Huston helped make those predictions come true by selecting Puerto Vallarta as the setting for *The Night of the Iguana*. Journalists who flew in to report on the progress of the movie and the love life of its stars began to gush over the quaint fishing village, and their reports started a trickle of tourists that turned into a torrent.

For a while, Puerto Vallarta seemed to be growing too fast. From north, south, and east, highways were pushed into a town that previously could be reached only by sea and air; local streets had a hard time handling the traffic. The airport never seemed big enough and was constantly expanding. On days when cruise ships put into port, the village was mobbed. All too often, hotels had more guests than rooms.

Most of these problems appear to have been resolved, although finding a parking spot can still be a challenge, and, even with a confirmed, prepaid reservation, it is wise not to arrive late in the day. Puerto Vallarta is still packing in the crowds.

EXPLORING PUERTO VALLARTA

There are three major parts to the Puerto Vallarta area: the village itself, the strip above the town, and the strip below it.

First seen by almost everyone is the strip above town. The airport is out this way (only five or ten minutes from many of the top hotels), as is the highway that comes from the north and links up with the road from Guadalajara. Here, too, is the marina where the cruise ships tie up.

Most of the luxury beachfront hotels are on this strip. Virtually every hotel is a self-contained resort whose management hopes that the guests will rarely leave the premises. All offer the ocean and magnificent pools, a bit of sailing and paraflying, informal cafes, specialty restaurants, music in lobby bars, and noise in discos. The highway leading to these hotels and into town is singularly unprepossessing, as if it were designed to encourage people to stay put.

Not many people stay put, however. Vacationers come to Puerto Vallarta because it is Puerto Vallarta and they want to see it.

The village begins where the pavement turns to cobblestones. The street, or *malecón,* is Calle Díaz Ordáz; it runs along a seawall with a rocky shoreline to one side and cafes, saloons, and a few boutiques on the other. It is almost a ritual to gather on the *malecón* an hour or so before sundown, stroll a bit, and seek the bar where the "happy hour" appears the happiest. Once dusk turns to darkness, the thing to do is poke about the shops on Díaz Ordáz and the streets leading into it. There are all kinds of fine restaurants in this neighborhood waiting for hunger pangs to strike.

The *malecón* twists past a lighthouse, changes its name to Madero, and runs up to the City Hall (where the local tourism office is), the main plaza, and the Church of Guadalupe with its steeple capped by a crown. This is the real downtown heart of Puerto Vallarta, a neighborhood not too many tourists wander into, although it is home to many resident Americans.

Gringo Gulch

The streets going up the hillsides lead to Gringo Gulch, an enclave of expatriots that dates back to before the filming of *The Night of the Iguana* (one reason Huston chose Puerto Vallarta is that he knew there were Americans who could act as extras).

Here it should be noted that "gringo" is not an insulting term any more than is Hoosier or Tarheel. How the term originated is the subject of much debate; suffice to say, it is the only word that describes a citizen of the United States. Mexicans, after all, are also Americans, even North Americans or *estadounidenses* (*"Unitedstatians"*), since they live in the *Estados Unidos Mexicanos,* but only a gringo is a gringo.

Now relatively few of the over one thousand gringos live in Gringo Gulch. In recent years, they have been opting for beachfront condos over houses on the hillside. Casa Kimberly is still the property of Elizabeth Taylor, but, when the star was last in town, she preferred a hotel suite. Huston's Puerto Vallarta home is on one of the bay beaches that can be reached only by boat.

Cuale River

Gringo Gulch tumbles down toward the Rio Cuale, which runs through the heart of Puerto Vallarta. The south side is the "other side of the tracks," where many budget hotels and cafes are found.

Two bridges, each handling one-way traffic, cross the river. Below them is Cuale Island, developed in the past decade or so as a tourist area, but fairly junky. There is a public market on the northern end of the upstream bridge where fileted fish, fruits, and vegetables are available at local prices. There is also a fair sampling of serapes and blankets at half the cost of those in the town shops.

The island has even more in the way of souvenirs—everything from embroidered shirts and dresses to stuffed iguanas. It also has a little museum that features pre-Columbian artifacts found in the region, including items of obsidian (volcanic glass). The museum is open weekdays from 10 A.M. to 5 P.M.

Several restaurants on the island serve seafood and Mexican dishes. There usually are some mariachis around in the evenings. It can be a lively spot, something like a fiesta going on every night. To be sure, a good many tourists are there, but most of them are Mexican.

Beyond the bridges is the only in-town beach, known locally as Playa de los Muertos (Deadmen's Beach), although Puerto Vallarta boosters would prefer it to be called Playa del Sol (Sunny Beach). The older, more morbid name supposedly dates back to the time when pirates and Indians fought a bloody battle on the spot, leaving the sands littered with corpses.

Fun-Filled Beach

Although this is the least attractive beach in the area, for many people, it is the most fun. There are several small inns about the neighborhood that are popular with less affluent travelers. In the area as well are a number of inexpensive cafes and bars. On the beach itself, however, pompano, robalo, snapper, and mackerel are skewered and roasted over coconut-husk fires. Accompanied by fruits and juices sold from nearby pushcarts, these make a tasty meal. Throughout the day, the beach is a gathering place for the young at heart.

The highway, which is a few blocks from the shore, runs south of town, out to Mismaloya where *The Night of the Iguana* set was built (after nearly a quarter of a century, one gets the impression that the making of the movie was the most exciting thing that ever happened in Puerto Vallarta). Along the road, condo units hug the hillsides, and a few towers soar up over beach coves. There are only a couple of luxury hotels on this side of the village; they have the disadvantage of being a long ride from the airport.

Those of an exploring nature may want to ride to Boca de Tomatlán (Mouth of the Tomatlán River), either by taxi or rental car. There are some good restaurants (open only for lunch) down this way, and the scenery is spectacular—a canyon gorge leading out to the sea.

PRACTICAL INFORMATION FOR
PUERTO VALLARTA

HOW TO GET THERE. By Air. Most international visitors arrive in Puerto Vallarta by air, many of them aboard charter flights. *Western Airlines* (800–843–9378) provides scheduled service from Los Angeles and Phoenix; *Northwest* (800–225–2525), from Memphis; *American* (800–433–7300), from Dallas/Fort Worth; *Continental* (800–525–0280) and *Aeroméxico* (800–237–6639), from Houston; *Mexicana* (800–531–7921), from Dallas/Fort Worth, Denver, Los Angeles, San Antonio, San Francisco, and Seattle. The two Mexican carriers operate domestic flights from many cities in the country.

By Bus or Car. Puerto Vallarta is about 1,200 miles from the Arizona border at Nogales, but less than 6 hours from Guadalajara.

By Sea. Carnival Cruise Lines' *Tropicale* sails weekly from Los Angeles year round, Admiral Cruises' *Stardancer* has weekly sailings October through May, and Sitmar Cruises' *Fairsea* calls frequently during the winter months. A car-carrying ferry makes an overnight crossing twice each week from Cabo San Lucas, Baja California. Accommodations on the ferry include sleeping cabins that cost little but are spartan. Tickets must be purchased at the ferry terminal on the day of departure.

TELEPHONES. To call Puerto Vallarta from the United States, dial 01152, the local area code (322), and the desired number. The number for the American consular agent is 2–0069; and for the Canadian consular agent, 2–0969. The number of the Tourism Office is 2–0242. The police may be reached at 2–0123; an ambulance, at 2–1533, and the regional hospital, at 2–4000. It should be remembered that personnel who answer probably do not speak English; therefore, emergencies are best handled through hotels.

HOTELS. As noted earlier, hotels are located above town, in town, and below town, and we indicate this in our listings. During the winter season, especially around Christmas and Easter, space is tight and arriving without a confirmed, prepaid reservation may mean sleeping on the beach (which is not allowed). Expect to pay $135 and above for a double room at a *Super Deluxe* hotel; $100–$135, *Deluxe;* $70–$100, *First Class;* $45–$70, *Moderate;* and under $45 in an *Inexpensive* inn.

Super Deluxe

Buganvilis Sheraton. Above town; 2–3000. With 501 rooms in 6 contiguous 14-story towers, this is the biggest resort in the area. With 5 tennis courts and 3 restaurants, it is regarded as one of Sheraton's top hotels anywhere.

Fiesta Americana. Above town; 2–2010. The design of this 282-room hotel is striking, especially its huge thatched cone roof over the lobby. Five tennis courts, a health club, 4 restaurants, and nightly entertainment are among its features.

Garza Blanca. Below town; 2–1023. Small, with a choice of beachfront suites, chalets, and villas (rates start at $150), this is the area's most exclusive resort and is fairly spread out. A good restaurant and an excellent beach.

Krystal Vallarta. Above town; 2–1459. The revamped **Posada Vallarta,** a complex of 501 rooms (not all with a sea view), 42 pools, lighted tennis courts, 8 specialty restaurants, and a private bullring.

Westin Camino Real. Below town; 2–0002. One of Puerto Vallarta's first luxury resorts, with 250 rooms overlooking a secluded beach, 2 pools, 2 lighted tennis courts, many special activities, and a video disco.

Deluxe

Holiday Inn. Above town; 2–1700. Adjoining towers, 1 with 236 suites, the other with 236 rooms, 2 tennis courts, swim-up bars in the pools, 3 restaurants, and live shows in the disco.

Playa de Oro. Above town; 2–0178. An older hotel, recently renovated and expanded to 392 units. Two pools, 3 restaurants, and a nightclub.

Plaza Las Glorias. Above town; 2–2224. Next door to the Plaza Vallarta and the Newcombe Tennis Club, with 243 rooms, 2 restaurants, and a weekly Mexican fiesta.

Plaza Vallarta. Above town, 2–4360. Cozy, with 375 rooms built in a village-like setting around the pool. Includes the John Newcombe Tennis Club with indoor and outdoor courts, a large shopping complex, several restaurants, and nightly entertainment.

First Class

Los Arcos. Olas Altas 380, in town; 2–1583. On the beach, with a pool, tennis court, coffee shop, restaurant, and a weekly Mexican fiesta. There are 10 suites with kitchenettes.

Buenaventura. Av. México 1301, in town; 2–3737. On the beach, but within walking distance of village attractions, with 210 large rooms, a large pool, scheduled activities, and a beachfront nightclub.

Conchas Chinas. Below town; 2–0156. Small, with 8 rooms and 32 housekeeping suites, a pool and beach, and *El Set,* one of the nicest restaurants in town.

Oro Verde. Rodolfo Gomez 111, in town; 2–1555. A renovated older hotel with 162 units on Playa de Muertos; by far the best hotel in the neighborhood. Two restaurants and a disco across the street.

Las Palmas. Above town; 2–0650. All 150 rooms have a balcony overlooking the ocean; handsome lobby, special entertainment most evenings.

Paraíso Perricos. Above town; 2–2325. On the highway with no beach (shuttles run to the seashore); 2 pools, 2 restaurants, and a nightclub. Lowest prices in this category.

Pelicanos. Above town; 2–2107. Not quite on the beach, but near it, with 220 rooms, 3 pools, a coffee shop, restaurant, and disco.

Moderate

El Conquistador. Above town; 2–2088. Popular with Mexican families, and the TV in the 108 rooms receives American programs. A walk to the beach.

Cuatro Vientos. Matamoros 520, in town; 2–0161. Tiny, with 16 rooms that are usually booked by guests who return year after year. No beach, and a stiff climb to reach the hotel, but the view is superb and the restaurant, *Chez Helen,* is wonderful.

Molino de Agua. Ignacio Vallarta 130, in town; 2–1907. On the south bank of the Cuale River, with 62 units facing the sea. Restaurant and bar plus 2 weekly barbecues.

Posada Rio Cuale. Serdan 242, in town; 2–0450. A lovely small hotel with just 24 rooms, a pool, bar, and very good restaurant.

Rosita. Díaz Ordáz 901, in town; 2–0133. Pretty much in the heart of town and somewhat noisy, with 111 rooms, a bar, restaurant, and pool, but no beach.

Tropicana. Amapa 227, in town; 2–0912. With 231 rooms, this is the largest hotel in town and fairly commercial. Not all rooms have a sea view, but there are a pool, bar, and restaurant.

Inexpensive

Encino. Juárez 122, in town; 2–0051. On the north bank of the Cuale River, with 75 rooms and a rooftop pool plus a restaurant.

Fontana del Mar. Dieguez 171, in town; 2–0712. Across the street from Los Arcos and the beach, with 37 rooms, 6 kitchenette suites, and a rooftop pool.

Marlyn. Av. México 1121, in town; 2–0965. Quite modest and rather noisy, with 37 rooms, not all of which are air-conditioned.

Marsol. Rodriguez 103, in town; 2–0865. Somewhat run down, but with kitchenettes in several of the 120 rooms, a pool, many shops, and restaurants near by.

Oceano. Galleana 103, in town; 2–1050. A landmark on the *malecón,* with 52 air-conditioned noisy rooms, a pool, and a very popular bar and restaurant.

Posada Roger. Basilio Badillo 237; 2–0836. A cozy, friendly 50-room inn, with a patio setting, nice bar, and pleasant restaurant.

 DINING OUT. Dining out in Puerto Vallarta usually means heading into town and sometimes hunting up back streets that are best found by taxi. The variety of restaurants is the greatest of any destination covered in this book; therefore, we are including only a few exceptional hotel food outlets among the restaurants listed. Expect to pay about $18 and above for a meal in a place listed as *Expensive,* $10–$18 in a *Moderate* establishment, and less than $10 in one that is *Inexpensive.* Much depends, of course, on whether chicken or lobster is ordered. Drinks and tips (15%) are extra. Most places accept Visa (V) and MasterCard (MC), but only an expensive few take American Express (AE) and Diners Club (DC).

Expensive

Capistrano. Mismaloya Highway below town; 2–2322. Mediterranean specialties served in an elegant thatched hut on a hillside. Dance music in the evening. AE, DC, MC, V.

Casablanca. Díaz Ordáz 570; 2–1723. Supposedly inspired by the Bogart movie, with a crowded ground-floor bar and more sedate international dining upstairs. AE, MC, V.

Cebolla Roja. Díaz Ordáz 822; 2–1087. Local version of the Red Onion, with food and atmosphere some rate as the best in Puerto Vallarta. Open kitchen and salad bar. AE, DC, MC, V.

Chez Elena. Matamoros 520; 2–0161. In the Hotel Cuatro Vientos, a gourmet rendezvous in a garden setting specializing in Indonesian dishes. Reservations advised. AE, DC, MC, V.

Daiquiri Dick's. Olas Altas 246; 2–0566. A long-time favorite on the beach, just south of the river. Especially lovely for dining under the stars and noted for its daiquiris. AE, DC, MC, V.

El Jardin. Díaz Ordáz 890; 2–0342. Right at the start of the *malecón,* serving seafood, good cuts of meat, and hearty drinks in a garden setting. AE, DC, MC, V.

La Jolla de Mismaloya. Mismaloya Beach, below town; no phone. Fun for lunch, delightful at sunset, romantic by moonlight, and the one place in town to see *The Night of the Iguana.* AE, MC, V.

Kamakura. Hotel Krystal Vallarta, above town; 2–1459. Authentically Japanese, with a chef from Osaka; teriyaki and teppanyaki tables. AE, DC, MC, V.

Mexican Joe's. Ecuador 1283; 2–4475. Not the easiest place to find, but worth the effort. Seafood and gourmet Mexican dishes are the specialties, and a guitarist sings at night. MC, V.

Mister Pepe's. Badillo 503; 2–2732. Reservations are a must at this rooftop rendezvous, where a pianist sings and Pepe himself supervises everything. Closed from July to September. AE, DC, MC, V.

Place Vendome. Playa las Glorias, above town; 2–4851. A bit of Belle Epoque Paris by the Pacific, with a French chef who learned his art at Maxim's. AE, DC, MC, V.

El Set. Mismaloya Highway, below town; 2–0302. Seafood and international fare on a bluff overlooking the sea. Considered very fashionable. DC, MC, V.

Tango. Hotel Krystal Vallarta, above town; 2–1459. Steaks cut and grilled in the Argentine manner, plus a nice choice of seafood. AE, DC, MC, V.

X.O. Pino Suarez 206; 2–3988. A Swiss chef presides at this Continental restaurant, where the bar is charming and the dining both indoors and out. AE, MC, V.

Moderate

Brazz. Morelos at Galeana; 2–0324. Local branch of a big Guadalajara chain, noted for its Mexican food, steaks, chops, beer, and mariachis. MC, V.

Carlos O'Brians. Díaz Ordáz 786; 2–1444. One of the Anderson chain of slightly whacky eateries, this is usually the most crowded place in town, with lines of people waiting to get in. A good place, but not worth the wait. AE, DC, MC, V.

Chico's Paradise, Chee Chee, and **El Eden,** Boca de Tomatlán, about 10 miles south of town, are 3 similar restaurants carved out of the jungle overlooking a river. Guests usually spend the afternoon, showing up for a swim, a drink, and a meal. MC, V.

Il Mangiare. Díaz Ordáz 644; 2–2486. As Italian as the name sounds, with homemade pasta and excellent veal dishes. AE, DC, MC, V.

Moby Dick. 31 de Octubre 128; 2–0655. Rather plain, but quite popular and generally regarded as the best seafood house in town. MC, V.

Las Palomas. Díaz Ordáz at Aldama; 2–3675. One of the lowest-priced restaurants on the *malecón,* hence always crowded. Open for breakfast. MC, V.

Pietro. Zaragoza 245; 2–3233. Around the corner from the Guadalupe church; run by an Italian who knows his pasta and pizzas. MC, V.

Señor Chico's. Pulpito 377; 2–3570. Chico Perez's special spot with 2 terraces, a breathtaking view, and international menu. MC, V.

Zapata. Díaz Ordáz 524 (upstairs); 2–1420. Sort of an American version of a Mexican restaurant. Mariachis play in the evening, which makes it fun. MC, V.

Inexpensive

Las Amapas, Punta Mita Highway above town; no phone. Wild game (venison, boar, armadillo, iguana, rattlesnake) cooked to order at a modest roadside shack. A good place to try *raisilla,* a more potent form of tequila. Dining here is an adventure.

Benitos. Juárez at Iturbide (no phone). A pizza and hamburger joint across from city hall; a spot everyone tries at least once. MC, V.

Cafe Franzi. Cuale River Island (no phone). South Seas atmosphere amid lush vegetation in a garden restaurant. Tops for breakfast; good for lunch.

ChiliWilly's. Cuale River Island (no phone). Open from 9 A.M. until midnight. Informal and fun; good for burgers, sandwiches, and tacos.

El Dorado. Playa de los Muertos (no phone). One of several seafood shanties along the town beach, this one is regarded by many people as the best.

 HOW TO GET AROUND. Volkswagen **vans** provide transportation from the airport at fixed prices, about $2 per person to hotels above town. Similar vans, as well as **buses,** run along the highway, going as far south as Mismaloya; while somewhat rattletrap, they can be fun and only cost a dime. **Cab** fare from most hotels into town is about $3.

 USEFUL ADDRESSES. The main local government offices, including **tourism** and **police,** are in the City Hall (*Presidencia Municipal*), Morelos at Zaragoza. The *Red Cross Hospital* is at Rio de la Plata and Rio Balsas and the *Regional Hospital,* on Carretera Libremiento, Km 1.5.

Several **banks** have offices on Av. Juárez, which is one block up from the *malécon.*

For **airlines** offices, *Aeroméxico* has its ticket office at Juárez 255, tel. 2–0031; *Mexicana,* at Juárez 202, 2–1707; *Northwest,* at the corner of Morelos and Rodriguez, 2–0267; *American,* 2–3787; *Continental,* 2–3096; and *Western,* 2–3919 have offices only at the airport.

The various **bus lines** have their terminals on or just off Calle Insurgentes on the south side of the river. All these terminals are within 3 blocks of each other.

Rental cars may be picked up from several firms at the airport or from *Avis,* tel. 2–1412; *Budget,* 2–2980; *National,* 2–2742; and *Quick,* 2–3505, all on the highway above town, and from *Hertz* in town at Díaz Ordáz 538, tel. 2–0024.

 TOURIST INFORMATION. The *State Tourist Office* in the City Hall (*Presidencia Municipal*) is well run and extremely helpful with everything from finding rooms when there seem to be none to handling complaints. It is open from 9 A.M. to 9 P.M. on weekdays and 9 A.M. to 1 P.M. on Saturdays; tel. 2–0242.

Hotel travel desks are another excellent source of information, especially when money is being spent.

 TOURS. While in Puerto Vallarta, almost everyone takes at least one bay cruise aboard one of the half-dozen yachts and sailing vessels making such trips. Prices range from $5 to $10, depending on the length of the voyage and whether lunch is included.

City tours lasting 3 hours may be taken in the morning or afternoon. The price is about $5 for an excursion that includes the main plaza, Gringo Gulch, the River Cuale and its islands, and Mismaloya beach, south of town.

More extensive is a 5-hour tropical tour that takes in both the city and some rural areas to the south. The jungle tour heads north into Nayarit state, with its mango and banana plantations. Both these outings cost about $8.

Something special is a 1-day tour of Guadalajara, in which you fly over in the morning, take in Lake Chapala, the Tlaquepaque craftsmen's village, and the famous Libertad Market, and return to Puerto Vallarta in time for a late supper. The cost is about $80.

Any hotel travel desk can make arrangements for these trips, or the following travel agencies may be contacted directly:

Servi Tours, Hidalgo 217; 2–4988.
Viajes Costa Norte, Agustin Melgar 140; 2–4754.
Promociones Tropicales, Independencia 231; 2–2926.
Contactur, Lázaro Cárdenas 219; 2–4640
Miller Travel Service, Av. de las Garzas 100; 2–1321.
Big Al Tours, Hamburgo at Lucerna; 2–0920.
Viajes La Jungla, Juárez 234; 2–4303.
Viajes Tortuga, Colombia 1438; 2–4509.
Viva Tours, Díaz Ordáz 652; 2–1003.

FIESTAS. The final two weeks of **May** mark *Puerto Vallarta's anniversary as a city* and are celebrated with bullfights, cockfights, charro rodeos, parades, and public entertainments. Even bigger doings take place in **December,** especially the week prior to Dec. 12, when the town holds the *Feast of Our Lady of Guadalupe* for whom the parish church is named. These festivities are along the lines of a classic Mexican fiesta, with processions, fireworks, and band concerts in the plaza.

BEACHES. *Playa Norte* (North Beach) stretches along the shore above town to the marina; this is where most of the big resort hotels are located.

Bucerias is farther up the bay in Nueva (New) Vallarta, across the Animas River in Nayarit State. The golf course is out this way, and this is the direction in which Puerto Vallarta is supposed to grow in the future.

Los Muertos (Deadmen's Beach), also known as *Playa del Sol* (Sunny Beach) is in town, just south of the Cuale River. Supposedly, it takes its name from the corpses left after a pirate-Indian battle. These days, it is where budget vacationers congregate and the place to munch on fish-on-a-stick.

Mismaloya, where the Mismaloya River meets the sea, is where *the* movie was filmed, but it has changed from what Tennessee Williams envisaged as "among the world's wildest and loveliest populated areas" into a tawdry clutter of shacks and huts.

Boca de Tomatlán, another river mouth, is not exactly a beach, but it is a wonderful place to swim where a jungle stream cascades among the rocks into the sea. Good restaurants are to be found in the neighborhood.

Las Animas and *Quimixto* are two Banderas Bay beaches that can be reached only by boat and are visited daily by tour yachts from Puerto Vallarta (see *Tours* section above). Quimixto has a lovely waterfall, but a bit of a hike is required to see it.

Yelapa may be more what Tennessee Williams had in mind when he wrote *The Night of the Iguana.* It has the feeling of being an island, with a few thatched restaurants and a tiny hotel, plus a few Americans who have made a home in the neighborhood. Here, too, the only communication with the outside world is by boat.

CHILDREN'S ACTIVITIES. During the summer months, many hotels, especially the big resorts, have special programs for children and often keep them busy throughout the day. Activities include everything from games and crafts to turtle races. Downtown, the River Cuale Island has several attractions designed to appeal to children. Baby-sitters are available at most hotels, provided sufficient notice is given, but they may not speak English.

SPORTS. Along with **swimming, sailing, windsurfing,** and **paraflying** (soaring in a parachute pulled by a speedboat) are the big activities along Puerto Vallarta beaches. *Chico's Dive Shop* at Díaz Ordáz 772 organizes **scuba** and **snorkeling** expeditions; prices start at $14 for snorkeling at Los Arcos (the arches) about a mile off shore and $28 for scuba diving at the same place. Arrangements can be made through your hotel.

Game fishing for billfish is good off Puerto Vallarta most of the year, and party boats take anglers out to blue water for about $40 per person. Cruisers from 38 to 42 feet may be charted from about $250 on up—a fee that includes a license, bait, tackle, and the services of a skipper. These boats carry between 4 and 6 people. Hotels make the arrangements.

Equestrians find Puerto Vallarta unmatched as a seaside resort. Both *Rancho Caballo Blanco* (2–0021) and *Rancho Ojo de Agua* (2–2165) arrange **horseback** tours into the back country that run anywhere from 3 hours to a full day.

Golf may be played at *Los Flamingos* (2–0959), an 18-hole course in Nuevo Vallarta, about a 30-minute drive from most hotels. Many hotels have tennis courts. For guests staying at those that do not, play can be arranged at the *John Newcombe Tennis Club* (2–4850), *Los Tules* (2–0617), the *Vallarta Tennis Club* (2–2767), and the *Puerto Vallarta Racket Club* (2–2526).

ENTERTAINMENT. Apart from bar and disco hopping, Mexican **fiestas, barbecues,** and **beach parties** are enjoyable ways to spend an evening. Almost every night, there is something going on somewhere; travel desks usually know, since they earn a commission selling tickets (which cost anywhere from $15 to $25).

Once a month, usually on a Sunday, there is a **cultural event** at the Camino Real, perhaps an opera singer or a chamber quartet. These events are staged for the local community but tickets for tourists usually can be arranged.

Bullfights are held Wednesday afternoons during the winter months at a ring across from the marina. Tickets, costing about $10, may be purchased at hotel travel desks or at Foto Taurina, Díaz Ordáz 524; 2–1158.

For a change of pace, a night might be spent at the **cinema.** Puerto Vallarta has 5 air-conditioned movie houses that often show English-language films with Spanish subtitles.

ART GALLERIES. Because it is so picturesque, Puerto Vallarta has inspired many artists and has several galleries to display their works. Best known of the local painters is the late Manuel Lepe, a primitivist whose work won international acclaim. Lepe's art, as well as that of others, may be seen and purchased at *Galeria Lepe,* Lázaro Cárdenas 239 (2–1777), *Galeria Uno,* Morelos 561 (2–0908), and *La Otra Galeria* at the Plaza Malecón Mall on Díaz Ordáz (2–4735).

Sergio Bustamante, a sculptor whose fantastic metallic animals have won him a reputation abroad, has his own gallery, *Studio Zoo,* at Morelos 522 (2–4736).

Other galleries of note are *Laura,* Lázaro Cárdenas 237 (2–1006), *El Dorado,* Morelos 631 (2–0745), *Bezan,* Lázaro Cárdenas 400 (tel. 2–4811), and *Estudio ETC,* Encino 60 (2–4811).

SHOPPING. Visitors often arrive in Puerto Vallarta with nearly empty suitcases, knowing they will find plenty of resort wear and much more to fill the suitcases for the trip home. Stores open in the morning usually from 10 A.M. to 1 P.M., close for siesta, and reopen from 4 or 5 until 8. Cruise-ship passengers hit the shops in the morning, but hotel vacationers usually wait for the cool of the evening after "happy hour" is over.

Díaz Ordáz (the waterfront avenue known as the *malecón*); Av. Juárez, which runs parallel a block inland; and the side streets connecting them are where the best boutiques are to be found, among them *Aca Joe,* Díaz Ordáz 588; *Ruben Torres,* Díaz Ordáz 592; *Designer's Bazaar,* Morelos 500; and *Ralph Lauren,* Aldama 109. All these specialize in wearables.

Good handicrafts are to be found at *Fonart,* Juárez at Zaragoza; *Casart,* Díaz Ordáz 680; *La Troje,* Juárez 614; and *Peggy,* Insurgentes 323.

Jewelry is another local specialty. Among the best shops are *La Azteca,* Juárez 360; *Arodi,* Juárez at Guerrero; and *Tane,* Díaz Ordáz 590.

The *Plaza Malecón,* about where Díaz Ordáz begins, is a mall with some 2-dozen shops selling resort wear, handicrafts, jewelry, and more.

Bargain hunters will want to explore the *public market* down by the Cuale River Bridge and the *stalls* on Cuale Island. Here bargaining is expected.

NIGHTLIFE. An evening in Puerto Vallarta is likely to start with a "happy hour" at one of the saloons along the *malecón,* followed by a tour of the shops, a leisurely dinner at one of the appealing cafes, and a visit to a disco or two. For variety, there are the hotels, many of which have happy hours of their own in lobby bars, specialty restaurants, discos, or show lounges.

Among the top discos are *Ciro's,* Díaz Ordáz at Allende (2–3000); *Capriccio,* Pulpito 170 (2–1593); *City Dump,* Ignacio Vallarta 278 (2–0719); *Sundance,* Lázaro Cárdenas 231 (2–2296); *Friday López* at the Hotel Fiesta Americana (2–2010); *La Jungla* at the Hotel Camino Real (2–0002); and *La Onda* at the Pelicanos Hotel (2–2107).

The Embarcadero at the Sheraton (2–3000); *El Pescador* at the Hotel Playa de Oro (2–0544), *Las Jaulas* at the Hotel Las Palmas (2–0650), *Tucanes* at the Buenaventura Hotel (2–3737), and *Isadora's* at the Holiday Inn (2–1700) all have live music for dancing.

MAZATLÁN

Affordable Pacific Resort

by
JIM BUDD

Lying on the mainland Pacific coast just south of the Tropic of Cancer, Mazatlán thrives as the major Mexican resort area closest to the United States. It also is the least expensive, doing a big business with college kids (who flock in during spring breaks and long weekends), pensioners (who often drive down to spend the winter), tour groups, and others who enjoy the hunting and the fishing.

Mazatlán is one of the few ports from which sailfish or marlin can be caught all year and ranks among the top 10 in the number of catches recorded. The average annual haul is 10,000 sailfish and 5,000 marlin. And these fish are big. A record 973-pound black marlin was pulled out of these waters, as was a 203-pound sailfish. Anglers in the backwaters south of the city catch rainbow runners, snook, ladyfish, barracuda, and milkfish.

Hunters also find lots of excitement. A long narrow island separates the Caimanero Lagoon from the sea and provides a fine feeding ground for wildfowl. Four species of duck, as well as quail, dove, and pheasant, are found in and around the lagoon. In the nearby hills are jaguar, ocelot, boar, mountain lion, deer, coyote, and rabbit.

Arrival of Sunseekers

Hunting and fishing are what originally brought tourists to Mazatlán, but it was not long before ordinary sunseekers discovered the city. And Mazatlán is a city—home to some 350,000 people and one of the largest ports on Mexico's west coast. Farming, shrimping, and shipping all are as important to the local economy as is the tourist industry.

Although it traces its roots back to preconquest times (Mazatlán is an Indian word meaning "Place of the Deer") and to a Spanish outpost established in the neighborhood in 1576, it is a fairly new city. It developed as a port of consequence with the coming of the railroad in the late 19th century.

The resort hotels lie along the beach away from downtown, and it is in this beach area where most of the action is. The beach is one of the longest unbroken stretches of sand along the Mexican Pacific, and there are parts where the surfing is great.

EXPLORING MAZATLÁN

Mazatlán is built on a wide peninsula with an excellent natural harbor on one side and the open Pacific on the other. Although the hotel zone along the Pacific is self-contained, most people enjoy at least one visit to the busy downtown area, which is not tourist oriented. The hub of the city is the main plaza dominated by the cathedral. Consecrated in 1937 after a century of construction, the church is of neo-Gothic design and sumptuous within. The only colonial church in Mazatlán is a few blocks away on a short street called Calle Campana.

The docks lie south of downtown along Avenida del Puerto. The fleet of shrimp boats anchor closest to the mainland. It is from here—near the gas station—that launches leave for Isla de Piedra (Stone Island) just across from the harbor. Shrimp boats are berthed first in the the main dock area; then come the cruise ships and merchant vessels. The ferries to La Paz utilize the end of the dock area nearest the ocean. By following the coast after the wharf, one reaches a narrow neck of land where the sportfishing fleet—the largest in Mexico—ties up. At the tip of this peninsula is the hill that leads 525 feet up to El Faro, highest lighthouse in the world this side of Gibraltar. It is a good half-hour hike up to the top, but the view is worth the effort.

A neighboring hill, Cerro de la Vigia (Lookout Point) has a road to the top for those who prefer riding. There is a weather station on this summit and a pretty good view as well. This hilltop road, as it runs down, is the beginning of one long street with many names. It starts out as Paseo Centenario and when it becomes Paseo Olas Altas, the tourist zone begins. Olas Altas turns into Paseo Claussen as it runs along the shoreline. Local high divers leap into the surf here whenever a large enough crowd gathers and the hat can be passed; the dives are especially impressive at night by torchlight. Landmarks on Paseo Claussen include the seedy-looking Casa del Marinero, which shelters wayward sailors, and what is called the Spanish Fort, with its lone rusting cannon. Not much of a colonial monument, the fort and its ramparts are a pleasant spot to pause and contemplate the majesty of the rocks and the sea.

Symbolic Monument

Rounding a curve, Paseo Claussen turns into Avenida del Mar along a gentle sweep of the bay. The hotels, shops, and restaurants become a bit more spiffy out this way. The landmark on Avenida del Mar is the Fishermen's Monument, something of the symbol of Mazatlán and worth a close look. The fisherman, net in hand, stands naked against a huge anchor behind which reclines an unclad beauty, her hand held out as if waiting for it to be crossed with silver.

Just off Avenida del Mar is Mazatlán's superb aquarium. A park, botanical garden, and small zoo are included in the complex. The baseball park is also in this area.

At Camarón Point, a rocky outcrop jutting into the sea atop which stands a gleaming white discotheque, Avenida del Mar becomes Calzada Camarón Sábalo and changes its name no more. Camarón Sábalo is the address for some of the best resort hotels in town (however, don't look for street numbers in these addresses since they're aren't any usually).

The *Zona Dorada,* or Golden Zone, starts where Avenida Loaiza cuts away from Camarón Sábalo at the Hotel Los Sábalos, passing by the Hotel Las Flores, the Hotel Playa Mazatlán, and more before rejoining Camarón Sábalo. The zone would appear as an oval on a map and is pretty much commercial. Sea Shell City, which calls itself a

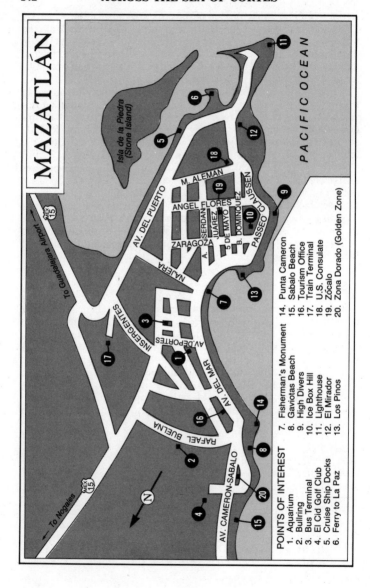

MAZATLÁN

POINTS OF INTEREST

1. Aquarium
2. Bullring
3. Bus Terminal
4. El Cid Golf Club
5. Cruise Ship Docks
6. Ferry to La Paz
7. Fisherman's Monument
8. Gaviotas Beach
9. High Divers
10. Ice Box Hill
11. Lighthouse
12. El Mirador
13. Los Pinos
14. Punta Cameron
15. Sabalo Beach
16. Tourism Office
17. Train Terminal
18. U.S. Consulate
19. Zócalo
20. Zona Dorado (Golden Zone)

museum (it displays shells from all over the world) is really two stories of items crafted from shells, all of which are for sale. Next door is the Mazatlán Arts and Crafts Center, which is another good place to stock up on inexpensive souvenirs.

Calzada Camarón Sábalo runs on to the Hotel El Cid, Mazatlán's largest resort property and the home of the golf course. It passes the Holiday Inn, the Oceano Palace and Westin Hotel's Camino Real—the last hotel on the avenue. What was a city street now becomes a country road, running over a bridge spanning the mouth of an estuary, then out toward a beach where condos sprout. At Cerritos Point, this 16-mile seaside boulevard of many names comes to an end at a couple of thatch-covered seafood shacks.

Countryside Trip

Still, there is life beyond Mazatlán. Going into the countryside for a while is part of the fun of a Mazatlán holiday.

A favorite trip is to the towns of Concordia and Copala. Both lie along Mexico 40 and are not far. Concordia dates back to 1565, and its colonial San Sebastian Church goes back almost to the era. The town is a crafts center noted for its leather goods, pottery, and furniture. Where other communities erect statues to war heroes and statesmen, the monument in the Concordia plaza is a huge chair. Copala, much smaller, once was a mining center; today it lives on its memories. Picturesque, sitting in the foothills of the Western Sierra Madre, Copala has a couple of quite good restaurants where tour groups stop for lunch.

Vacationers who are interested in seeing a bit of jungle head south on Mexico 15. Usually, they stop at Rosario, another one-time mining center noted for its 18th-century plateresque church, which, at one point in its history, was moved stone by stone to its present location. Next comes Tecapa, a fishing village with a shrimp-packing plant. Here the jungle begins, teeming with wild flowers, birds, and tree iguanas in the mangrove swamplands. Beyond, the beaches at Las Cabras and La Tambora have good sand and are nice spots for a swim.

PRACTICAL INFORMATION FOR MAZATLÁN

HOW TO GET THERE. By Air. *Western Airlines* flies in from Los Angeles and Phoenix; *Mexicana,* from Denver, Los Angeles, San Francisco, and Seattle; and *Aeroméxico,* from Houston and San Diego (Tijuana Airport). The two Mexican airlines link Mazatlán with a number of Mexican cities as well.

By Car. From Nogales at the Arizona border, the drive to Mazatlán is nearly 750 miles; at least one overnight stop should be planned because motoring in Mexico after dark is not advisable. The bus line making the trip is *TNS.*

By Rail. Trains come from Mexicali and Nogales, both on the border, but service is not good. Porters may literally have to be bribed if reservations are to be honored, sleeping cars are dirty, and rest rooms are filthy.

By Sea. Admiral Cruises' *Stardancer* and Carnival Cruises' *Tropicale* visit Mazatlán once a week while vessels of Sitmar Cruises and Princess Cruises call during the winter months. An overnight ferry connects Mazatlán with La Paz in Baja California. Cabins with berths are available and fares are low. The ferry also carries cars at bargain rates. Tickets must be purchased at the ferry terminal on the day of departure.

TELEPHONES. To call Mazatlán from the United States, dial 01152, area code 678, and the local number. The number for the *U.S. Consulate* is 1–2905 and the Canadian Consulate, 3–7320. *Police* may be reached at 1–3939, the *Red Cross* ambulance service at 1–3690, and the *hospital* at 1–4874, but personnel who answer usually do not speak English. Emergencies are best handled through hotels. The *State Tourist Office* number is 3–2545.

HOTELS. In Mazatlán, hotels are widely available in all price ranges, and even the most costly are less expensive than are similar establishments elsewhere in the country. In this listing, *Deluxe* resorts charge about $75 for a double room; *First Class,* $50; *Moderate,* $35; and *Inexpensive,* $25.

Deluxe

El Cid. Camarón Sábalo; 3–3333. One of the biggest resorts in the country and growing. On the beach, with more than 600 rooms, 11 bars, restaurants, an elegant disco, 17 tennis courts, 18 holes of golf, and 6 swimming pools.

Los Sábalos. Loaiza 100; 3–5409. Among the newer hotels in town in the heart of the *Zona Dorada* and on a great beach. Big with convention groups, the hotel has 185 rooms, 5 bars and restaurants, tennis courts, and a health club.

Westin Camino Real. Camarón Sábalo; 3–1111. One of the first posh resorts in town and showing its age, the 170-room Camino Real has a lovely pool but a small beach (which requires a hike to reach), 2 tennis courts, and 3 good restaurants.

First Class

Aqua Marina. Av. del Mar 110; 1–7085. Nice enough, with 100 rooms, a restaurant, and bar, but across the street from the beach and a bit of a walk to the action spots.

Aristos. Camarón Sábalo 51; 3–4611. Three hotels combined into one, with 393 rooms and suites and several bars and restaurants. On a nice stretch of beach, near the *Zona Dorada.*

Belmar. Olas Altas 166; 1–4299. Close to downtown and on one of the better surfing beaches, with 196 rooms, a bar, restaurant, and pool.

Caravelle Beach Club. Camarón Sábalo; 3–0203. A 115-room beachfront hotel with a heavy stress on activities (fishing, sailing, scuba, etc.). Good restaurant and popular disco.

Costa de Oro. Camarón Sábalo; 3–5344. Pleasant, with 200 rooms, restaurants and bars, a pool and a fine beach; near the *Zona Dorada.*

Las Flores. Loaiza; 3–5033. On a fine beach in the heart of the *Zona Dorada,* with a bar and restaurant; 122 nice rooms.

Hacienda. Av. del Mar and Flamingos; 2–7000. A 95-room hotel with nightly entertainment; nice except for the beach.

Holiday Inn. Camarón Sábalo 696; 3–2222. A favorite with tour groups; 200 rooms, nightly entertainment, and lots goings on. Good beach, but a bit of a walk to the *Zona Dorada.*

Oceano Palace. Camarón Sábalo; 3–0666. A full-service hotel with 167 rooms, a good beach, and nightly entertainment, but somewhat far from the *Zona Dorada.*

El Pescador. Camarón Sábalo at Atun; 3–0377. Lots of evening entertainment and on a nice beach, but a bit of a walk to the *Zona Dorada.*

Playa Mazatlán. Loaiza 202; 3–4444. A big rambling old favorite with much activity, on a great beach, and right in the *Zona Dorada.*

Suites Las Sirenas. Av. del Mar 1100; 3–1866. Small, with just 72 suites but all services, including tennis. The drawbacks are a rocky beach and its distance from the *Zona Dorada.*

Torres Mazatlán. Calzada Cerritos; 3–6360. Isolated at the end of the hotel zone and small with just 60 rooms. The beach is nice, but the surf can get rough.

Moderate

Las Arenas. Av. del Mar; 2–0000. Small hotel, with 57 rooms, a pool, and restaurant; beach across the street.

De Cima. Av. del Mar 48; 2–7300. Not as elegant as it once was, but with 150 large rooms, 2 illuminated tennis courts, a beach, pool, and top nightclub.

El Dorado. Av. del Mar 177; 1–4718. Another small hotel, with 41 rooms, on a good beach with a nice pool, tennis courts, a coffee shop, and a restaurant. Not close to anything.

Posada Don Pelayo. Av. del Mar 1111; 3–1888. A favorite in this price category. The beach is rocky, but the hotel disco gets wild and the *Zona Dorada* is close by.

Inexpensive

Arlu. Albatros 2, Colonia Gaviotas; 3–5212. Intimate, with just 11 air-conditioned rooms and a restaurant. Not close to any beach.

Marcos Suites. Av. del Mar 1234; 3–5998. Nearly as small, with 12 semi-suites, all air-conditioned. The beach is rocky, but it is better nearby. The *Zona Dorada* is a bit of a hike.

Playa Mar. Av. del Mar 139; 2–0833. Largest hotel in this category, with 61 air-conditioned rooms and a beach across the street.

Suites Caribe Mazatlán. Av. del Mar 1020; 3–1844. Nice for a long stay, with 21 reasonable air-conditioned suites. The beach is rocky, and the *Zona Dorada* is not too close.

 DINING OUT. Steak and seafood are the local specialties; Pacífico is the highly regarded beer brewed in Mazatlán. The price of a seafood meal will run as high as $15, depending on how many drinks accompany it; steak or chicken dinners run from $10 to $12. Visa and MasterCard are accepted almost everywhere, but relatively few establishments take American Express or Diners Club. In Mazatlán most visitors eat a large, late breakfast; snack at midday; and splurge on a big dinner. Many restaurants are open from 1 P.M. to 11 P.M. and serve anytime, but the fashionable hour for the evening meal is 8.

Aha Toro. Camarón Sábalo; 3–6646. Elegantly masculine decor, with brass and polished wood, serving steaks and lobster to celebrating fishermen.

Beverly Grill. Av. del Mar 556; 2–1127. The idea is that this is an enclave of Beverly Hills in Mazatlán. Along with dining, there is dancing to disco music.

El Camarón. Av. del Mar; 1–6626. An informal spot where guests are welcome either for a drink and a snack or a fine meal from the international menu.

Casa de Bruno. Camarón Sábalo; 3–6241. "Mucho fiesta" promised here, along with steaks, lobster, and shrimp. Strolling musicians add to the atmosphere.

Casa Loma. Av. Gaviotas 104; 3–5398. Subdued elegance in what was once a private home. On the menu are international specialties. Closed from June to September.

Doney. Mariano Escobedo at Cinco de Mayo; 1–2651. Mexican specialties, along with seafood and steak at reasonable prices. Mariachis play on weekend evenings.

Fellini's. Camarón Sábalo 333; 3–7767. Something of a pub, with good hamburgers, steaks, and seafood plus "music to sooth your soul."

Le Gourmet. Av. Loaiza 403; 3–5009. In spite of its name, this is simply another steak and lobster house, but quite good in its way.

Mamucas. Simón Bolivar Poniente 404; 1–3490. Downtown and generally regarded as the best of the Mazatlán seafood houses. Portions are huge and prices are reasonable.

El Marinero. Cinco de Mayo 530, just off Paseo Claussen; 1–7682. A long-established seafood house where mariachis play.

Mesón del Cobre. Camarón Sábalo; 3–7692. A casual place; open from 7 A.M. until midnight.

El Parador Español. Camarón Sábalo; 3–0767. Spanish specialties, such as paella, are served here, and Spanish cuisine is quite different from Mexican.

El Patio. Av. del Mar 30; 1–7301. The decor is Mexican colonial and mariachis often drop in, but the cuisine is Continental.

Los Pelicanos. Av. del Mar 553; 2–6839. An attractive place to dine on 2 levels with good food, lively music, and a friendly staff.

Señor Frog. Av. del Mar; 1–4367. Wild and crazy, something of a singles bar, where people come to eat and end up dancing on the tables.

Señor Pepper. Camarón Sábalo; 3–1111. One of the more elegant dining spots in Mazatlán, featuring large portions, a subdued setting, and piano serenades.

Shrimp Bucket. Olas Altas Sur 11; 1–6350. The acorn from which the Carlos Anderson collection of casually stylish restaurants grew. Ribs and seafood are good here.

Tequila Charlie's. At the Arts and Crafts Center; no phone. Fairly inexpensive; open for breakfast and has music at night.

Tres Islas. Camarón Sábalo; 3–5932. One of the better seafood shacks, built on the beach; nice for lunch and romantic in the evening when trios croon.

HOW TO GET AROUND. From the airport, it is about a 40-minute ride to most hotels; a seat in a **minibus** costs $3 per person while **taxis** make the trip for about $7. In town, **buses** run along the coastal avenues all the way to the main plaza; the fare is about 10¢. A fun way to see the city is aboard a *pulmonia* ("pneumonia"), as the open-sided **scooter cabs** are called. These vehicles are unique to Mazatlán; the fare from most hotels into town is $3, about what a regular taxi would charge.

TOURIST INFORMATION. The best sources of information on what is going on are hotel travel desks, which have area maps and promotional flyers. To be avoided are the information booths in the *Zona Dorada;* their main purpose is to peddle time-sharing condos.

TOURS. Three-hour bay cruises aboard the yacht *Fiesta* are popular and inexpensive (about $5). Perhaps more interesting are the picnic cruises to Isla de Piedra, where passengers debark for a swim. Best of all is a morning or afternoon sail aboard the *Tam-Tam,* which charges $30 for the cruise and carries only 20 persons.

Highly recommended is a half-day city tour that takes in the downtown market as well as all the sights; there is much to see in Mazatlán. A favorite full-day excursion is to Concordia and Copala; Concordia, in the foothills of the Sierra Madre, is noted for its pottery, leather, and cabinetry, and Copala, once a mining center, is now pretty much a ghost town, with a couple of charming restaurants. The price of this trip is about $25.

Twice a week, 12-hour journeys are made south of Mazatlán to the jungles of Nayarit down to San Blas. The trip includes a boat ride up the Tovara River and a visit to an old fort and a mission. Although this $40 (lunch included) excursion adds up to a long and tiring day, it is a memorable one as well, going into the rain forests, past pineapple plantations and mango orchards.

Hotel travel desks will book any of these tours. Those who prefer going alone in a car should call *Mazatlán's Private Guides* at 3–9837.

USEFUL ADDRESSES. Airlines. *Aeroméxico,* Av. del Mar 117; 1–3096; *Mexicana,* Paseo Claussen 101B; 2–7722; *Western,* Camarón Sábalo; 3–2709. **Car Rentals.** *Avis* (3–6200), *Budget* (3–2000), and *Hertz* (3–4955) have booths at the airport and offices along Camarón Sábalo. **Consulates.** *United States,* Circunvalación Poniente 6; 1–2905 and 1–4488; *Canadian,* Albatros 705; 3–7320. **Postoffice,** downtown on the main plaza at Av. Juárez.

SEASONAL EVENTS. *Carnaval,* the week before Lent (either in **February** or **March**), is a Mardi Gras that rivals those in Rio and New Orleans; hotel space usually is booked months in advance, but rooms in private homes may be available. The festivities include parades with floats, street dancing, fireworks, and much more. *Mazatlán Fishing Tournament,* in late **August** or early **September,** attracts sports people from several countries.

BEACHES. Keep in mind that the seashore in Mexico is federal property; there are no private beaches and hotels have no control over the sands that front their property. Few beaches have life guards.

Las Gaviotas, which starts at Camarón Point (Valentino Disco is the landmark), is backed by the *Zona Dorada* and many hotels, making it the most popular tourist beach. It is wide and long, protected from heavy seas by several small islands. A launch, known as the *SuperPato* (SuperDuck), runs out to one of these islands every couple of hours, departing from in front of the Hotel Las Flores and charging about $3 for the round trip. The island has Hobie Cats, Windsurfers, waterskiing boats, and scuba diving equipment.

Playa Norte is the stretch of beach running along Avenida del Mar from Camarón Point back to the Fishermen's Monument. The hotels here are across the street, so this sandy strip is where many budget travelers who are staying at beachless hotels choose to congregate. There are some rocky bits, but generally the sands are inviting; the many seafood shacks make lunch no problem.

Olas Altas, means high waves, and it was here that Mazatlán's first beachfront hotels were built. The beach is fairly small; the sands shift from one point to another with the season. During the summer months, Olas Altas is where the surfers congregate. The beach is within easy walking distance of downtown and has many appealing restaurants across the street. Where the sands turn into a rocky coastline is where the Mazatlán high divers leap into the surf.

Playa Sábalo is the location of the Camino Real, Holiday Inn, Oceano Palace, and several other hotels, as well as a trailer park. It is less crowded than the other popular beaches but has plenty in the way of water sports.

Cerritos, last stop on the bus line, is a good white-sand beach fairly far out. A couple of hotels and several condo developments have gone up, and the betting is that this will be Mazatlán's resort area of the future.

Isla de Piedra, (Stone Island), which is a short boat ride from the harbor, is where the locals congregate on weekends. Picnic cruise boats stop here, too. There are several seafood shacks, live music, and lots of fun. The sand is nice on the island and the tranquil water is fine for swimming.

Brujos (Witches' Beach) is a lovely spot that often is empty on weekdays but attracts locals on weekends, when a small seafood restaurant is open and musicians show up to serenade.

Escondida (Hidden Beach) lives up to its name. Fringed by palms, it might be the shore of a desert island, obviously a good place for a couple who want to be alone.

Delfin is a beach with one hotel and not much more. The hoteliers apparently thought this area would be further developed, but that has not happened.

PARTICIPANT SPORTS. Fishing. Although Mazatlán has the biggest sportfishing fleet in all Mexico, part of its appeal is its uncrowded waters. Off many U.S. points, there may be as many as 1,000 boats at one time; off Mazatlán, there are rarely as many as 100.

Striped marlin run from November through May, when the blue and black marlin come in, which stay through December. The season for sailfish and dolphin is April to November. Several tournaments are held during the year; the big one is either in late August or early September.

In all, a dozen fishing fleets operate out of Mazatlán. They range from 3 to 14 boats and all are docked at the foot of Lighthouse Hill. Hotels will help book charters, or the skippers may be contacted directly. Among the most reputable are the *Star Fleet* (2–3878), *Faro Fleet* (1–2824), and *Perla Fleet* (1–7211). Rates start at about $200 per day, depending on the size and capacity of the craft.

Mike's Fleet (2–4977) operates party boats, charging $45 per person for a chair and a line plus bait and 2 beers; passengers are insured.

To be avoided are touts soliciting customers on the beaches or sidewalks.

Hunting. Several species of duck, along with white-wing doves, morning doves, and quail, abound in the Mazatlán area. The season runs from October through April. *Aviles Brothers,* Box 222, (1–6060), is the most experienced outfitter, arranging everything from licenses to the rental of firearms. The cost of a 6-hour hunt will run about $80, including transportation, boat, retriever, and English-speaking guide.

Golf. The 18-hole course at *El Cid* is open to the public, as are the 9 holes at the *Club Campestre de Mazatlán,* which is a bit out of town.

Water sports. Windsurfing, parasailing, waterskiing, and navigating a Hobie Cat are among the favorite activities along Mazatlán's beaches. For those who want to learn, lessons are available. Scuba diving is growing in popularity and courses are available at resorts. A scuba trip will cost about $40.

SPECTATOR SPORTS. Bullfights are held most Sunday afternoons between December and Easter; technically, bullfighting is not considered a sport but a spectacle—a test of a *matador's* skill and daring against what is, after all, a killer bull. Still, with lots of blood, bullfights are not for everyone. Those who wish to see one can obtain tickets at almost any hotel and take a taxi for the short ride to the ring.

Charreadas (charro rodeos) are often held Sunday mornings at the *Lienzo* on Insurgentes near the rail depot, but have your hotel check before you go. *Charreadas* usually are competitions between 2 associations of amateur but highly skilled riders, complete with bronco riding, steer wrestling, and bareback riding. Tourists are warmly welcomed and usually enjoy the show.

Winter baseball is played at a stadium on the airport road just off Av. del Mar. The minor league teams often include Americans who hope to break into the big time.

SIGHTSEEING. Mazatlán has many places besides beaches that are worth seeing, which sets it apart from other Mexican seaside destinations. Many of these sights are included in city tours, but some visitors prefer seeing them on their own.

Aquarium, Av. de los Deportes 111, a block or so from Av. del Mar, should not be missed, although with all the sharks and piranas, it might be left for the last day or so. This aquarium is one of the most attractive of its kind in all Mexico, teeming with fascination. The admission price is about $1. For information, call the State Tourist Office, 3–2545.

Lighthouse Hill and *Lookout Hill,* otherwise known as *El Faro* and *La Vigía,* are two landmarks that offer wonderful views of the area. Bookings for both boats can be made at hotel travel desks. The lighthouse is the highest in the Western Hemisphere, but it can be reached only by walking; a paved road goes to the top of Lookout Hill.

The harbor, which can be appreciated from either of the two hills, can be seen even better aboard the *Fiesta,* which cruises the bay, or one of the boats that goes to *Isla de Piedra* (Stone Island). One can also drive along the shore, past the sportfishing docks to the piers, where freighters and cruise ships tie up, and down to where the shrimp boats put in.

The cathedral and the *plaza* are in the heart of downtown Mazatlán. The cathedral, consecrated only half a century ago, is quite new as Mexican churches go, but very much a local landmark. Nearby is the postoffice, public market, and the many small shops and stores of a typical Mexican city.

SHOPPING. The **Zona Dorada,** which is the area off the beach between Blvd. Camarón Sábalo and Av. Loaiza, is brim full of boutiques as well as hotels and restaurants. The *Mazatlán Arts and Crafts Center,* which pretty well started it all, is a bazaar full of stalls selling everything from turtle oil to piñatas. Almost next door is *Sea Shell City,* whose name tells its story. *Designers Bazaar, Boutique Nueva,* and the local *Beneton* and *Ralph Lauren* franchises are good places to look for resort wear. *Casa Pacífico* is noted for its jewelry and *Galeria Indio,* for its decorative items. *Galeria de Arte Moderno* has a nice selection of contemporary Mexican paintings and sculpture.

Downtown, the public market carries a wide range of handicrafts; negotiating a price is the way to strike a deal. *Plaza Nueva* is a mall where local folk shop, and prices are said to be considerably lower than in the *Zona Dorada.*

NIGHTLIFE. Discos are alive and thriving in Mazatlán; the lines are longest outside *Valentino's, Frankie O's* and the *Caracol* at El Cid. Others are *El Navegante* at the Hotel de Cima and *Roxy's* at the Oceano Palace. Many hotel lobby bars and several restaurants have live musical entertainment. Almost every night, there is a Mexican fiesta at one of the hotels; those at the *Camino Real, Playa Mazatlán, Los Sábalos,* and *Costa de Oro* are worth checking out.

MANZANILLO

Commercial Port on the Pacific

by
JIM BUDD

For vacationers, Manzanillo is known more as an airport than as a city. Nearly 20 miles from town, the airport is a gateway to several self-contained resorts—vacation hideaways where guests rarely leave. That sets the area apart from the other holiday destinations in northwestern Mexico.

The city of Manzanillo is a big commercial port, and a grubby one. It has a certain waterfront character, but one quick visit is enough for most people.

About 150 miles down the coast from Puerto Vallarta, Manzanillo has been a settlement of some size since Spanish colonial times. Near here, Miguel López de Legaspi sailed west to conquer the Philippines. In more recent years, the coming of a railroad made Manzanillo Mexico's principal port for trade with the Orient.

Trains made Manzanillo easy to reach in an era, not so long ago, when road travel was uncomfortable and airplanes were frightening. At one time, there were more hotels here than in Puerto Vallarta. Investors and developers saw a great future for Manzanillo. Many of them still do.

Best known of these dreamers was the South American Croesus, Anteñor Patiño, who funded the you-have-to-see-it-to-believe-it Hotel Las Hadas, a vacation club called Maeva, condos, a golf course, a marina, and, according to some, the jet-sized airport. There were other dreamers as well, although they worked on a somewhat smaller scale. Among them was a group of Americans from the Denver area who started the Club Santiago before Patiño's time, and some titled Europeans who had great plans for the Costa de Careyes, or Turtle Coast, which is up the shoreline in the state of Jalisco.

It would be wrong to say that none of these projects materialized. But they did take some unexpected twists. Manzanillo has yet to turn into another Acapulco, as many people expected, but several individual resorts have prospered. Las Hadas, which is now run by Westin Hotels, is booked solid most of the year, and the Club Med on the Turtle Coast is a winner. Maeva is doing pretty well, and Fiesta Americana, one of Mexico's biggest chains, operates a resort at Tenacatita that is doing well. It is just that between these places there is not very much.

EXPLORING THE MANZANILLO AREA

A city of some 90,000 inhabitants, Manzanillo is bunched between the mountains and the sea. Railroad tracks crisscross the city, running right down to the docks. The town is cluttered and jumbly, only worth walking about to satisfy your curiosity. Except for the lively plaza, the *zócalo,* there is little of interest to see.

The harbor, to be sure, has a certain fascination, as most harbors do. Usually, freighters are tied up at the docks, along with a few small ships of the Mexican Navy. This is one place where fishing boats may be chartered and where yachts depart on bay cruises.

Across the bay is Playa Azul, a lovely beach on Manzanillo Bay. The waters tend to be tranquil along some parts of the beach and the surf is moderate at others. The shape of the bay protects bathers from the big waves.

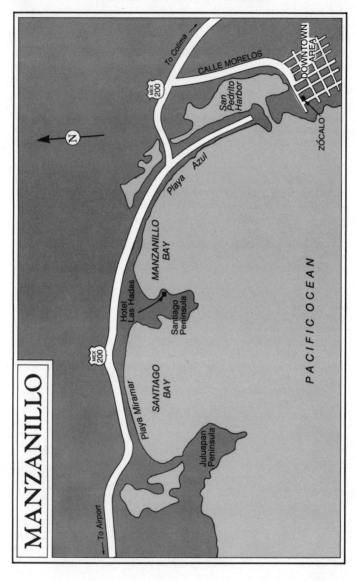

The upper arm of the bay, known as the Santiago Peninsula, is where Las Hadas stands. The 200-room hotel is something of an Arabian Nights fantasy, said to be inspired by a Moorish village, although the Moors never saw anything like it. The peninsula has a golf course and several condo developments. It has been built up with ecological good sense, housing units spaced out and surrounded by plants and flowers.

Across the peninsula is Santiago Bay, wide and lovely, with hotels and condos along its shore. The highway, Mexico 200, passes by a little settlement called Salahua—directly inland from the peninsula—and Santiago, both of which really are part of Manzanillo proper, but much more attractive. There are a few restaurants along this stretch, as well as stores and a shopping center. Beyond, the highway cuts along shoreline wilderness.

The airport is 20 miles up the coast; a little farther along, over the Jalisco state line, are the twin hamlets of Barra de Navidad and San Patricio Melaque.

A tiny fishing village, Barra de Navidad once was a getaway for vacationers who truly wanted to drop out for a while in the Mexican tropics. Of late, it has been changing and has a development of its own, Pueblo Nuevo. A hotel and condo project, Pueblo Nuevo has a pool, tennis courts, shopping center, and marina. Most of its customers are well-to-do folk from Guadalajara, which is less than a five-hour drive away.

The town manages to retain its laid-back flavor, visitors and fisherfolk mingling easily on the cobbled streets. The inns here are modest but clean and comfortable. Most of the restaurants are open-sided affairs serving little but seafood. Oysters spiced with diabla sauce (garlic, butter, and chili) are the great local delicacy.

Almost next door, San Patricio Melaque—usually known simply as Melaque—is more of a town, with some 5,000 inhabitants. Here, too, is a selection of modest hotels and restaurants.

Tenacatita, perhaps an hour's drive farther, is another fishing village, once favored by the late muralist José Clemente Orozco. Here Fiesta Americana has its big resort, Los Angeles Locos (which means the Crazy Angels; it does not mean that Los Angeles, CA, is insane). Nearby is El Tecuan, another resort hotel, which is independent of any chain.

Costa de Careyes (the Turtle Coast) is perhaps 15 miles farther along. European developers had splendid schemes for this area, but, thus far, all that has emerged is one rather quiet Italianate resort and a wild and swinging Club Med.

PRACTICAL INFORMATION FOR
THE MANZANILLO AREA

HOW TO GET THERE. By Air. The international airport is located roughly midway between Manzanillo proper and Melaque. *Aeroméxico* (800–237–6639) flies in direct from Houston and Los Angeles, while *Mexicana* (800–531–7921) provides direct service from Dallas/Fort Worth. Between them, these two airlines fly in from numerous points in Mexico. Ground transportation is provided by Volkswagen vans and tends to be relatively inexpensive, with prices rising when only one or two passengers are headed for a specific destination.

By Car. Manzanillo is about 1,500 miles from the Arizona border at Nogales and is 200 miles from Guadalajara. *Tres Estrellas de Oro* provides bus service along both routes to Manzanillo, Barra de Navidad, and Melaque, but the buses do not drive into the individual resort hotels, which are often 2 or 3 miles from the highway.

By Rail. The train from Guadalajara is quite good but slow; the trip takes about eight or nine hours.

TELEPHONES. The area code for this region is 333; to call from the United States, first dial 01152. Outside the towns, telephone service is poor or nonexistent. The number for the **tourism office** is 2–2090 in Manzanillo and 7–0100 in Melaque; **police,** 2–0181 in Manzanillo and 7–0080 in Melaque; **hospital,** 2–0029 in Manzanillo. Except for those in the tourism offices, however, personnel are unlikely to speak English.

HOTELS. The Manzanillo area has a wide range of hotels and prices, but even the least costly are clean, comfortable, and often cater to American tourists. Those in more remote locations frequently do not have good telephone service. In this classification, a double room in a *Super Deluxe* establishment will cost about $135 and above; a *Deluxe* room, $100–$135; *First Class,* $70–$100; *Moderate,* $50–$70; and *Inexpensive,* less than $50. Since the properties in this region are quite spread out, we list them by location.

MANZANILLO

Las Hadas. *Super Deluxe.* Santiago Peninsula; 3–0000. Managed by Westin Hotels, this fairyland (Las Hadas means the fairies) of a resort put Manzanillo on the jet-set map. The hotel has 206 rooms and 204 condo suites plus an 18-hole golf course, 10 tennis courts, and all water sports.

Club Santiago. *Deluxe.* Playa Santiago; 3–0413. Two miles of beach, 9 holes of golf, 6 tennis courts; accommodations in studios, condo apartments, and villas.

Las Hadas Club. *Deluxe.* Santiago Peninsula; 3–0081. A condo development under separate management from the hotel but offering many of the hotel's facilities, including golf, tennis, a beach, and restaurants.

Playasol. *Deluxe.* Playa Azul; 3–0309. On the beach at Manzanillo Bay, the 120 units are spacious condo apartments; a pool, restaurant, and disco.

Roca del Mar. *Deluxe.* Playa Azul; 2–0805. A small bungalow complex on the Manzanillo Bay beach, with 29 units overlooking the sea; a pool, shop, bar, and restaurant.

Villas del Palmar. *Deluxe.* Playa Azul; 3–0575. A complex on Manzanillo Bay, with 186 units, pool, all water sports, tennis, and golf facilities.

Charles y Willie. *First Class.* Santiago Peninsula; 2–2906. Fairly new and a good spot to make friends, with 40 rooms (U.S. programs on TV), a pool, restaurant, and bar.

Club Maeva. *First Class.* Playa Miramar; 3–0595. A vacation club complex, with 514 units in villas, a huge pool, tennis, water sports, and a busy activities program. Quite spread out, but a big favorite with Mexican families.

El Pueblito. *First Class.* Santiago Peninsula; 3–0550. A condo complex, with 60 suites in 9 hillside villas and a pool. Charming, but there are many steps to climb, and the beach is far away.

Playa Santiago. *First Class.* Playa Santiago; 3–0270. Once the grandest resort in the area, now a bit run down, with 100 units, 2 pools, tennis, and miniature golf.

Colonial. *Moderate.* Av. México 100, downtown; 2–1080. An older commercial hotel, with 38 rooms and a congenial bar but no pool or beach.

Las Brisas. *Moderate.* Av. Cárdenas; 2–1951. A big favorite with repeat visitors; many of the 66 rooms have kitchenettes and some are cooled by fans.

Motel Star. *Moderate.* Avenida Cárdenas; 2–2400. On Manzanillo Bay, with 42 units, a pool, coffee shop, and good parking.

La Posada. *Moderate.* Playa Azul; 2–2404. Owned by an American who started the place in 1957; 24 rooms, a nice pool, and breakfast included in the room rate.

Savoy. *Moderate.* Carillo Puerto 60, downtown; 2–0754. A 24-room commercial hotel with a good view of the port from the top floors and a restaurant that never closes.

BARRA DE NAVIDAD

Cabo Blanco. *First Class.* Armada at Puerto Navidad; 7–0182. Part of the Pueblo Nuevo complex, with 125 rooms, 3 restaurants and bars, several pools, all water sports, and fishing.

Barra de Navidad. *Moderate.* Carranza at Legaspi; 7–0122. Some of the 60 rooms are air-conditioned; others have ceiling fans.

Sands. *Moderate.* Morelos 24; 7–0018. All 44 rooms are cooled by fan; the hotel overlooks a lagoon and has a pool, restaurant, bar, and disco.

Tropical. *Moderate.* Av. Legaspi 150; 7–0020. On the beach, with a choice of air-conditioned or fan-cooled rooms (there are 57); a pool, bar, and restaurant.

Delfin. *Inexpensive.* Morelos 23; 7–0063. A small hotel with 23 fan-cooled rooms, a pool, and a coffee shop.

Karelia. *Inexpensive.* Av. Legaspi; 7–0187. Ten bungalows with kitchenettes, on the beach.

COSTA DE CAREYES

Club Mediterranée Playa Blanca. *First Class.* 2–0005, or in the United States, 800–258–2633. One of the many Club Meds around the world. Guests check in for a week (membership required); meals and most activities are included in the price.

Plaza Careyes. *First Class.* 2–0018. An Italian-style resort sharing the same bay as the Club Med, but considerably more sedate; 97 rooms.

SAN PATRICIO MELAQUE

Azteca. *Moderate.* Av. Avante; 7–0150. A complex of 13 fan-cooled bungalows on the beach. Pool.

Club Nautico. *Moderate.* Madero 1; 7–0239. Fairly new, with 29 rooms, some of which are air-conditioned, a restaurant and a bar.

Melaque. *Moderate.* Paseo de la Primavera; 7–0001. On the beach; the biggest hotel in town, with 185 fan-cooled rooms, a pool, and a restaurant.

Las Brisas. *Inexpensive.* Gomez Farias 102; 7–0108. Small, with bars; fans in the 22 rooms.

Posada Pablo de Tarso. *Inexpensive.* Gomez Farias 408; 7–0117. A combination of 11 rooms and 16 bungalows, some air-conditioned; on the beach, pool.

TENACATITA

Los Angeles Locos de Tenacatita. *Deluxe.* 7–0221. An elegant, new Fiesta Americana property, with 200 rooms overlooking a quiet bay beach.

TECUAN

El Tecaun. *First Class.* 7–0132. A secluded hideaway, with just 40 rooms on the beach; pool, tennis court, water sports, and surf fishing.

DINING OUT. In Manzanillo, there is a growing choice of places to dine, but elsewhere, the choice is more limited. Expect to pay about $15 in a place listed here as an *Expensive* place, around $10 in a *Moderate* establishment, and roughly $5 in one that is listed as *Inexpensive.* AE indicates that American Express cards are accepted; DC, Diners Club; MC, MasterCard; and V, Visa. Many places, especially those outside Manzanillo, accept no cards at all.

MANZANILLO

Expensive

Manolo's. Main Highway, Salahua; 3–0475. International cuisine served in a garden setting. Open for dinner only. AE, DC, MC, V.

Osteria Bugatti. Main Highway, Santiago (no phone). Oysters and other seafood specialties prepared in the Italian manner. Open for lunch and dinner. AE, MC, V.

L'Récif. Av. Olas Altas; 3–0624. A Continental-style seafood restaurant, with a superb menu and a wonderful view of the ocean. Open for lunch and dinner. AE, DC, MC, V.

Moderate

Aldea Bruja. Main Highway, Santiago (no phone). A large thatch-covered place specializing in seafood. Open for breakfast, lunch, and dinner. MC, V.

Carlos n' Charlies. Main Highway, Santiago (no phone). One of the Carlos Anderson chain of informal, slightly whacky, beaneries, known more for its fun than its food. AE, DC, MC, V.

La Chiripada. Colonia Las Brisas; 2–0722. Steaks and seafood; live music and dancing at night. MC, V.

México Lindo. Main Highway, Salahua (no phone). Mexican specialties, quail, seafood, and steaks; music during the lunch and dinner hours. MC, V.

Tio Juan. Main Highway, Santiago; 3–0619. A good place for breakfast. Open for lunch and dinner, too, serving meats and seafood. MC, V.

El Vaquero. Crucero Las Brisas; 2–2727. Steaks and chops, with some cuts sold by weight. Name means cowboy. MC, V.

Inexpensive

La Hamburgesa. Davalos 25, downtown; 2–1429. Hamburgers, as the name implies, and other light fare.

El Plato. Main Highway, Santiago. A thatch-roof roadside seafood shack that turns out some pretty good dishes.

Savoy. Davalos at Puertos, downtown; 2–0754. A hotel coffee shop, nice to know about since it never closes.

BARRA DE NAVIDAD

La Palapa. *Expensive.* Cabo Blanco Hotel; 7–0182. International specialties and seafood at the best restaurant in town. AE, MC, V.

El Manglito. *Moderate.* Av. Veracruz. A little place by the lagoon; noted for its oysters.

Marisco Natcho. *Moderate.* Av. Legaspi 49. Grilled fish and other seafood.

Pancho. *Moderate.* Av. Legaspi 53; 7–0176. A lively seafood spot by the ocean with an imaginative cook.

Bananas Grill. *Inexpensive.* Av. Veracruz. An outdoor eatery that is popular with Americans; a good spot for breakfast or a light lunch.

Eloy. *Inexpensive.* Morelos 47; 7 0365. A seafood shanty jutting out over the lagoon.

SAN PATRICIO MELAQUE

Kosonoy. *Moderate.* Punta Melaque. A favorite gathering place after sundown. Seafood and Mexican specialties.

La Tropicana. *Moderate.* Punta Melaque. A daytime hangout with a good bar and Mexican food.

Aurora. *Inexpensive.* Carillo Puerto 53. Excellent Mexican cooking but not much seafood.

Rincon Tropical. *Inexpensive.* López Mateos 34. Open for breakfast, lunch, and dinner, serving Mexican food.

 HOW TO GET AROUND. Taxis are plentiful, but since distances are great, they can be expensive. **Buses** are one alternative, but many hotels are a long hike from bus stops. **Rental cars,** although costly, often are the best answer. They can be picked up at the airport or in Santiago, where *Avis* (3–0194), *National* (2–0302), and *Hertz* (3–1018) have offices.

 TOURIST INFORMATION. In Manzanillo, the **tourism office** is hidden away on the fourth floor at Av. Juárez 244 (2–0181); in San Patricio Melaque, the office is in the Hotel Melaque (7–0100). These offices are open weekdays 9 A.M.–3 P.M. and 5–7 P.M., only in the mornings on Saturdays, and not at all on Sundays. Sadly, the information they provide is scanty.

 TOURS. City **sightseeing** ($5), excursions to Barra de Navidad ($15), and air tours to Guadalajara ($80) can be arranged by hotel travel desks in Manzanillo or by calling *Viajes Bahias Gemelas* at 2–1818 or *Recorridos Turisticos* at 3–0055. Morning and sunset **cruises** depart from the Manzanillo docks; call 2–2262 for further information (price is about $5).

In Barra de Navidad **boats** are available for about $8 per hour to tour the lagoon and bay or cross over to Colimilla for a snack and a swim. The tour desk at the Hotel Cabo Blanco (7–0182) puts together **coconut plantation** tours that include a chance to do a bit of cape work with a small bull; these run about $10 per person.

SEASONAL EVENTS. *Carnaval,* the pre-Lenten Mardi Gras, usually in **February,** is celebrated both in Manzanillo and Barra de Navidad/Melaque with parades, dances, beauty queens, and fireworks.

SPORTS. Manzanillo bills itself as the **sailfishing** capital of the world, the season running from October into early May with tournaments in November and February. In Barra de Navidad, there is an international tournament in mid-January. In Manzanillo, cruisers may be chartered from about $250 on up, depending on their size; prices are lower in Barra de Navidad. Charters include the services of a skipper, necessary licenses, gear, bait, and sometimes refreshments. Arrangements may be made at the waterfront, but it is preferable to work through a hotel, since hotel personnel know which skippers are the most reliable.

The 18-hole **golf** course at Las Hadas, designed by Roy Dye, and Larry Hughes's 9 holes at Club Santiago usually are open to the public. These hotels and several others also have **tennis** courts.

Scuba diving is becoming popular in this area. *Aguamundo* (3–0000) and *Eureka* (3–0413) run diving trips in Manzanillo, and the sports center at the *Cabo Blanco Hotel* (7–0182) makes arrangements in Barra de Navidad. Prices start at about $40 for a one-tank boat dive.

Waterskiing costs about $15 for 30 minutes; **Windsurfers** rent for about $12 per hour.

BEACHES. A lovely strip of golden sand, *Playa Azul,* runs along Manzanillo Bay to the Santiago peninsula where Las Hadas is located. The beach on the peninsula is *La Audiencia,* so called because a few centuries ago a local chief granted Spanish explorers an audience. On the other side of the peninsula are Santiago Bay and *Santiago Beach.* Farther along the bay are *Playa Olas Altas* (high waves) and *Miramar,* where there is a bit of surf, but not enough to make swimming dangerous. Most of the smaller hotels are located along Playa Azul and are fairly close together, while the resorts on Santiago Bay are larger and more spread out.

San Patricio Melaque looks out on a very nice beach, and there is another beach farther along toward the tip of the peninsula that divides the bay from the lagoon. Between these two, the water is rough and the currents strong, making swimming dangerous. About two miles east of Melaque is a picturesque bay, *Cuastecomate,* with an exceptionally good beach and a few seafood shanties. Farther up the coast are the beaches at *Tenacatita, Tecuan,* and *Costa de Careyes,* all of which have nice hotels and good places to eat. The beaches themselves are federal property and not owned by any hotel.

SHOPPING. The *Plaza Santiago,* along the main highway, is perhaps the best place in the **Manzanillo** area to find a selection of resort wear and handicrafts, although better-quality goods at higher prices may be found at the stores at the mall in *Las Hadas.* Downtown, *Hugo's* at Juárez 25, *El Caracol* at Juárez 42, and *Casa Colorada* at Av. México 231 have a nice selection of resort clothing at reasonable prices. In **Barra de Navidad,** the best place to pick up a swim suit or T-shirt is the *Hotel Cabo Blanco. Curiosidades del Mar,* where some rather imaginative items are made from sea shells, is the most interesting shop in **Melaque.**

NIGHTLIFE. The fanciest discos are at *Las Hadas* and *Club Maeva,* although *Caligula,* on the main highway in Santiago (3–0706), can be great fun. In Barra de Navidad, *Mar y Tierra,* at the Cabo Blanco Hotel, often has live as well as recorded entertainment. *El Galeon* is the disco at the Sanda Hotel; *La Giff* at Legaspi 44, is more popular, but the crowd occasionally gets rough. The same can be said for *Sibonay* on the outskirts of Melaque; *Albatros,* López Mateos 58 (7–0083), is a bit more refined.

THE COPPER CANYON

Mexico's Wild West

by
MARIBETH MELLIN

Baja is Mexico's coastal wilderness; the Copper Canyon is its Wild West. The ferry from La Paz in Baja Sur to Topolobampo in Sinaloa links the peninsula to the mainland; the train from the coast through the Sierra Madre Occidental and Chihuahua connects Mexico to the United States. It sounds simple, but the Chihuahua-Pacific Railway took almost 100 years to complete. Today, the railway, from sea level through the Sierra Madre, with its 39 bridges and 86 tunnels, is a popular trip for tourists, engineers, and railroad buffs. It is only since 1961 that tourists have been able to travel this 400-mile route, going from the fertile sea-level farms around Los Mochis up 9,000 feet to the

caves of the Tarahumara Indians and down again to the city of Chihuahua, the center of Mexico's Wild West.

The Southern Route from Los Mochis

Travelers from Baja begin their Copper Canyon journey in Topolobampo, where the ferry from La Paz arrives on Sundays, Mondays,
Wednesdays, and Thursdays (subject to change). The harbor is one of
the deepest in the world; the town is small and used by travelers mainly
as a base camp for fishing and hunting excursions. Topolobampo is said
to be an Indian word meaning "the lion's watering place," referring to
the abundance of sea lions in the bay and ocean. Isla El Farallon is a
breeding ground for the sea lions and attracts flocks of seagulls. On the
mainland, lagoons, estuaries, and the Fuerte River are famous for their
wildlife and frogs' legs, clams, oysters, scallops, and crabs. The inner
bay has miles of shallow beaches, good for shell hunting and beach-
combing.

Travelers bound for the Chihuahua Pacific Railway treat Topolobampo as a suburb of Los Mochis, just 15 minutes inland. Day trips
to the beach from the city are common; those making the early morning
train trip usually prefer to stay in Los Mochis for convenience.

Los Mochis is an agricultural boomtown; its location near the harbor
and railroad makes it an export center for the state of Sinaloa, which
produces much of Mexico's basic crops. Tractor dealerships and mechanics' shops line the road to town from the airport. Unlike most
Mexican cities, Los Mochis sprawls without relation to its center.
There is no old main plaza or park; most people point to the new Plaza
Fiesta shopping center by the country club as the town's major attraction.

Benjamin Johnston, builder of the Ingenio Azucarero, or sugar refi-
nery, is credited with being the town's founder. Johnston collected
plants from around the world; the grounds of his home near the country club are now a botanical garden. Both the club and garden are open
to tourists, and tours of the city's factories can be arranged through the
major hotels.

Like Topolabampo, Los Mochis is a base camp for hunters and
fisherfolk. The hunting season runs from November through February.
It is said that 1.6 million game birds migrate to Sinaloa in the winter;
the hunters who follow them are particularly fond of quail, white-
winged dove, duck, and geese. Most hunters either hire a guide through
their hotels or stay at one of the hunting lodges outside Los Mochis,
where guns, ammunition, and licenses are provided. Fisherfolk head
for Topolobampo and smaller coastal towns in search of corvina, yellowtail, red snapper, and cabrilla. The Hidalgo Dam, 50 miles from Los

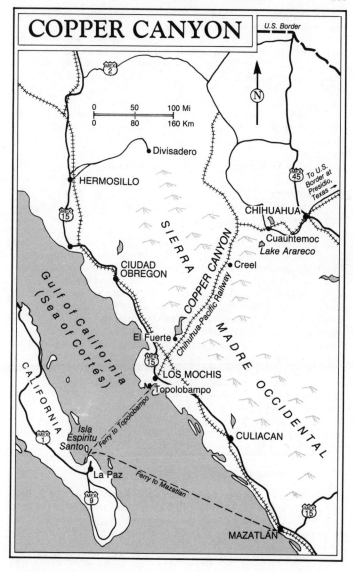

COPPER CANYON

U.S. Border

MEX 2

N

| 0 | 50 | 100 Mi |
| 0 | 80 | 160 Km |

Divisadero

HERMOSILLO

MEX 45

To U.S. Border at Presidio, Texas

MEX 15

CHIHUAHUA

Cuauhtemoc
Lake Arareco

SIERRA

CIUDAD OBREGON

Creel

COPPER CANYON

Gulf of California (Sea of Cortés)

El Fuerte

Chihuahua-Pacific Railway

MADRE OCCIDENTAL

CALIFORNIA

MEX 15

LOS MOCHIS

Topolobampo

MEX 1

Isla Espiritu Santo

Ferry to Topolobampo

CULIACAN

La Paz

Ferry to Mazatlán

MEX 9

MEX 15

MAZATLÁN

Mochis near the colonial town of El Fuerte, is the place to catch catfish, largemouth and black bass, and carp.

El Fuerte, unlike Los Mochis, is a quaint colonial town, named for the fort built there by the Spaniards in the 1600s. Centuries-old homes are built around central patios; the nearby Misión de Cerocahui was founded in 1690. The El Fuerte Valley is picturesque; 70 percent of its arable land is under irrigation, and fields of tomatoes, rice, sugarcane, and winter vegetables are interspersed with vast cattle ranges.

The town of Cerocahui is located about 15 miles from the Bahui-chivo station of the Chihuahua-Pacific Railway, and is often the first layover for train travelers. The Urique Canyon, first of the chain making up the Copper Canyon region, is about 15 miles from town; day trips by foot, horeseback, and truck can be arranged through hotels. Hot springs, gold mines, missions, Indian caves, and waterfalls are all within a 30-mile radius.

The Chihuahua-Pacific Railway

In 1872, a young engineer from the United States, Albert Kinsey Owen, had the dream of building a U.S. farming community around Topolobampo and a railroad to Texas. In 1893, Benjamin Francis Johnston continued Owen's work by building a sugar mill and organizing the community with churches, public buildings, and roads in the area that would later become Los Mochis and the fertile Valle del Fuerte. Arthur E. Stillwell, builder of the Kansas City Southern Railway and the Kansas City, Mexico and Orient Line, enacted the northern version of Owen's dream in 1898 by building 1,000 miles of railroad from the United States through Chihuahua and into the Sierras. In 1912, his company went broke.

The Mexican government completed the Chihuahua-to-Texas rail line in 1928, but it wasn't until 1961 that the last southern stretch to Los Mochis, through 85 miles of spectacular canyons and mountains, was finally finished. Engineers throughout the world said it couldn't be done; now railroad buffs travel the route regularly, marveling at the magnitude of it all.

Took Century to Build

This incredible railway, often called "The World's Most Scenic Railroad," took about 100 years to build. Its importance as a freight route from the Sea of Cortés to the U.S. Southwest kept engineers, entrepreneurs, and explorers busy plotting new ways to blast through the Sierras. The final burst of construction began in 1953 and ended eight years later with 39 new bridges and 86 new tunnels snaking through the vast series of canyons four times longer than the Grand Canyon. Although the entire route is often called the Copper Canyon Railroad, the Chihuahua-Pacific Railway travels through more than six different canyons, the most important of which are Urique, Cobre (Copper), Batopilas, Tararecua, and Sinforosa. These canyons are often called *barrancas,* rather than *cañones,* because of their shallow configuration.

The entire railway runs 570 miles from Los Mochis to Ojinga, across the border from Presidio, Texas, but the most scenic portion is the 400-mile span between Los Mochis and Chihuahua. The Los Mochis train station, the railway's southernmost departure point, is about 15 minutes from downtown Los Mochis. The station is a plain, dingy building with a small cafe, a ticket counter, and little information about the train ride. The first-class train normally leaves while it is still dark, around 7 A.M. Those who've traveled the railway often say it is best to start in Los Mochis rather than Chihuahua, to get the full visual benefit of the ride. It is inevitable that some part of the 13-hour (at best) ride will be in the dark; traveling north offers more daylight during the canyon segment of the ride.

Hookup at Sufragio

Sufragio, about an hour northeast from Los Mochis, is the connecting point for the Chihuahua-Pacific Railway and the Pacífico Railroad, with trains to Mexicali, Nogales, Guadalajara, and Mexico City. At this point, it is just getting light, and the view is of a vast scrub desert, with towering saguro cactus and stunted oaks, pine, and juniper. Before long, the Urique and Septentrion rivers cut long canyons in the hillside, and the train travels over its longest bridge, El Fuerte, and through its longest tunnel, Descanso. From there, the line twists, sometimes doubling back on itself as it climbs through the Sierra foothills to Temoris. There is a time change when the train crosses the state line between Sinaloa and Chihuahua. The tunnels and bridges here are so close to each other that sometimes the front of the train is in one state while the rear is in another. Some say this is the most spectacular stretch of the trip, particularly in the spring, when the rivers are high and waterfalls flow through crevices in the canyon walls. Pine forests appear above grassy foothills and oak savannahs. The 305-foot-high bridge over Rio Chinipas gives one the feeling of being suspended in space; looking back across canyons to the tracks you just were on gives a sense of the awesome work it took to carve this path through the wilderness.

The valleys and hills are dotted with the pink blossoms and cotton pods of the amapa trees, and ferns grow through moist crevices in the canyon's rock walls. At Temoris, a small lumbering town in a deep-set valley, the train crosses the Santa Barbara Bridge. A huge sign commemorating the 25th anniversary of the railway looms over the town, next to a steep waterfall. The train turns 180 degrees inside a long tunnel just north of Temoris, then climbs the side of the canyon. The Bahuichivo station, next in line, is the departure point for those going to Cerocahui, about 20 minutes from Bahuichivo, near the Urique Canyon. In San Rafael, the train stops for a few minutes to change crews; delays are common here, and there's not much to see except the railyard and a few humble homes.

Where the West Begins

The sense of the Wild West begins here, as the train climbs once again past apple orchards, a few small farms, and the beginnings of pine forests. As you reach the Continental Divide, the train stops for 15 minutes in Divisadero on the upper edge of the Urique Canyon. Here the Tarahumara Indian women sell their baskets and carvings along the train tracks, against the backdrop of the spectacular canyon. The Urique river flows through subtropical valleys 7,500 feet below. From the lookout at the canyon's edge, you can see across three canyons— Cobre, Urique, and Sinforosa—and possibly spot a tiny Tarahumara settlement far down the hills. There are two hotels at Divisadero (the train stops for the first shortly before reaching the Divisadero station), with hiking and horseback tours into the canyon to Indian cave dwellings, waterfalls, and picturesque forests and valleys. A small cafeteria and food stands sell burritos, tacos, hot dogs, and apples near the station. If you get off to shop, sightsee, or take pictures, be sure to listen for the train whistle. The train will leave without you.

Top of the Sierras

On its way toward Creel, the next major stop, the train climbs to over 8,000 feet at the top of the Sierras. Snow is common here in the winter months, and the train may be delayed. The canyons are visible from both sides, and the tracks are lined with piles of logs and fresh-cut planks. At 7,500 feet, Creel is a fair-sized lumbering town, with lots of dirt roads and paths leading into the forests and canyons. It is a cowboy town, with saloons, cafes, and curio shops lining the main dirt street, López Mateos. Two churches stand at the main plaza, which is not much more than a cement court with steps and benches. Music blares from the town's only movie theater across from the churches. Horses and pickup trucks share the narrow, sometimes muddy, streets; Tarahumara Indians sit in clumps outside the shops, averting their eyes from the tourists. A short drive outside town there is a Tarahumara cave settlement, where tourists can sample the Indians' way of life, but these caves are not truly representative of the canyon dwellers; they are much too full of cardboard and plastic castoffs from town.

From Creel, one can visit the 1,000-foot-high Basaseachic waterfall, one of the largest in North America. With a guide, you can skirt the falls and go halfway down to a spot called La Ventana (the window) for a spectacular view. The falls can also be reached from Cuauhtemoc, farther up the rail line toward Chihuahua. Lake Arareco, about 20 minutes from Creel on dirt roads, is good for rainbow trout and black bass fishing. Most hotels can arrange horseback, hiking, or van trips through the canyon to rock clusters resembling frogs and elephants, down into Batopilas Canyon or to the town of Batopilas, founded for silver mining in 1720. Creel is a far-from-luxurious spot and can be very cold in the winter, but from here, one gets a real Wild West sense of the vast expanse of the mountains and canyons. The Indians hold their famous Easter celebrations at Misión San Ignacio, near Creel; it is the one time when travelers can see the Tarahumara of old, dressed in traditional costumes following ancient rituals.

Descent to Chihuahua

The train descends from the mountains toward Chihuahua. Farms, cattle ranches, and wood-pulp processing plants dot the rolling hills and plateaus. Cuauhtemoc, two hours from Chihuahua, is the commercial center for the Mennonites. In the 1920s, a large group of Mennonites from the United States, Europe, and Canada emigrated to Mexico. They later made an arrangement with the Mexican government that allows them to farm the land in isolated communities, practice their religious beliefs without interference, and run their own schools. Because of their beliefs, the Mennonites are pacifists and are forbidden to serve in the military or hold political office. Between 15,000 and 60,000 Mennonite farmers live on about 300,000 acres outside Cuauhtemoc; they are credited with making the state of Chihuahua a leading producer of oats, cheese, and meats. Their cheeses and sausages are excellent, and are sold at shops around Cuauhtemoc. The Mennonites, who are distinguishable by their blond hair, blue eyes, and German language, travel to town only when they must, and are private people who shun both their Mexican neighbors and tourists. Most Mennonites do not speak Spanish and marry only among themselves. Because of their customary large families, they are running out of farmland, and some have left for Paraguay and Belize. Many still wear the traditional costume of dark suits for the men and long calico dresses for the women, but some have adapted to coveralls and jeans. Horse-drawn wagons are common, although there are some pick-up trucks, since the religion does not preclude mechanical devices or electricity. It is possible to visit their communities, but it is best to do so on an organized tour. The roads to the farms are barely passable, even with a four-wheel drive vehicle. Tours to Mennonite settlements are available through hotels in Cuauhtemoc and Chihuahua. The Mennonites, who have grown accustomed to tour groups, are willing to discuss their lifestyle and will allow you to take photographs; however, some will hide their faces from the camera.

End of the Line

The train ride ends in Ciudad Chihuahua, the capital of the state of Chihuahua—Mexico's largest and wealthiest state. The city was founded in 1709; even though it is large and modern, it still has a frontier feeling. Chihuahua is the center of a vast ranching, timber, and silvermining region and lies just east of the Sierra Madre mountain range. The large Baroque cathedral on the city's main plaza is one of the few outstanding colonial buildings in northern Mexico; construction of the cathedral began in 1724, but battles between the Spaniards and the Indians held up its completion until 1826. Padre Miguel Hidalgo, one of Mexico's foremost national heroes, who launched Mexico's struggle for independence from Spain, was held prisoner by the Spaniards in Chihuahua. The building where he was imprisoned, now called the Palacio Federal, houses government offices. The building where he was executed in 1811 is now the Palacio de Gobierno, housing state government offices; its walls are filled with murals depicting Mexico's history. The Church of San Francisco, built by Franciscan monks between 1717 and 1789, is another example of colonial architecture. Underground passages connect the church and the cathedral.

Home of Pancho Villa

On the north end of the city is Quinta Luz, the former home of General Francisco Villa—better known as the bandit Pancho Villa. The house was headquarters for Villa's "Golden Ones" during the Mexican Revolution. After Pancho Villa was assassinated in 1923, Luz Corral de Villa won a court battle against other women claiming to be Pancho Villa's wife and was awarded the home. She converted the house into a museum filled with Pancho Villa's firearms, cartridge belts, and personal effects. On display is the bullet-ridden car Villa was driving when he was ambushed and killed. The museum is famous throughout Mexico and is considered by some to be a kind of national shrine. When Dona Luz died in 1981, Quinta Luz was taken over by the Mexican Government and is now called the Museum of the Revolution. A monument to Pancho Villa, officially named Monumento a la

División del Norte (for Pancho Villa's army), dominates the traffic circle of Avenida Universidad and Avenida División del Norte.

A mansion built as a replica of Tara in *Gone With the Wind* is located on Calle Cuauhtemoc; it is a private home and can be viewed only from the outside. Hacienda de Quinta Carolina, just outside town, is a fine example of the luxurious lifestyle of Chihuahua's wealthy residents in the 1800s. The Museo de Arte Popular on Avenida Reforma has a permanent exhibition of the Tarahumara culture and examples of their crafts. The famous Chihuahua dogs can be purchased throughout the city; be careful what you buy—those that have been allowed to roam the streets may be wild and mean.

The Tarahumara

Although the mountains through which the Chihuahua-Pacific Railway travels are officially called the Sierra Madre Occidental, within the region they are more commonly referred to as the Sierra Tarahumara. The Tarahumara Indians were the original residents of these mountains; in the 1700s, Spanish explorers and missionaries began herding the Tarahumara into communities in mission settlements. Those who resisted were driven deeper into the canyons. Mexico's Law of Colonization in 1825, which encouraged Mexicans to settle in remote areas on land that would be free to them, brought even more interlopers into the Tarahumara's lands, and the Indians withdrew even farther, relinquishing the best mountain farmlands. The Tarahumara now occupy a 25,000-square-mile portion of the Sierra Tarahumara, mostly in the western remote foothills and canyons.

About 45,000 Tarahumara are estimated to live in these mountains. They are asocial and nomadic, living in small settlements tucked so deeply in the wilderness that one hardly realizes they are there. The Tarahumara live in caves and humble wooden shacks close to riverbeds and arable fields. Their communities are small—fewer than 12 families will live in the same region, probably because of the shortage of farmland. They exist through subsistence farming and goat herding and resist assimilation. The Tarahumara are short of stature and have a short life span of 40 or 45 years.

The Tarahumara rely on their feet for transportation, thinking nothing of climbing for days up the canyons for supplies. From birth, they are trained to walk and run long distances and climb steep mountains. They are called the Raramuri, the foot runners, for their fame as some of the best long-distance runners in the world. They also are known for their kickball races, called *rarahipa*. These races can last for several days and nights as teams of runners chase small wooden balls down cliffs, over streams, and through rocky trails to the finish line. Other runners light the trail with pine torches when night falls.

Impact of Missionaries

Missionaries have had an impact on the lifestyle of the Tarahumara; many of the children now attend mission schools and are learning Spanish. The Tarahumara have combined the Christian beliefs of the missionaries with their more traditional rituals, celebrating Christmas with religious processions and Christian services followed by feasting, drinking *tesguino* (corn beer), and nightlong Matachine dances. The dancers, all male, wear elaborate headdresses and carry wooden rattles and wands; musicians play handcrafted violins and guitars. At Easter, the Tarahumara enact a Holy Week pageant in which the soldiers are pitted against the Pharisees. Those playing the Pharisees paint their faces and bodies and carry drums as they march; the soldiers wear the traditional Tarahumara loincloths, shirts, and head scarves. The pageant culminates in a procession and religious ceremony. The traditional pre-Christian Yumari fiestas are "curing" ceremonies, held to cure sick people and animals, prevent disease, bring rain, bless fields, and remove the spirits of the dead. Chanters, dancers, and musicians or matachine dancers (depending on the season and reason) follow ritualistic routines throughout the night, culminating in a feast.

The Tarahumara believe the devil inhabits the bodies of those who are not Tarahumara; thus, they avoid outsiders. Those who display and sell their crafts at the railroad stations and tourist hotels appear unfriendly; that may be due to this belief, combined with the sight of hordes of strangers taking their pictures and bartering in English. The sellers are mostly women and children dressed in long skirts, their heads wrapped in scarves, their feet practically bare (even in the snow) except for thin sandals with narrow straps wrapped around their ankles. They sit in clusters of two or three on the pavement along the train tracks with their wares laid out on blankets; in the evening, they wrap their wares in the blankets, tie them on their backs, and descend silently into the canyons.

Crafts Are Simple

The Tarahumara crafts are simple and rustic—baskets woven from bear grass and pine needles; rustically carved pine animals, spoons, and bowls; wooden dolls dressed in Tarahumara fashion; simple unglazed pottery vases and bowls; brightly colored woven belts; and violins, drums, and guitars made of pine, ash, willow, and redwood. Few items cost more than $5; many are under $1. The women do not barter or chat with strangers; indeed, they avert their eyes and take the money silently when a purchase is made. Although tourists commonly take photos of these Indians, they won't get any smiles or poses from these basically shy people who protect their privacy and traditions zealously.

It is possible to join tours at the mountain hotels to Tarahumara settlements. Those closest to the hotels can be disappointing, since the caves and huts are often filled with the throw-aways of civilization. The Tarahumara are resourceful people; they collect what others discard, fashioning sardine cans into ladles, tequila bottles into canisters, and discarded clothing into dolls' dresses. In the wilderness, this skill is exhibited in plows made from oak limbs and mortars molded from rocks. Here they eat over 200 varieties of herbs, vegetables, and plants that grow in the mountains; catch fish by stunning them with herbal poisons mixed in the stream waters; and hunt deer by chasing them through the canyons. The farther you go into the canyons and mountains, the less evidence of civilization you see; instead, there are families living in caves above steep cliffs or log houses without ceilings beside a simple garden patch. Tours often include a visit to a mission school; these school children are more accustomed to strangers, and some enjoy being photographed.

PRACTICAL INFORMATION FOR
THE COPPER CANYON

HOW TO GET THERE. By Air. Los Mochis can be reached on *Aeroméxico* and *Aero California* by flights within Mexico from La Paz, Tijuana, Guadalajara, and Mexico City and from Texas and New Mexico on *Pan-American Airlines.* Chihuahua can be reached by flights from Ciudad Juárez, Tijuana, Guadalajara, and Mexico City. The only way to get from Los Mochis to Chihuahua is on the Chihuahua-Pacific Railway. (See *How to Get Around* below.)

By Ferry. The ferry from La Paz docks at Topolobampo, 15 miles from Los Mochis, on Sundays, Mondays, Wednesdays, and Thursdays.

By Train. Sufragio, north of Los Mochis on the *Chihuahua-Pacific Railway,* is accessible by passenger train from Mexicali, Chihuahua, and Guadalajara. Chihuahua can be reached by trains from Texas.

TELEPHONE. The area code for Chihuahua is 641 and for Los Mochis, 681.

HOTELS. There are many good hotels in Los Mochis and Chihuahua, but along the railroad route there are few options. It is always wise to make reservations for hotels along the train route through travel agencies in Los Mochis and Chihuahua. In this listing a hotel in Los Mochis or Chihuahua rated as *Expensive* costs about $35 per night; *Moderate,* about $20; and *Inexpensive,* about $10. There are few inexpensive places along the train route; sometimes families will allow tourists to stay in their homes for a negotiated price.

CEROCAHUI/BAHUICHIVO

Hotel Misión. *Expensive.* About 15 miles from the Bachuichivo train station; reservations through the Santa Anita Hotel, Los Mochis; 2–00–46. American plan (meals included), 28 rooms with fireplaces, dining room, craft shop, and large game room with Ping-Pong, billiards, and cards. Tours to the Urique Canyon.

Cabanas Barrancas de Urique. *Moderate.* 25 miles from the train station at Bahuichivo; 21 cabins, bus tours to canyons and Tarahumaras. Reservations: Box 622, Chihuahua, MX.

CHIHUAHUA

Expensive

Castel Sicomoro. Ortiz Mena 411; 3–5445; Centrally located and very popular; 128 rooms, a pool, travel agency, 2 bars, restaurant, cafeteria, and cable TV.

Exelaris Hyatt. Av. Independencia 500, downtown; 6–6000. Centrally located, with 190 rooms, a cable TV, travel agency, car rental, bar, restaurant, disco, cafeteria, and nightclub.

Motel Mirador. Universidad 1309; 3–2205; Large motel, with 87 rooms, a pool, travel agency, car rental, bar, restaurant, and cafeteria.

El Presidente. On the central plaza at Libertad 9; 6–0606; High-rise hotel with 84 rooms, a pool, 2 bars, restaurant, cafeteria, and Penthouse disco.

Moderate

Hotel Apolo. Juárez and Carranza; 6–1100. Air-conditioning, cafeteria, bar, and parking.

Posada Tierra Blanca. Independencia and Niños Héroes 100; 5–0000; 108 rooms, a pool, bar, restaurant, cafeteria, and disco.

Victoria. Juárez and Colón; 2–8893; A nice older hotel, with 121 rooms, a pool, bar, disco, and restaurant.

Inexpensive

Motel Maria Dolores. Niños Héroes 901; 2–2544; 25 rooms, restaurant close by.

Roma. Libertad 1015, 2 blocks from downtown; 2–7652; 23 rooms.

San Juan. Victoria 823 near downtown; 2–8492; 61 rooms, a bar, and a restaurant.

CREEL

Parador de la Montana._Expensive._ Calle López Mateos 41; phone 75; Reservations: Allende 114, Chihuahua, 2–2062. A motel arrangement on the edge of town, with 36 rooms, a restaurant, bar, lobby fireplace, and tours to Tarahumara caves, lakes, and canyons.

Cabañas del Cobre (Copper Canyon Lodge). _Moderate._ 30 minutes from the Creel station; no phone. Reservations through the Hotel Santa Anita, Mochis, Box 159, Los Mochis, Sinaloa, MX; 2–0046; in Chihuahua, 2–8893. A 25-room lodge, with fireplaces and kerosene lanterns, a game room, van tours to Indian dwellings and nearby lakes and canyons.

Hotel Nuevo. _Moderate._ Across the street from the train station. Tours to Indians, lake, and canyons. Small establishment with new clean rooms.

Hotel Korachi. _Inexpensive._ Across the tracks from the Creel station; no phone. Tours to Indians, lake, and canyon.

CUAUHTEMOC

Rancho La Estancia. _Expensive._ Hunting lodge on the outskirts of town. Reservations: Box 986, Chihuahua, MX; 2–2282. Tours to the Mennonite settlements and Basaceachic waterfall.

EL DIVISADERO

Hotel Cabañas Divisadero Barrancas. _Expensive._ On the edge of the canyon at the Divisadero station. Log-cabin lodge and adjoining buildings, with central dining area, fireplace, and bar. Some of the 35 rooms have fireplaces and canyon views. Hiking and horseback tours into the canyon and to Tarahumara dwellings. Reservations through the Hotel Colinas in Los Mochis or the Hyatt Exelaris Chihuahua or write Aldama 407, Box 661, Chihuahua, MX; 12–3362. Rooms on the American plan, with 3 meals costing an extra $15 per person (it's the only place other than taco stands for meals).

Hotel Posada Barrancas. _Expensive._ About 5 minutes before the Divisadero station. The train stops here briefly to let off hotel guests. A mountain lodge near the canyon's edge; 35 rooms with fireplaces, dining room, bar, and disco. Tours into the canyon and to Indian dwellings. Reservations in Los Mochis, Hotel Santa Anita, Box 159, Los Mochis, Sinaloa, MX; 2–0046. American plan.

EL FUERTE

Hotel Posada. _Expensive._ Hidalgo 101; 3–0242; reservations in Los Mochis, 2–0046. A converted colonial mansion with 27 units, some with balconies; a pool, restaurant, bar, and disco; hunting and fishing tours.

LOS MOCHIS

Expensive

El Dorado Motel. Leyva and Valdez, 5–1111. On the main street, close to shops and restaurants, with 90 air-conditioned rooms, a pool, restaurant, coffee shop, and parking.

Hotel Colinas. Carretera International 15 and Blvd. Macario Gaxiola, A.P. 600, Los Mochis, Sinaloa, MX; 2–0101 or 2–0242. A Best Western high-rise tourist and convention hotel on a hill overlooking Los Mochis. Two pools with a long twisting water slide, hot tub, restaurant, bar, dancing; plans for a miniature golf course and fitness facilities. Connected with hotels along the train route and can reserve rooms for your trip.

Santa Anita. Leyva and Hidalgo; Reservations: Box 159, Los Mochis, Sinaloa, MX; 2–0046. Popular older hotel, with 130 air-conditioned rooms, a bar, good restaurant, and travel agency. Part of the Balderrama chain, with hotels along the train route. Hunting and fishing tours are available through the hotel desk as well. The Santa Anita is the informal information center for much of what's happening in Los Mochis.

Moderate

America. Allende Sur 655; 2–1355. Not far from the bus station, and has a guarded lot for recreational vehicles.

Beltran. Hidalgo 281 and Zaragoza; 2–0710. 42 air-conditioned rooms, plain and simple.

Motel Plaza Inn. Calle Leyva and Hidalgo; Reservations: Box 1159, Los Mochis, Sinaloa, MX; 2–0075; 42 rooms, a swimming pool, cable TV, and hunting and fishing tours.

Motel Posada Real. Leyva and Buelna; 2–2179. A motel on the edge of town, with air-conditioning, a pool, restaurant, and bar.

Inexpensive

Los Arcos. Allende Sur 534; 2–3253. Around the corner from the bus station; the pleasant clean rooms fill up quickly.

Hotel del Parque. Obregón 600; 2–0260. Near the sugar mill; small and simple.

Los Mochis Trailer Park. On Av. Gabriel Leyva at the far north end of town; no phone. A large, landscaped park; gets crowded in the winter.

TOPOLOBAMPO

Yacht Hotel. *Expensive.* On the waterfront. Reservations: call Los Mochis 2–3862. Small hotel, with 20 rooms, no telephone or TV, and restaurant and bar with water view.

DINING OUT. Along the coast, in Los Mochis and Topolobampo, lobster, shrimp, frogs' legs, and fresh fish are plentiful; some of the best restaurants specialize in dozens of fish preparations. Beef is the other specialty throughout Sinaloa and Chihuahua. Along the train route, your dining options are limited. The major Copper Canyon hotels often have the only kitchens in sight; they normally work on the American plan and serve generous, delicious Mexican meals family style. At a few of the stops along the train route, children board the train briefly and sell burritos and sodas; some stops have taco stands along the tracks. Meals in the cities and train stops, not including tips and drinks, are considered *Expensive* at about $10; *Moderate,* about $6; *Inexpensive,* under $5. Most of the expensive places as well as the moderately priced ones accept major credit cards.

CHIHUAHUA

Expensive

Robin Hood Pub. Talavera 208; 5–3769. Meat cuts, incredible sandwiches, crab, smoked salmon, rainbow trout, good bakery, video shows with rock music on one side of the restaurant and romantic music on the other.

Los Vitrales. Av. Juárez 2116; 2–0915. Good Cantonese and Mexican dishes in a pleasant large hacienda. Live music.

Moderate

Ajos y Cebollas. Colón 207; 6–3102. A cafe and art gallery, specializing in the dishes of rural Chihuahua.

La Calesa. Av. Juárez 3300; 2–8555. Mexican dishes; live music on weekends.

La Olla de Chihuahua. Av. Juárez 3331; 6–2221. A good restaurant with 3 branches; specializes in meats and basic Mexican meals. Live music on weekend nights.

Los Parados de Tony Vega. Juárez 3316, 2–4141. Specializes in beef, seafood, and international dishes. Separate bar with live music; popular with the city's residents.

Inexpensive

Hosteria 1900. Independencia 903B; 6–1990. Crepes and Mexican dishes; video bar next door.

La Parilla. Aldama 1105; 6–6322. Good Mexican meat dishes and tacos.

Pizza del Rey. Universidad 2918; 4–0908. Traditional pizzas with salami and pepperoni, Italian wines, live music.

LOS MOCHIS

El Bucanero. *Moderate.* Allende 828 and Rafael Buelna; 2–9767. A good fish restaurant a bit out of the way; lots of families.

El Farallon. *Moderate.* Obregón and Flores; 2–1428. Nautical decor, murals, seafood.

El Trigal. *Moderate.* In the Hotel Colinas, at Carretera Internacional and Blvd. Gaxiola; 2–0101. A coffee shop on one side and more elegant dining area on the other; good Mexican dishes.

Madrid. *Inexpensive.* Obregón 414 and Leyva; no phone. Mexican cooking, plain and cheap.

Mexico-Español. *Inexpensive.* Hidalgo Poniente 281; 2–2983. Spanish cooking.

HOW TO GET AROUND. Taxis are abundant in Los Mochis and Chihuahua. Elsewhere along the Copper Canyon, you must rely primarily on tour vans from your hotel or hike to what you want to see.

By Car. Driving around Los Mochis and Chihuahua is not hard, but getting into the canyons or valleys can be extremely difficult without a four-wheel drive vehicle. The dirt roads are not marked; it is best to have a guide. **Rental cars** are available from *Hertz* and *National* at both the Los Mochis and Chihuahua airports.

By Bus. The Los Mochis bus station is at Obregón 61; 2–1757. Buses travel up and down the coast and into the mainland from here. In Chihuahua, the bus station is at Progreso 1204, 5–9555.

By Rail. The Los Mochis train station is about 15 minutes outside town on Blvd. Castro. The Chihuahua-Pacific Railroad runs from Los Mochis to Chihuahua, covering 410 miles of rugged mountains and canyons in about 13 hours. Various passenger trains link Los Mochis and Chihuahua. The most popular with tourists is the *Vista Tren,* a 2-level domed car that provides the best scenery, with a snack bar, comfortable seats, and small private sitting rooms. Seats are about $35 each way. The Vista Tren is supposed to leave Los Mochis at 6 A.M. on Thursdays, Fridays, Saturdays, and Sundays, but occasionally it doesn't arrive or is booked by a private group. The passenger train leaves daily from Los Mochis and Chihuahua at 7 A.M. and arrives at the opposite end, if all goes well, at 8:30 P.M.

There are two classes on the passenger train; *especial numerada,* with padded seats, heat, and air-conditioning, and *primera general,* more crowded and uncomfortable. Rates are about $15 and $8, respectively. Most passenger trains have dining cars with limited menus.

It is next to impossible to reserve seats on the train, although some travel agencies can inform you about what cars are running when and how much the price will be. It's a good idea to get to the station early because the cars fill up quickly and you'll want a window seat. Since the train often arrives later than expected, inform your hotel of the day you will arrive at the station and have them send a taxi or van for you.

Please note that all rates and schedules are subject to change without notice.

TOURS. Most of the major hotels in Los Mochis and Chihuahua can arrange reservations for you along the train route. Some travel agencies specialize in Copper Canyon packages that include the train fare, hotels, meals, and other transportation.

CHIHUAHUA

Viajes Cañon Del Cobre. Av. Juárez and Colón; 2–5353. Specializes in Copper Canyon trips.

Viajes Gulliver. Exelaris Hyatt Hotel; 6–1270. Copper Canyon and Mennonite tours.

LOS MOCHIS

Agencia Flamingos. Around the corner from the Santa Anita Hotel at Leyva and Hidalgo; 2–1613. The only agency in town that can actually sell tickets on the Chihuahua-Pacific Railway. Good information and brochures on the surrounding area.

Viajes Granados. Leyva 326; 2–0273. Copper Canyon packages.

IN THE U.S.

Baja Adventures. 16000 Ventura Blvd., Suite 200, Encino, CA 91436; 818–906–2252, or 800–345–2252 in California, 800–543–2252 outside California. Full-service tours of Baja and the Copper Canyon, including air and train travel, hotels, and side trips.

SEASONAL EVENTS. In late **March** or early **April,** the Tarahumara hold lavish Easter celebrations and pageants during *Holy Week,* which can be seen on special tours from hotels along the Copper Canyon railroad line.

MUSEUMS. In Chihuahua, there is a good exhibit of Tarahumara life and crafts at the *Museo de Arte Popular.* Av. Reforma 5; 13–31–19.

SPORTS. Hunters flock to the Los Mochis area when an estimated 1.6 million game birds migrate south. The hunting season runs from November through February; quail, white-winged dove, duck, and geese are the most common targets. Most of the major hotels in Los Mochis can arrange guides and tours for hunters.

Topolobampo's harbor is a popular departure point for **sportfishing** trips year round. From November through April, yellowtail, wahoo, bonito, toro, and red snapper are plentiful, June through October is the season for sailfish and marlin. The Fuerte River and Hidalgo Dam are popular for trout and bass fishing.

Hunting and fishing tours are available through hotels and through *Viajes Flamingo* at the Santa Anita Hotel, 2–1613; *Motel Plaza Inn,* Box 159, Los Mochis, Sinaloa, MX 2–0075.

USEFUL PHRASES AND VOCABULARY

Spanish is a relatively easy language to learn. Here are a few basic rules on pronunciation.

		as in:	example:
1) **Vowels** are pronounced precisely, with exceptions noted below:			
a		father	mas
	exception: ai/ay	life	aire, hay
	au	out	autobós
e		then	necesito
	exception: ei	weigh	seis
	eu—no equivalent word in English, but sounds like:	eh-oo	neumático
i		police	repita
	exeption: before a, e, o, u	yes	viaje, bien, edificio, ciudad
o		none	noche
	exception: oi	boy	oigo
u		good	mucho
	exception: before a, e, i, o	was	cuarto, puedo, cuidado, acuoso
	(silent when used with: qui, que, gul, gue)		aquí, queso, guía, embrague
2) **Consonants** are pronounced similarly to English, except:			
c before a, o, u		kick	casa, poco, película
before e, i		see	dice, décimo
g before a, o, u		go	gazpacho, langosta, gusto

before e, i	house	gerente, ginebra
gu	before a	guava agua
h(silent)	Esther	hablo
j	hill	mejor
ll	young	llame
ñ	onion	señor
q (always followed by silent "u")	pique	mantequilla
rr rolled	thr-r-ee	arroz
x as in English, except in a few proper names when between vowels or beginning a proper name	hut	México, Oaxaca,
	zest	Xochimilco Xochicalco
y before vowels	yet	ayer
when meaning "and"	me	y
z	lose	azul

3) **Accent marks** are used to indicate which syllable is stressed, or to distinguish between two words, i.e., el (the) or él (he).

General

Good morning/good day.	Buenos días.
Good afternoon.	Buenas tardes.
Good evening/good night.	Buenas noches.
I am glad to see you.	Mucho gusto en verle.
I don't speak Spanish.	No hablo español.
Do you speak English?	Habla usted inglés?
A little bit.	Un poquito.
How do you say in Spanish?	Cómo se dice en español?
Do you understand me?	Me entiende usted?

I understand.	Entiendo.
I don't understand.	No entiendo.
What did you say?	Cómo dice?
More slowly, please.	Más despacio, por favor.
Repeat, please.	Repita, por favor.
Write it down, please.	Escriba, por favor.
I don't feel well. I am sick.	No me siento bien. Estoy enfermo.
I need a doctor.	Necesito un médico.
How are you?	Cómo está usted?
Fine. And you?	Perfectamente. Y usted?
Very good.	Muy bien.
I have the pleasure of introducing Mr.	Tengo el gusto de presentarle al señor . . .
Pleased to meet you.	Mucho gusto en conocerle.
The pleasure is mine.	El gusto es mío.
Pardon me. Excuse me.	Perdóneme. Con permiso.
Do you have a match?	Tiene usted un fósforo?
Can I take your photo?	Puedo tomar su fotografía?
Where is the . . . ?	Dónde está . . . ?
I don't know.	No sé.
Where can I change my money?	Dónde puedo cambiar mi dinero?
Where do you come from?	De dónde es usted?
Can you tell me?	Puede usted decirme?
What do you wish?	Que desea usted?
What is the matter?	Que pasa?
Sit down, please.	Siéntese, por favor.
You are very kind.	Usted es muy amable.
It doesn't matter.	No importa.
Call me/phone me.	Llámeme por teléfono.
Is Mr. . . . in?	Está el Señor . . . ?
What is your name?	Cómo se llama usted?
Let's go.	Vámonos.
Good-bye.	Adiós.
Till we meet again.	Hasta la vista.
Until later/so long.	Hasta luego.
Many thanks.	Muchas gracias.
Don't mention it/You're welcome.	De nada

address	dirección
American	americano
aspirin	aspirina
better	mejor
boat/ship	barco
book	libro
bookstore	librería

boy	niño, muchacho
building	edificio
bullfight	corrida de toros
bullfighter	torero
business	negocio
chair	silla
church	iglesia
cigarette	cigarro
clean	limpio
cleaning	limpieza
come here	venga acá
come in	entre
depart	salir, partir
do	hacer
dry	seco
dry-clean	lavado en seco
expensive	caro
eye	ojo
eyeglasses	lentes, anteojos
few	pocos
film	rollo, película
find	encontrar
forbidden	se prohibe
from	de
garden	jardín
gentlemen	caballero, el señor
girl	niña
go	ir
good	bueno
guide	guía
handbag	bolsa de mano
hard	duro
heavy	pesado
high	alto
hospital	hospital
house	casa
husband	esposo
know	saber
lady	la señora, dama
look	mire, vea
look out	cuidado
lost	perdido
man	hombre
more	más
me	mi
my	mio, mia

name	nombre
new	nuevo
no more	nada más
no/non-	no
of	de
office	oficina
old	viejo
painting	pintura
please	por favor
policeman	policía
pretty	linda, bonita
quick	rápido, pronto
rain	lluvia
school	escuela
see	ver
single	solo, sencillo
smokers	fumadores
smoking	fumar
suitcase	maleta
sweet	dulce
there is, are	hay, son
thick	grueso
thin	delgado
time	tiempo
too	también
trip	viaje
United States	Estados Unidos
up	arriba
very	muy, mucho
wallet	cartera
watch	reloj
water	agua
weather	clima
welcome	bienvenido
wet	mojado
wife	esposa
with	con
with me	conmigo
without	sin
woman	mujer
yes	sí
young lady	la señorita
your	su

Calendar

Months (meses):

January	enero
February	febrero
March	marzo
April	abril
May	mayo
June	junio
July	julio
August	agosto
September	septiembre
October	octubre
November	noviembre
December	diciembre

Days (días):

Monday	Lunes
Tuesday	Martes
Wednesday	Miércoles
Thursday	Jueves
Friday	Viernes
Saturday	Sábado
Sunday	Domingo

Year (año)

next year	el año que viene (or; el año próximo)
last year	el año pasado

Seasons

winter	el invierno
spring	la primavera
summer	el verano
fall	el otoño

Time (tiempo)

At what time?	A qué hora?
What time is it?	Qué horas son?
It's 10 A.M.	Son las diez de la mañana.
It's noon.	Son las doce.
It's 1 o'clock.	Es la una.
It's 3:15.	Son las tres y cuarto.
It's 4:30.	Son las cuatro y media.

It's 5:45.	Son las seis menos cuarto.
It's 6:50.	Faltan diez para las siete.
At 8 o'clock sharp.	A las ocho en punto.
About 9 o'clock.	Cerca de las neuve.
At 10 P.M.	A las diez de la noche.
It is midnight.	Es la medianoche.
I will be a little late.	Llegaré un poco tarde.
Whenever you please.	Cuando guste.
In a little while.	Dentro do poco.
minute	minuto
hour	hora
ago	hace
2 days ago	hace dos días
today	hoy
tomorrow	mañana
day after tomorrow	pasado mañana
yesterday	ayer
day before yesterday	antier
morning	mañana
afternoon	tarde
night	noche
for tonight	para esta noche
last night	anoche
week	semana
next week	semana próxima
next week	semana pasada
when?	cuándo?
now	ahora
late	tarde
early	temprano
next time	la próxima vez
how long	cuánto tiempo?
always	siempre
in a minute	al momento

Hotel (hotel)

Where is the hotel?	Dónde está el hotel?
Where is a first-class hotel?	Dónde está un hotel de primera clase?
Where is a motel?	Dónde está un motel?
Where is the inn?	Dónde está la posada?
I would like a single room	Quiero un cuarto sencillo.
I would like a double room.	Quiero un cuarto para dos.
I would like a room with twin beds.	Quiero un cuarto con camas gemelas.

I would like a room with double bed.	Quiero un cuarto con cama matrimonial.
I would like a room with bath.	Quiero un cuarto con baño.
I would like a room with shower.	Quiero un cuarto con regadera.
I would like a room with a bathtub.	Quiero un cuarto con tina.
I would like a room with a view.	Quiero un cuarto con vista.
I would like a room with air conditioning.	Quiero un cuarto con air acondicionado.
I would like a quiet room.	Quiero un cuarto tranquilo.
What is the price?	Ciál es el precio?
Is there a garage?	Hay garage?
Is there a laundry of dry-cleaning service?	Hay servicio de lavandería o tintorería?
Is there a pressing service?	Hay servicio de planchar?
Is there a drugstore?	Hay una farmacia?
Is there a beauty shop?	Hay un salón de belleza?
Is there a barbershop?	Hay una peluquería?
I would like a haircut.	Quiero un corte de pelo.
I would like a shampoo and set.	Quiero un champú y peinado.
May I use your telephone?	Me permite usar el teléfono?
Where is the phone?	Dónde está el teléfono?
Where is the ladies' room?	Dónde está el baño de damas?
Where is the men's room?	Dónde está el baño de caballeros?
Open the door.	Abra la puerta.
Will you please sent the baggage up?	Favor de hacer subir el equipaje.
Will you please send the baggage down?	Favor de hacer bajar el equipaje.
Put it here.	Póngalo aquí.
This isn't working.	Esto no funciona.
Close the window.	Cierre la ventana.
Keep the change.	Quédese con el cambio.
My bill, please.	Mi cuenta, por favor.
key	llave

Restaurant (restaurante)

Where is a good restaurant?	Dónde hay un buen restaurante?
I reserved a table for two.	Reservé una mesa para dos.
A menu, please.	El menú, por favor.
I am hungry.	Tengo hambre.
I am thirsty.	Tengo sed.
What do you wish?	Qué desea usted?
Bring me . . .	Tráigame . . .
I like my meat . . .	Quiero la carne . . .

medium rare	media cocida
rare	tierna, cruda
well done	bien cocida
I would like a little more of that.	Un poco más, por favor.
The check, please.	La cuenta, por favor.

Breakfast (desayuno)

Juices (jugos)

tomato	de tomate
orange	de naranja
grapefruit	de toronja
pineapple	de piña

Eggs (huevos)

Mexican style	a la mexicana
Mexican ranch style	huevos rancheros
soft-boiled	tibios
poached	pochados
scrambled	revueltos
with sausage	con chorizo
hard-boiled	cocidos
fried	fritos
omelet	omelet
with bacon	con tocino
with ham	con jamón

Bread (pan)

rolls	bolillo
sweet rolls	pan dulce
toasted	tostado
butter	mantequilla
syrup	jarabe, miel
corn griddle cakes	tortillas
crackers, cookies	galletas
French toast	a la francesa
marmalade	mermelada
honey	miel de abejas

Beverages (bebidas)

coffee	café
black	negro
with cream	con crema
without milk	sin leche
Sanka	Sanka

Expresso	café express
tea	té
iced tea	té helado
chocolate	chocolate
milk	leche
bottle of pure water	botella de agua pura
mineral water	agua mineral
mineral water,	agua mineral,
uncarbonated	sin gas

Lunch (comida) and Dinner (cena)

Appetizers (entremeses)

marinated fish	ceviche
refried beans with melted cheese topping	frijoles refritos con queso
smoked salmon	salmón ahumado
fruit cocktail	coctel de frutas
baby cactus	nopalitos
avocado dip	guacamole
herring	arenques
shrimp cocktail	coctel de camarones
olives	aceitunas

Soups (sopas)

bean (spicy)	frijoles, picante
chick pea	de garbanzos
lentil	lentejas
cold veg.	verduras
consommé	caldo
pea	chícharo
garlic	ajo

Fish & Shellfish (pescados y mariscos)

salmon	salmon
trout	trucha
tuna	atún
crayfish	langostino
clam	almeja
oysters	ostiones
eels	angulas
red snapper	huachinango
bonito.	bonito
lobster	langosta
crab	cangrejo, jaiba

shrimp	camaron
snails	caracoles
halibut	lenguado
smoked codfish	bacalao

Meat & Poultry (carne y aves) Mexican Specialties:

tamales with beef	tamales con carne
tacos, Enchiládas, and Tostadas with chicken or beef	con pollo; con carne
chopped meat, creole style, fried green bananas and rice	picadillo a la criolla
meatballs	albóndigas
stuffed peppers	chiles rellenos
tortillas with meat, cheese and sauce	enchiladas
chicken and rice	arroz con pollo
chicken or turkey in Mexican chocolate sauce	mole poblano or mole de pavo (or; de guajalote)

Vegetables (legumbres)

potatoes	papas
fried	fritas
with cheese	con queso
spinach	espinaca
beans	frijoles
string beans	ejotes
peas	chícharos
asparagus	espárragos
mushrooms	champiñónes, hongos
carrots	zanahorias
lettuce	lechuga
radish	rábano
celery	apio
garlic	ajo
corn	elote
sweet potatoes	camotes
tomato	jitomate
rice	arroz
squash	calabaza
beets	betabeles
cabbage	col
onion	cebolla
eggplant	berenjena
cauliflower	coliflor
sauer kraut	choucrut

artichokes	alcachofas
avocado	aguacate

Desserts (postres)

cheese	queso
Spanish cream	natillas
custard	flan
ice cream	helado
sherbet	nieve
cake	pastel
fruit salad	ensalada de frutas
stewed fruit	compota
fruit tart	pastel de frutas
candy	dulces
pudding	pudín

Fruit (frutas)

apple	manzana
banana	plátano
strawberries	fresas
raspberries	frambuesas
pineapple	piña
coconut	coco
lime	lima
lemon	limón
papaya	papaya
melon	melón
mango	mango
guava	guayaba
grapes	uvas
watermelon	sandía
fruit cocktail	coctel de frutas
plums, prunes	ciruelas

Beverages (bebidas)

cactus plant drinks:	Tequila, Mezcal, Pulque, Margarita, Tequila cocktail
beer	cerveza
Bohemia	(light, native)
Carta Blanca	(light, native)
Dos Equis XX	(dark, native)
brandy	coñac
champagne	champaña
cider	sidra
gin	ginebra
wine	vino

white	vino blanco
red	vino tinto
Spanish wine punch	Sangría
rum	ron
soda	soda, Tehuacán
sherry	jerez
liquor	licor
soft drinks	refrescos
ice	hielo

Miscellaneous

sugar	azúcar
salt	sal
pepper	pimienta
mustard	mostaza
oil	aceite
vinegar	vinagre
butter	mantequilla
knife	cuchillo
fork	tenedor
spoon	cuchara
teaspoon	cucharita
sauce/gravy	salsa
tip	la propina
waiter	el mesero
waitress	la mesera; señorita
sour	agrio
spicy	picante

Mail (correo)

post office	oficina de correos
stamps	timbres, estampillas
airmail stamp	timbres, estampillas de correo aéreo
register	registrado
letter	carta
postcard	tarjeta postal

Getting Around

By car (por carro)

How do you get to . . . ?	Cómo se va a . . . ?
Where are you going?	A dónde va usted?
How far is it to . . . ?	Qué distancia hay a . . . ?
It is near/very near.	Está cerca/Está muy cerca.

It is far/very far.	Está lejos/Está muy lejos.
Which way?	Por dónde?
This way/that way.	Por aquí/Por allí, Por allá.
Go straight ahead.	Vaya usted derecho.
Turn right/left.	Doble usted a la derecha/a la izquierda.
Keep to the right.	Tome su derecha.
When are you returning?	Cuándo volverá usted?
Is the road paved?	Está pavimentado el camino?
No parking.	Se prohibe estacionarse.
Maximum speed.	Velocidad máxima.
Go ahead.	Siga
Stop	Pare, alto

By Air (por Avión)

We want a reservation.	Queremos una reservación.
One way.	Viaje sencillo.
Round trip.	Viaje redondo
When does the plane leave?	A qué hors sale el avión?
When does the plane arrive?	A qué hors llega el avión?
Is the plane on time?	Llega el avión a tiempo?
Is the plane late?	Llega tarde el avión?
No smoking.	Se prohibe fumar.
Check my luggage, please.	Revise mi equipaje, por favor.
airline	línea aérea
airport	aeropuerto
flight	vuelo

By train (por tren)

Where is the railway station?	Dónde está la estación de ferrocarriles?
train	tren
timetable	itinerario
conductor	conductor
What is the fare?	Cuá es la tarifa, por favor?

Index

FODOR'S TRAVEL GUIDES

Here is a complete list of Fodor's Travel Guides, available in current editions; most are also available in a .
British edition published by Hodder & Stoughton.

U.S. GUIDES

Alaska
American Cities (Great Travel Values)
Arizona including the Grand Canyon
Atlantic City & the New Jersey Shore
Boston
California
Cape Cod & the Islands of Martha's Vineyard & Nantucket
Carolinas & the Georgia Coast
Chesapeake
Chicago
Colorado
Dallas/Fort Worth
Disney World & the Orlando Area (Fun in)
Far West
Florida
Fort Worth (see Dallas)
Galveston (see Houston)
Georgia (see Carolinas)
Grand Canyon (see Arizona)
Greater Miami & the Gold Coast
Hawaii
Hawaii (Great Travel Values)
Houston & Galveston
I-10: California to Florida
I-55: Chicago to New Orleans
I-75: Michigan to Florida
I-80: San Francisco to New York
I-95: Maine to Miami
Jamestown (see Williamsburg)
Las Vegas including Reno & Lake Tahoe (Fun in)
Los Angeles & Nearby Attractions
Martha's Vineyard (see Cape Cod)
Maui (Fun in)
Nantucket (see Cape Cod)
New England
New Jersey (see Atlantic City)
New Mexico
New Orleans
New Orleans (Fun in)
New York City
New York City (Fun in)
New York State
Orlando (see Disney World)
Pacific North Coast
Philadelphia
Reno (see Las Vegas)
Rockies
San Diego & Nearby Attractions
San Francisco (Fun in)
San Francisco plus Marin County & the Wine Country
The South
Texas
U.S.A.

Virgin Islands (U.S. & British)
Virginia
Waikiki (Fun in)
Washington, D.C.
Williamsburg, Jamestown & Yorktown

FOREIGN GUIDES

Acapulco (see Mexico City)
Acapulco (Fun in)
Amsterdam
Australia, New Zealand & the South Pacific
Austria
The Bahamas
The Bahamas (Fun in)
Barbados (Fun in)
Beijing, Guangzhou & Shanghai
Belgium & Luxembourg
Bermuda
Brazil
Britain (Great Travel Values)
Canada
Canada (Great Travel Values)
Canada's Maritime Provinces plus Newfoundland & Labrador
Cancún, Cozumel, Mérida & the Yucatán
Caribbean
Caribbean (Great Travel Values)
Central America
Copenhagen (see Stockholm)
Cozumel (see Cancún)
Eastern Europe
Egypt
Europe
Europe (Budget)
France
France (Great Travel Values)
Germany: East & West
Germany (Great Travel Values)
Great Britain
Greece
Guangzhou (see Beijing)
Helsinki (see Stockholm)
Holland
Hong Kong & Macau
Hungary
India, Nepal & Sri Lanka
Ireland
Israel
Italy
Italy (Great Travel Values)
Jamaica (Fun in)
Japan
Japan (Great Travel Values)
Jordan & the Holy Land
Kenya
Korea
Labrador (see Canada's Maritime Provinces)
Lisbon
Loire Valley

London
London (Fun in)
London (Great Travel Values)
Luxembourg (see Belgium)
Macau (see Hong Kong)
Madrid
Mazatlan (see Mexico's Baja)
Mexico
Mexico (Great Travel Values)
Mexico City & Acapulco
Mexico's Baja & Puerto Vallarta, Mazatlan, Manzanillo, Copper Canyon
Montreal (Fun in)
Munich
Nepal (see India)
New Zealand
Newfoundland (see Canada's Maritime Provinces)
1936 . . . on the Continent
North Africa
Oslo (see Stockholm)
Paris
Paris (Fun in)
People's Republic of China
Portugal
Province of Quebec
Puerto Vallarta (see Mexico's Baja)
Reykjavik (see Stockholm)
Rio (Fun in)
The Riviera (Fun on)
Rome
St. Martin/St: Maarten (Fun in)
Scandinavia
Scotland
Shanghai (see Beijing)
Singapore
South America
South Pacific
Southeast Asia
Soviet Union
Spain
Spain (Great Travel Values)
Sri Lanka (see India)
Stockholm, Copenhagen, Oslo, Helsinki & Reykjavik
Sweden
Switzerland
Sydney
Tokyo
Toronto
Turkey
Vienna
Yucatán (see Cancún)
Yugoslavia

SPECIAL-INTEREST GUIDES

Bed & Breakfast Guide: North America
Royalty Watching
Selected Hotels of Europe
Selected Resorts and Hotels of the U.S.
Ski Resorts of North America
Views to Dine by around the World

AVAILABLE AT YOUR LOCAL BOOKSTORE OR WRITE TO
FODOR'S TRAVEL PUBLICATIONS, INC., 201 EAST 50th STREET, NEW YORK, NY 10022.